CONTENTS

D1756565

*This book is dedicated to all those in rugby
who did – and who didn't – make it through
those troubled times*

FOREWORD

This book tells of the major (and some minor) rugby matches played during, despite and sometimes even due to, World War Two. It is written to fill in some detail the perceived gaps in the history of Rugby Union football, during 1939-1946, when amateur 'rugger' was still played by schoolboys, students, clubmen and international players (both former and yet to be), of whom many also took part in the greater contests against Germany, Italy and Japan.

Just as in World War One, many did not survive, and while I have tried to record all the international players who died (in the order of the date of death), there are many more great players mentioned here who suffered either death or injury.

While soccer of a sort carried on, rugby 'got by', with both oval codes having wartime international matches for which caps were not generally awarded, although France did so. A story from a Welsh player pictured wearing an international cap was that one teammate, Les Manfield, had been capped pre-war and he passed it around for each man to have his picture taken, as Wales would not buy fourteen more!

As in a previous book – *The King's Cup 1919* – both Phil Atkinson and I have tried to make this to an extent a world of rugby book, with the inclusion of the contribution of overseas players. There will, doubtless, be games missed, but we hope that we have included the main ones played in the UK in particular between 1939-40 and 1945-46.

Without the help of Ray Ruddick, in particular, we would have struggled for programme images, though naturally – mainly due to the calls of war or travel

difficulties within Britain – the teams due to play were often altered at the last moment.

The rank of a person in the services often changed: for example, Haydn Tanner's differed from programme to programme. Also, players' clubs changed as many turned out for several outfits in quick succession.

Some players switched to Rugby League pre-war and others transferred post-war. When a player's club is not shown, it is because it had seemingly not changed from a previous match.

So, here we go: with * denoting that a player had gained a full cap pre-war and + denoting that a full cap was gained post-war. Note that 'RL' denotes Rugby League and 'NZ' denotes New Zealand (as in NZ Services, etc.) in team lists etc., to save space.

Howard Evans
Cardiff, 2019

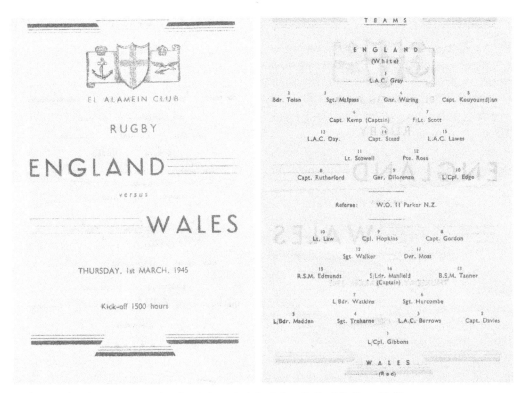

A date in the desert - an 'England v Wales' clash in Cairo, St David's Day, 1945

FOREWORD

Even more so than with our pleasingly well-received previous publications on *The King's Cup 1919 and The Wizards: Aberavon Rugby 1876-2017,* I have to emphasise that all the 'heavy lifting', the detailed player and game research for this later foray on *War Games 1939-46* has been undertaken by the indefatigably enthusiastic and knowledgeable Howard Evans: well done, sir!

My role has been largely confined to background and linkage: placing his efforts into a context and providing brief historical settings for his hard-won gems of statistics and reportage. As the decades pass since 'the war my father fought', it is hopefully helpful and important to recall and record in these pages some of the recreations which helped to raise funds, morale and the hope of a successful return to normality, following those often dark days of 1939 and afterwards.

The commemorations of the 80th anniversary of the Second World War will reveal both the genuine interest in and, often, unfortunate ignorance of the events of 1939-45. The intention behind War Games is to provide, for posterity, a record of 'the great game' during the war years, and of those embroiled in the conflict who held a deep passion for rugby and sought every opportunity to play the game.

I am extremely honoured that Howard invited me to assist him in editing War Games, and would like to thank Ashley Drake of St. David's Press for enabling Howard's unsung work and endless search for accuracy to be published. It is important that Howard's tireless investigation and painstaking recording of rugby detail during this period, researched over many decades, should see the light of day and be made available to both rugby and military historians around the globe, and to the families of the men who gave their all for their country, and on the field of play, especially those who did not return.

Phil Atkinson
Newport, 2019

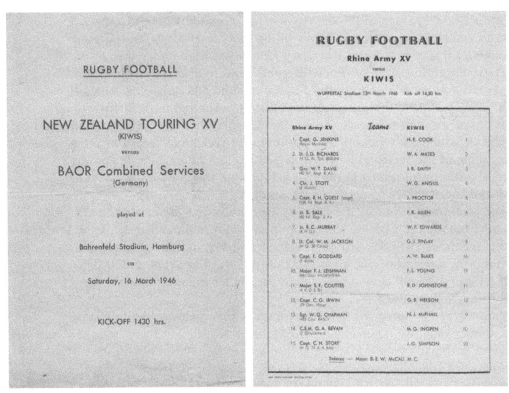

The 'Kiwis' in Germany 1946: v BAOR Combined Services and v the Rhine Army XV

PREFACE

Thanks to Them All

The idea for this book came to me in the middle of a night. I could clearly see them all speaking to me, yet none of them was with us any longer. Who? The great rugger players to whom I hold clear memories of talking, long after they had played their last games in this greatest of sports and long after they had fought in the war.

The memories of both would never leave them. Nor would they leave me: as a young boy in an Anderson Shelter or then as a grown man, talking to them, reminiscing of great days on and off the field. I had been dreaming of them, but woke at 4.00am that cold, Welsh morning, thinking of and hearing them all. I got up and began typing. They would have wanted it.

It was RUGGER then. Amateur rugger, but the very highest class of RUGBY that they played. Some were even paid to play the other code. But, in wartime, they all played together. For example, a young Bleddyn Williams often found himself in between professionals like Gus Risman (centre) and Willie Davies (fly half). What a way to learn and reach the top level of the game......

When I was fifteen I attended an interview for a clerical job in Cardiff's City Hall. I sat opposite the City Treasurer, Mr. R.L. Davies, and his deputy, Mr. John Murray Bowen. "I see you went to Cardiff High School, young Evans," said the impressive Mr Bowen. "Yes, sir." Tick, tick on their papers. "And did you play Rugger for the school?" "Yes, Sir." Tick, tick again. "Then we are pleased to offer you the job of junior clerk in the Rates Hall." No other questions!!

I was lucky enough to have an uncle (Wickham James Powell) who had played four times in 1920 for Wales, scored against England and France and then moved to Rochdale Hornets Rugby League Club.

Uncle Wick was shrewd. He kept paying his dues to Cardiff Athletic Club when he was 'Up North' and years later became captain of the Cardiff Athletic Bowls section and a County bowler, as well as being mine host at the City Arms Public House opposite

Wickham Powell

the Arms Park. When David Watkins and Colin Dixon (both with Salford RL) were refused entry, Uncle Wick smiled. He was never refused and indeed Rex Willis (a 1950 British Lion) often helped him across Westgate Street to home.

I loved talking to great players. Maybe it began when Uncle Wick and Auntie Blanche had the Cardiff Cottage Hotel in St Mary Street. One night I was asleep high above the bar where Rugby League greats such as Jim Sullivan, Johnny Ring, Jerry Shea, etc had gathered. A regular said: "Mr Sullivan, you surely did not need to knock young Bleddyn (Williams) that hard today, did you?" Jim sipped his pint and said: "I had never seen him before, but I had read about him and of his brilliant side-step and I don't buy side-steps!!"

As a six-year-old I chased Jack Matthews along Porthcawl beach on a Sunday afternoon. "Mr Matthews, Sir, could I have your autograph?" Dr Jack put the baby (probably Peter Matthews) under his arm like a rugby ball. "Of course you can," he said. He scribbled his autograph with my mother's pencil and I was glowing. Then, up came Bleddyn, Haydn Tanner, Billy Cleaver and most of the Cardiff backs to discuss tactics no doubt.

Bleddyn and Jack were one of the greatest-ever centre pairings. They kept in touch with Tjol Lategan (part of the great Springbok partnership with Ryk van Schoor). Tjol even came from South Africa to a Michael Rayer benefit. He was a lovely man. Jack once said, with Bleddyn grinning, that it was all wrong in newspapers. "I could run faster than Bleddyn. I was a Schools sprint

Bleddyn Williams & Jack Matthews (courtesy of Williams family).

champion." Bleddyn added: "But I tackled harder than Jack." History had it the other way around!

On another day, I was with Bleddyn, Jack and Billy Cleaver when ex-Welsh hooker Maldwyn James came up hobbling on his stick. Bleddyn touched me to say: "For Pete's sake never mention Maldwyn's penalty miss in front of posts right at the end of Cardiff's match with the Kiwis." It had cost the draw. "Why did he take it?" Jack smiled and said: "He wanted to, so we let him. It wasn't his fault, but he believed it cost us the game." I got to know Maldwyn and after he died I wrote an obituary in the Western Mail. His daughter sent me a lovely letter of thanks, which I still have.

I met Ossie Williams (Llanelli and Wales forward) at his home in Rogerstone. "I moved from Llanelli as work ran out down there," he said. I countered: "You were always a dirty forward as I remember." Ossie said: "Yes, I used to hit Bleddyn when he played for Cardiff against us. It was the only way to stop him! But, I always took care of him when we played for Wales together!"

I spoke to a smiling Les Manfield (Wales pre and post-war) and said: "The Cardiff pack were so clean." "Who were you watching?" he replied. "We had to do some dirty things at times to give Bleddyn and Co. the ball!" His smile has always stayed with me.

I met the Kiwis (2nd NZEF) in the 1990s when the NZ Army brought them back. They were all there except Johnny Simpson, who stayed in the Angel Hotel with influenza. There came the famous answer by Fred Allen (later knighted) when I asked why they did not go straight back to their loved ones in NZ after the war ended. "Rugby was more important," he replied and they all nodded approval.

"Come on. Let me show you the spot on the pitch where Deans reckoned he scored in 1905," said a young WRU official, who admitted he had never heard of the Kiwis. "No thanks mate," said Fred. We have played out there several times. It's cold and we prefer to talk to these people in here." The WRU man went red and said quietly: "Could you spare one of your brochures for me?"

Billy Darch was a lovely man. Billy left Cardiff despite having a superb half-back partnership with Billy Cleaver. "Why? You

Fred Allen

were always so popular with the Arms Park crowd." Darch said: "When Tanner came I knew I would never get in. I knew Emlyn Davies of Aberavon and Wales and I was renting near Port Talbot, he asked me to go there and I spent a happy season before work took me to Alaska for several years."

I was with Harry and Jackie Bowcott at Harry's house in Wenvoe. Jackie had driven from Porthcawl to see me. "Would you have ever considered going to Rugby League?" I asked. "Good gracious, NO, I was an amateur," retorted Harry. Jackie caught my arm: "I would have. But nobody ever asked me!"

Walter Vickery (Aberavon and Wales) was the son of George Vickery (Aberavon and England). Walter had played four times for Wales (1938-1939). He and George were unique, as George had won an England cap in 1905. When I met Walter he was aged 90, but his brain was still very active.

Living alone (his wife had predeceased him), he greeted me in his Duke Street (Port Talbot) house with an outstretched left hand. We went in and he said: "Do you know why I shook hands left-handed?" I said I could see that several fingers of his right hand were in a position in the palm of his hand that could not be moved, and one finger on his left hand was likewise.

His father had come from Chard in Somerset to Port Talbot where he became a police officer. He had played for Bath and then Aberavon from whom he won a cap against Ireland in Cork four years before Walter was born. Walter never saw his dad play and at the age of 91, George died, but had seen Walter, a docker, come from Central School in Port Talbot through the ranks of Taibach, British Steel and Cwmavon to join their beloved Aberavon.

In 1939, Walter was in the Wales side at Twickenham. England led 3-0 when Walter suffered a terrible blow to the knee – one he was to suffer for the remainder of his life. "I was playing for Wales for the fourth time and Wilf Wooller passed me the ball with 20 yards to go, but my leg had gone and I had already been off the field. In those days there were no replacements so I had to come back you see, but three English players caught me in the corner as I could not get there, running virtually on one leg. But for that I would have scored."

The War soon followed, but Walter, who skippered Aberavon in 1936-37, returned when hostilities ended to lead them again in 1945-46. "I was not really fit enough, as I had lost too many good years to the war and though I had a few war-time games, it was six years before I was back in Aberavon colours. "I knew I was not right, but had to give it one last go, and yes, despite it all, if I had have known how that would have left my fingers and knees in later life, I still would have done it. It was all worth it – JUST TO PULL ON THAT RED JERSEY FOR WALES."

Walter showed me a dirty old bandaged boot that he had kept near an outside coal shed and said: "I wore this one at Twickenham in 1939!" In the following year, April 2000, this fine gentleman died, though not before he admitted to playing just one game for Aberavon's deadly rivals – Neath! The boot was thrown away.

I twice went to my hero's house – Wilf Wooller. You loved him or hated him and I suspected that Wilf encouraged the latter. I loved him. So much so that I taped one interview. That tape I have never played. It sits alongside me on my desk but I have never, ever played it. I do not know why.

Wilf Wooller beats Scotland at Cardiff, 1939

My father thought the world of Wooller – as a man, player of cricket and rugby and as a Conservative. I told Wilf that I had traced and coloured his beautiful Cardiff picture from the book of Rugby Football by Cliff Jones. I sent it to him and Wilf had replied saying: "You are a clever boy, Master Howard. Best wishes from Wilfred Wooller." I had not even sent a return envelope. I still have it. It was 1948, just after Wilf had led Glamorgan to the County Cricket Championship.

I told him that my father was at the 1935 Wales-NZ game and reckoned that the winning try was scored by Geoffrey Rees-Jones because Wilf had been fouled. Wilf, though, thought a lot of New Zealand people, and shook his head: "No, Mike Gilbert did not foul me. It was icy. I kicked over him but the bounce beat us both and we landed in the straw over the goal-line. Rees-Jones was the slowest and behind us and he was up to score as we lay there."

He recollected the cricket match against South Africa that Glamorgan won on August Bank Holiday Monday 1951 at Swansea. "We had left them 148 to win and they were 54-0. Then Jim McConnon and Len Muncer started spinning them out. In came Clive van Ryneveld. He was a South African but played for Oxford University and was capped at rugby as a centre for England.

Being a Cambridge Blue myself, I did not like Clive too much. But he was a good player and I knew we must get him. I went and stood at silly mid-on. I could see him thinking that he would kill me with a big hit."

I added: "I saw the photo. You took a brilliant catch two-handed and seemed to be dancing." Wilf sat back, smiled and said: "He smashed it at me. I thought it would knock my balls off so I put two hands out and it stuck. I was hopping around, just so glad it had not maimed me!

I reminded Wilf of the first-ever Wales win at Twickenham by 7-3 on 1933 with a Ronnie Boon try and drop goal. "Ronnie was a cheeky chappie. He dropped the goal with two or three of us clear outside ready to touch down." What was the most enjoyable game? Wilf immediately said: "Playing in a great British Army side that walloped France in Paris. Best side I ever played in."

I nearly cried when I stood by Wilf in the pouring rain at a Glamorgan photo-call. Vivian Richards had just joined Glamorgan. The players ran for cover, except two. Matthew Maynard brought Viv over to us. Viv took off his cap and shook hands, saying: "I am so pleased to meet you, Mr Wooller." How did Viv know who Wilf was? Well, he did and it brought tears to my eyes. It was a memorable moment.

Graham Hale (who died in January 2018, aged 97) told me of the Cardiff 1939 Middlesex Sevens win at Twickenham. "We went up by train with six of us having never played Sevens and having no chance. Wilf, who had played Sevens for Sale, was alone during the time, except when the second semi-final was on. He sat next to me and said that Bruce Lockhart was the man to stop in the final. We did stop him and we raced back to Paddington. The train was starting to move out of the station when Wilf lumbered up the platform with the Cup. We got back and a surprised staff had to open up the bar at the Arms Park for us."

Albert Fear was a lovely man whose debut at Murrayfield was at open-side wing forward. Scotland were out to get fly half Cliff Jones but Albert made sure they did not. So much so, that years later when I met him at his son's house in Pencoed, Albert looked in his jacket and produced a letter sent by Cliff's mother that said: "Thank you for looking after my son at Murrayfield." It never left Albert's pocket until he died.

The daughter of Tyssul Griffiths told me how Tyssul's father switched on the radio with 20 minutes gone at Murrayfield in a Victory International. At half-time he was still amazed that the commentator had not mentioned his son. It turned out that Tyssul had been taken off injured in that first quarter before the radio broadcast had started.

These are the stories of players from before, after and during the war-time era. As you will see, they played, fought, played again then fought again: and in some cases, died just days after playing. These were the greatest of men, who helped people like myself love both them and 'Rugger': as Edward Humphrey Dalrymple Sewell called his 1944 book – *Rugger, The Man's Game*.

It was the sport for men of all classes in those dreadful, wonderful years – and even the RFU had to relent once more and let the league men back in, for a while, during the war!

Middlesex Sevens, 1939

1

Before the War

1919: and the Versailles Treaty with beaten Germany. A deal much hoped – and much hyped – as bringing an end to the 'war to end all wars', but which did a great deal to help ensure another was only two decades away, was signed in June. A few short weeks earlier, the New Zealand Services side had become worthy winners of the six-sided King's Cup tournament with their win over the Mother Country at Twickenham, as rugby celebrated the peace with some style and silverware.

The victors toured South Africa, without any 'Test' games, on their lengthy trip home, and in the next few years the real All Blacks were to host the Springboks for the first time, travel to Australia on 'missionary' work better received in New South Wales than the rugby league-bound Queensland, and return to the British Isles and France in 1924 for an invincible tour – without even one blot, as controversially applied by Wales in 1905.

The South Africans meanwhile grew into the other southern hemisphere giant, whose rivalry with the New Zealanders at home and away tended to provide the effective 'World

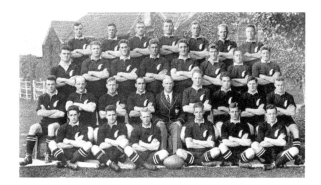

NZ Invincibles, 1924

NZ 1924-5 Tour Autographs

1

Pontypool beat both these touring sides

South Africa at Swansea, 1931

Champions' long, long before the Rugby Unions would countenance such an official tourney and title. The Springboks toured the British Isles in 1931 for the first time since 1906, while a Maori squad (no chance of an invite to South Africa) had visited in 1926-7, as had the 'Waratahs' of NSW – effectively Australia – in 1927-8.

Some – sadly, fairly meaningless – Olympic rugby took place in 1920 at Antwerp and 1924 in Paris, the winners being the USA, beating France on both occasions in the 'finals' but only having to play three games in total to do so. Post WW1, France played in the Five Nations Championship with the Home Countries until concerns over suspected professionalism saw them 'exiled' after 1931.

The old pattern had returned in 1920-1 and in the '20s in particular, it was England and Scotland, often stiffened by talent from the Dominions at university, medical school and business who stood out. The RFU and other IRB countries were less inclined to adopt ideas, law changes and bids for representation from the South, though, despite the far from strong showing of a poorly prepared 'Lions' outfit in S Africa in 1924.

Scotland built their impressive new ground at Murrayfield and Ireland battled through their contemporary batch of troubles and partition to remain and grow as a significant force united in rugby, playing at both Dublin and

USA warm up at Devonport, 1924

Olympic Final USA v France, 1924

Olympic Rugby Programme

1924 Memorabilia

Belfast. Whether at Cardiff or Swansea, though, it was Wales, much more the home of the working-class game, which struggled most in those years.

Jobs and income fell as post-war slump and General Strike were followed by world depression, as the 1929 Wall St Crash in the USA chop-tackled the planet's leading economy and saw bad ball rapidly passed backwards to Europe and beyond, fuelling a mass Welsh exodus to the car plants of Coventry,

Lions SA Souvenir, 1924

the factories of Slough, the staffrooms of England or, for the suitably talented, the rugby league fields of Wigan, St Helens, Rochdale and the like.

It also fuelled the rise to power of the Nazis in a Germany which was to throw off the bonds of Versailles and regain its natural strength under a vengeful Hitler: and meanwhile, ironically, to play some rugby amongst the few worthy opponents of 'banished' France in the 1930s. Mussolini's Fascist Italy, meanwhile, used rugby and images of it as a propaganda tool and exemplar of unity and determination.

When knocked back by the navel-gazing IRB, Italy also helped France found FIRA, 'European' rugby's governing body, but she and her potential and real allies in the 1930s

Italian Rugby Card, 1930s

Italian Fascist Poster, 1930s

also got a cartoonist backlash, in at least one case employing a rugby metaphor.

Meanwhile the rise of rugby in the grammar schools of Wales, a trend already enjoyed by the more prosperous middle classes of England, with consequent growth of their club game, was to help the Welsh national XV regain some performance and pride, finally beating their Twickenham bogey in 1933 and – fittingly, with Wilf Wooller to the

Anti-Fascist Cartoon , 1930s

fore – taking another giant stride with the further defeat of the All Blacks of 1935-6.

England, with the aid of Russian prince Alex Obolensky's immortal myth-making try-scoring, many decades before Grannygate, Faletau, the Vunipolas and residency rules – also beat New Zealand. Obo was to die in his training aircraft, preparing to fight for his adopted land, in 1940.

Meanwhile the round of Club, County, Barbarian and Oxbridge rugby, often very well-attended, continued. The British Lions, still travelling by sea, still wearing blue jerseys, still unable to win a series in NZ in 1930 or S Africa

1935-6 All Blacks Souvenir

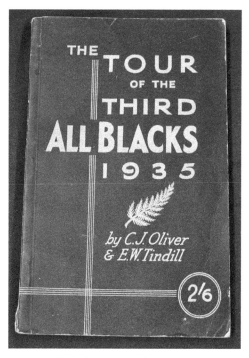

1935-6 All Blacks Tour Book

London Transport Poster, England
v NZ, 1936

Prince Obolensky, Oxford
University, mid 1930s

(still picking only white players) in 1938, kept up links with those juggernauts, between whom the Boks generally had the 30s upper hand.

Then at last, in 1939, it was time for Australia, the Wallabies, to return to the shores of what many still saw as the Mother Country. Sadly the invitation was as well timed as the worst of hospital passes. International tensions had risen in the late 30s, with Germany's flouting of the Versailles terms and her moves into Austria and Czechoslovakia, Italy's expansionist moves in Africa, the Spanish Civil War, for which more than one Welsh rugby man volunteered, and Japan's aggression in the Pacific.

Appeasement in Europe gave an impression of bringing breathing – and recruitment – space after 1938. Rugby proceeded as normal, with a three way tie in the Championship, Scotland the unlucky wooden-spooners. France had been promised a provisional return to the fold for 1940. Naturally, impartiality prevents us pointing out that under today's rules Wales would have been sole champions!

England's 9-6 Calcutta Cup win in Scotland on 18th March was to

Poster for Catalonia's first international, 5-5 v.
Italy, 1934

*Cigarette card depictions of 11 British Lions: First row - B E Nicholson,
C W Boyle, R Leyland; Second row - S Walker (Capt), H Tanner, J L Giles;
Third row - W G Howard, S Couchman, A H G Purchas; Fourth row -
R Alexander (died in WW2), P L Duff*

Radio Times previews: Rugby in March, War in September

Scotland v England Programme, 1939

prove the last international game before the Second World War. Although seven would return to international rugby after it, six players who took part in the game, four of them airmen, would lose their lives on active service.

Both fullbacks were to fall, Scotland's George Roberts as a Japanese PoW in 1943 and England's Ernest Parsons from NZ, whose only test was that Murrayfield clash. He was a bomber pilot who won the DFC but was to die over Italy in 1940, just one day before England prop and airman Derek Teden.

From the back rows, Scotland's Donald Mackenzie, RAF, and England's Robert Marshall, Navy, DSC and bar, were to perish in 1940 and 1945 respectively, while Scotland scrum-half Tommy Dorward was to prove another RAF fatality in 1941.

For as September 1939 dawned, Germany had invaded Poland and appeasement was at an end. After a long sea voyage (with some training), the Australian tourists under skipper 'Vay' Wilson arrived in Penzance on September 2nd, due to play 28 matches in ten months: the next day, war was

Skipper 'Vay' Wilson　　　　　　　　　*Ill-fated 1939 Wallabies train at sea*

declared. After three weeks of filling sandbags and a royal reception, these unluckiest of tourists were back at sea for a six-week voyage home, dodging German U-boats on the way.

2
1939

June 1 to December 31
   There were no international matches played in the UK during this period: and in fact there were no 'full' international matches until early 1947.

   That Australian touring team, then, sadly but inevitably found that all their matches were cancelled, and nine of the party never got to play Test rugby. They returned home, playing en route one match again st Bombay Gymkhana Club, in which all the 'new' players were used.

Australia's 'non-playing' tourists, 1939

The Wallabies' tour squad was –
   Backs: M. Clifford, R. Rankin, D. J. Carrick, L. H. Smith, P. K. Collins, V. Richards, C. Ramalli, E. de C. Gibbons (vice-captain), B. J. Porter, J. D. Kelaher (all NSW); L. S. Lewis, W. P. J. Ide, V. M. Nicholson (all Queensland); M. G. Carpenter (Victoria).
   Forwards: A. W. M. Barr (Victoria); W. M. McLean, V. W. Wilson (captain), B. D. Oxlade, C. I. A. Monti, J. C. McDonald (all Queensland); J. H. Malone, A. J. Hodgson, J. F. Turnbull, K. M. Ramsay, B. B. Oxenham, K. S. Windon, A. H. Stone (all NSW); G. A. Pearson, S. Y. Bisset (both Victoria).

   Pearson and Stone were in the tour party, though some lists omitted them. The manager of the team was Dr. Wally F. Matthews, the Mayor of Orange, who had been manager of the A.I.F team of 1919 and also of the Wallabies in South Africa in 1933-34. The Victorian members of the team had boarded the 'Mooltan' in Melbourne, and the secretary of the

NSW RU, Joseph Noseda, who acted as team secretary, had joined up in Adelaide.

Their captain was Vayro William Wilson (5 tests 1937-1938), from Queensland. He was born at Gympie, 18/1/1912 and died in Perth (Australia), 2/4/1962, at 50. Reports suggest he went back to Australia, then returned and he was certainly in Britain in December 1939, as he was selected to play for the Barbarians against Cardiff in a game called off due to bad weather. He later joined Nottingham University and also played for Rosslyn Park. In 1941, as a Sub-Lieutenant in the RNVR, he was awarded the DSC.

Amongst his team, 'Nicky' Barr, born in Wellington (NZ), became a fighter pilot who on one day alone, flew six operational missions. He was shot down on 26/6/1942, made a Prisoner of War, but escaped and became a resistance fighter, later being a wing-commander in the RAAF. He was awarded the MC, DFC and bar and later the OBE and lived until he was 90.

Vauxhall Nicholson was taken Prisoner in Malaya while serving with the Eighth Division. 'Steak' Malone came through the war with the RAAF, but died in a motorcycle accident in 1947 while escorting trucks.

Ide and Ramalli

Winston 'Blow' Ide, the son of a Japanese-born printer who was interned in Australia, joined the 2nd Field Regiment of the Eighth Division and was taken prisoner at Singapore, working for three years on the Burma-Siam railway. In 1944 he was being shipped to the Japanese coal mines on the 'Raduyo May' when it was torpedoed by an American submarine. He refused to join an overcrowded raft and drowned.

Cecil Ramalli (his real name was Ali Ram), a lance-corporal in the Signaller's Eighth Division, Australia's first Aboriginal and Asian Wallaby was also captured in Malaya, sent to Changi Camp and then to help build the Burma-Siam Railway. He was working in the Nagasaki mine when the atomic bomb was dropped above him and when he came to the surface the city had virtually vanished.

Stan Bisset (and his brother Hal) went from fighting in the Middle East to Papua New Guinea with the 2/14 Battalion. Stan was the battalion's intelligence officer and his brother was a platoon commander who was killed by machine-gun fire. Stan was awarded the Military Cross for valour

Stan Bisset

Bill McLean

and leadership, and later gained the Order of Australia Medal. He died at the age of 98 and is the subject of a recent admiring biography, *'Kokoda Warrior'* by Andrew James.

Mick Clifford was in the RAAF and was killed just off New South Wales in a 1942 training flight.

Kenelm ('Mac') Ramsay was taken Prisoner near Rabaul and while on a Japanese prison ship he was killed by a torpedo from an American submarine off Luzon in the Phillipines in 1942. Len Smith survived the war, though he saw action with the AIF in Palestine, Egypt and Syria before switching to RL where he gained two caps for Australia.

Ron Rankin joined the Royal Air Force in Britain and won an England Services cap. He gained the DFC and bar as well as the Croix de Guerre, having taken part in a raid on St Nazaire.

Bill McLean became a commando who, fittingly, survived to return to Britain to skipper the next Australian tourists of 1947-48.

Back in 1939, rugby was soon suspended, amid real early fears of bombing and invasion. (It was two years later that I was born and Phil Atkinson a further decade on. My early days were often spent in an Anderson shelter at the back of the house, which had the railings taken and melted down for the war effort. The house had all its windows blown in by a bomb landing 75 yards away which flattened several houses and killed some of our neighbours, plus hundreds in a shelter at the end of the street, including many servicemen on their way from Cardiff Docks towards the town itself).

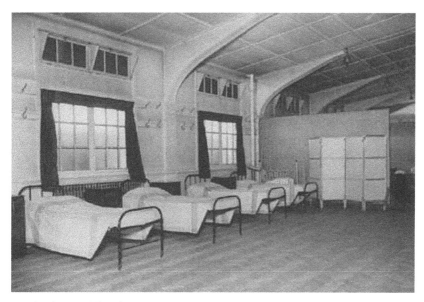

Twickenham, Civil Defence Unit

Twickenham Stadium had been quickly requisitioned for official war use. In the event of a chemical attack on London the Stadium was to have special responsibilities as a decontamination centre. In the West Stand the Civil Defence Unit took over the dressing rooms and restaurants, elsewhere there were coal and allotments. No matches were played there for several years, while many pre-war players were to be killed or wounded in the bigger conflicts which loomed further afield.

However there was to be some rugby played in the UK during the war: in particular, by schools, some clubs, and more officially in the series of Red Cross, then Services, and finally 1945-6 Victory 'Internationals', uncapped by most countries. France, however, did award some full caps at the time, while almost 70 years later Wales were to award some of its so-called 'President's Caps' for the 'Victory' games. What exactly they were supposed to mean, though, is perhaps best known to the Welsh Rugby Union.

The Red Cross Match, 1939

As the 'phoney war' – before France was invaded – dragged on (dubbed by the Germans the 'sitzkrieg' or sitting down war, as opposed to the 'blitzkrieg' or lightning war to come), the biggest game by far of late 1939 was staged near London.

December 16th 1939 – THE RED CROSS MATCH:
ENGLAND/WALES 17 SCOTLAND/IRELAND 3 (at Richmond Athletic Ground).

England/Wales XV, 1939

England/Wales – *Vivian G. J. Jenkins (W); *E. Jim Unwin, *Peter Cranmer (both E), *E. Claude Davey (W), *Prince Alexander S. Obolensky; *Gus A. Walker (capt), *Jack Ellis; *Robin E. Prescott (all E), *+W. ('Bunner') Travers, *W.E.N. ('Wendy') Davis (both W), Stanley R. Couchman (Old Cranleighans/GB), *T. Fred Huskisson, *Dudley T. Kemp, *Derek E. Teden, *John K.Watkins (all E).
   Tries: Teden, Obolensky, Unwin, Cranmer. Con/Pen: Jenkins.
Scotland/Ireland – *W.N. (Bill) Penman (S); *Maurice J. Daly (I), *+W.C.W. ('Copey') Murdoch (S), *Harry R. McKibbin, *C. Vesey Boyle (both I); *Rab B. Bruce-Lockhart, *William R.C. Brydon (both S); *John Megaw, *Charles Teehan (both I), *+Ralph W.F. Sampson (S), *R. Blair Mayne (I), *George B. Horsburgh (S), Archie W.B. Buchanan (Army/London Scottish), *H.J. Mike Sayers (I, capt), *P. Laurie Duff (S).
   Try: Sampson.
   Referee: Cyril H.Gadney (Leicester).

Scotland/Ireland XV, 1939

Scotland centre *Duncan J. Macrae was forced to withdraw after selection and 'Copey' Murdoch came in. Only Stanley Couchman, a GB tourist to the Argentine, and Archibald W.B. Buchanan were uncapped. Ireland forward Mike Sayers brought the other 29 players together and the gate receipts went to the Red Cross.

On a bitterly cold day the teams were introduced to General Sir Walter Kirke, Commander-in-Chief of the Home Forces. Richmond's highest crowd for years watched the game.

Both Sayers and Viv Jenkins missed with penalty efforts, but when the latter's kick was fumbled it was Jack Ellis who gathered to send Derek Teden over for the first score. Jenkins missed the conversion but soon placed a penalty.

Harry McKibbin and Sayers failed with further penalties and at the interval England/Wales led by 6-0. Soon after the restart Prince Alex Obolensky scored a try that Jenkins converted. Scotland/Ireland replied with Ralph Sampson scoring a try from a forward rush and then both Jenkins and Bill Penman missed further penalty shots.

It was England/Wales who finished strongest, as Gus Walker kicked ahead for Jim Unwin to score before the final try was added by Peter Cranmer in the follow-up to his own kick. Neither try was converted.

Duncan Macrae

Obolensky: Uniform (and boots!)

Duncan Macrae was awarded a Military Cross fighting with the 51st Highland Division, but was captured and made a Prisoner of War in June 1940, then served as a Medical Officer at Stalag VIII-B, Lamsdorf, one of so many prison camps where makeshift rugby was played. He later became a doctor in Scotland and died in 2007, aged 92 having won 9 caps (1937-39) and being a GB tourist to South Africa in 1938.

Obolensky was to die in that 1940 plane crash and Teden, Penman and Sayers were all killed in action. As we shall see, Walker lost an arm in the war and Brydon spent five years as a prisoner of war of the Germans.

Other late 1939 matches of note included:

Sep 6 – NZ Maoris 4 Fiji 14 (at Rugby Park, Hamilton). The Maoris included the All Black forward Everard Jackson, whose father was the controversial 'Frederick Jackson' (probably Welshman Ivor Gape), who had played for Leicester, Cornwall and the 1908 Anglo-Welsh (GB) team.

Oct 18 – Army 9 Navy 3 (at Portsmouth).

Army – Tries: Bond, Darewski, Robinson.   Navy – Try: H. C. Lyddon (later knighted).

Nov 1 – Wilfred Wooller's XV 57 (11 tries) RAF 3 (at Arms Park, Cardiff).

Nov 18 – Oxford University 3 R. V. Stanley's XV 8.

Oxford – Try: Gerry A. Hollis. Stanley's XV – Tries: Horsburgh, Obolensky. Con: Sayers.

George Brown Horsburgh discarded his kilt just prior to the kick-off to don his shorts and play in an almost-fully international side. He played 9 times for Scotland (1937-39) and for London Scottish, Surrey and the Barbarians. In 1940 he turned out for the British Army against the French Army but soon after was reported as 'missing'. However, he was found alive and eventually died in London 10/3/1986, having been born in Stirling 20/7/1910. He was a tailor and a company director.

Nov 18 – Munster 8 Leinster 3 (at Lansdowne Road, Dublin).

Nov 29 – Cambridge University awaited the arrival of St Bart's Hospital, but the latter did not turn up.

Dec 2 – Cardiff's first match of the season. They beat Neath 8-0, but Cardiff's international prop ('Wendy') Davis and Neath's hooker Denver Evans were ordered off following 'a dispute' after only 10 minutes of play. Glamorgan cricketers Wilf Wooller and Willie E. Jones were on opposing sides.

Dec 6 – Cambridge University 3 Oxford University 15 (at Grange Road, Cambridge).

Cambridge – Try: E.J.H. Williams (wing). Oxford – Tries: Luyt, Davies, R.M. Osborne. Con: Phillips. DG: Luyt. Referee: Bernard C. Gadney (Leicester).

Blues were not awarded, with Oxford playing in the Greyhounds' jerseys and Cambridge in those of the LX Club. For the first time since the 1870s, the match was played at the ground of one of the Universities.

Oxford included +E. Keith Scott (full back), Hollis, J.N. Matson from New Zealand University, H. Muller from Pretoria University and the Rondesboch centres R.E. Luyt and *Michael John Davies (Wales, 2 caps, 1939). Hollis, Luyt, Muller and P.C. Phillips were the only Old Blues.

Sir Richard Edmonds Luyt GCMG KCVO DCM was born in Cape Town 8/11/1915 and died 12/2/1994. He was the Colonial Governor of British Guiana in 1964-66, returning to South Africa in 1967 as principal and vice-chancellor of the University of Cape Town, until 1980. He was a Rhodes Scholar and during the war he fought against the Italians in Ethiopia and was awarded the DCM.

Cambridge included E. Ronnie Knapp, *John H. Steeds (later England) and the South African forwards C. L. Newton-Thompson, D. Barnes and M. G. Webber (later a Sub-Lieut. on the 'Prince of Wales' when it was sunk), as well as centre P. G. Henwood (also later a Sub-Lieut.).

Chris Newton-Thompson had taken over as captain when wing *John Gordon Scott Forrest (Scotland, 3 caps, 1938) left for military duties in the Navy. Forrest was killed in action on 14/9/1942 at the age of 25. Steeds and Newton-Thompson were the only Old Blues.

Dec 30 – England Schools v Scotland Schools (at Richmond) was cancelled due to bad weather, but England had included Kenneth A. N. Spray of Oundle School (and later Newport and Cambridge University) at centre; +Philip Brian Cecil Moore (later Lord Moore) from Cheltenham College at full back (though he won an England cap in 1951 from the back-row!); +Graham Alexander Wilson in the second row from Oundle School (Scotland, 3 caps, 1949) and +Geoffrey Robert D'Aubrey Hosking of Cheltenham College in the back row (England, 5 caps, 1949-1950).

Scotland had included wing T. G. H.Jackson of Cheltenham School (Scotland, 12 caps, 1947-1949); centre E. C. K. Douglas of Fettes School, later a Services international, and hooker J. A. R. Macphail of Edinburgh Academy (Scotland, 2 caps,1949-51), who also played for the Barbarians and died at Pitlochry 10/6/2004, aged 80.

John Alexander Rose Macphail was born in Singapore 14/10/1923 and went to South Africa for his early education. The son of a stockbroker, he moved to Edinburgh in 1932 and was educated at Edinburgh Academy where he shot for the school at Bisley. During the War he served with the RAF, mainly in the Aden Communication Flight. He captained the school XV 1940-41 and Edinburgh 'Accies' in 1948-49.

After qualifying as a chartered accountant, he entered the whisky industry in 1949 and he became a director of Arthur Bell & Sons, Perth. He left in 1962 to become an executive director (then chairman) of Robertson & Baxter and Highland Distilleries, held the chairmanships of North British Distillery, the Clyde Bonding Co and The Robertson Trust and was one of the founder directors of the Scotch Whisky Heritage Centre in Edinburgh, serving as its first chairman from 1987-94.

He became a member of the Council of the Scotch Whisky Association in 1964 and became chairman in 1983, also being made the first grandmaster of the Keepers of the Quaich (1988-89). His Scholarship helps fund two young Scotland players each season.

Dec 30 – Cardiff v Barbarians (at Cardiff Arms Park) was also cancelled just before the kick-off due to that weather. The side had been due to be:

Barbarians – *W.M. Penman (S); *D.G. Cobden (NZ), *Louis Babrow (SA), *E.C. Davey (W), *E.J. Unwin; *+T.A. Kemp (both E), *+H. Tanner (W); *R.E. Prescott (E), *+W. Travers, *M.E. Morgan (both W), C.L. Newton-Thompson (Cambridge University), *H. F. Wheatley (E), *H. J.M. Sayers (I), *G.B. Horsburgh (S), *E.E. Dunlop (Aust).

Late changes saw Cobden, Prescott and Newton-Thompson replace *Prince A.S. Obolensky, *D.E. Teden (both E) and that ill-fated Australian 'skipper', *V.W. Wilson.

'Jock' Wemyss' book on the Barbarians claimed that *+W. B. (Bill) Young (S), *Arthur M. Rees (W) and G.F. Smith (Blackheath) were due to play and not Horsburgh, Wheatley and Newton-Thompson.

Australian international Ernest Edward Dunlop (2 caps, 1932-34), of St Mary's Hospital, later became a Prisoner of War in Japan and was knighted in 1967. Known as 'Weary' due to Dunlop – 'tired'. Showed great leadership in captivity and in his subsequent medical career.

Brass relief of E E Dunlop

Pilot/Officer Donald Gordon Cobden (RAF), the NZ international wing, died on his 26th birthday, 11/8/1940, when his plane was shot down; his body was washed ashore at Ostend.

Both Penman and Sayers were killed in action in 1943. Derek Teden had met the same fate in 1940 and Obolensky's death we have recorded.

Amongst further items of rugby interest from the year:

On June 22 the Welsh Rugby Union announced profits of £332 with assets placed at £49,116. Other assets went north, though, in August, W.T.H. 'Willie' Davies moving from Swansea to Bradford Northern. Lee Griffiths was his replacement at Swansea, partnering Haydn Tanner, the cousin of Davies.

On Sept 11th, 14th and 24th respectively, the Scottish, English and Welsh Unions had cancelled all official fixtures due to the war., while Murrayfield and Blackheath closed their grounds. Some clubs, though, still hoped to continue with much-amended fixture lists. The latter included Harlequins, Wasps, Rosslyn Park, Guy's Hospital and King's College Hospital.

Derek Teden, 1939

Oblolensky Memorial, Ipswich

On Sept 30th some rugby had begun and results included: Rosslyn Park 11 Harlequins 5 at Old Deer Park; Guy's Hospital 30 Catford Bridge 9; and Bridgend 18 RAF XV 3, though on Oct 4th Leicester decided not to play any games.

Most of the rugby played was between school or senior sides in the London area, while matches also began with and between Services sides. Rosslyn Park were prominent and energetic in organisation, encouragement and administration, though quite often the players selected withdrew at the last moment due to the emergency nature of the times.

Still available, several clergymen were also playing rugby, notably Rev H.C.C. Bowen in the pack for Llanelli (then still spelt as Llanelly) and the Rev H.M. Hughes at centre for Gloucester.

Wasps included Harry M. Bowcott, the 1930 GB tourist to NZ and Australia and pre-war Wales cap, at fly half against Guy's Hospital and Cheltenham College included three future stars in (P.B.C.) Moore (at full back and captain), (T.G.H.) Jackson (wing) and (G.R.) D'A. Hosking (forward).

Rugby League and some soccer continued, though the touring New Zealand RL team returned home after two matches. Some Welsh clubs attempted to play games within their own area, while London Irish and London Welsh combined to play as the 'Shamleeks', for whom young Welsh fly half Glyn Davies and the lively Irish forward J.C. Daly turned out in, apparently, scarlet and emerald quartered jerseys.

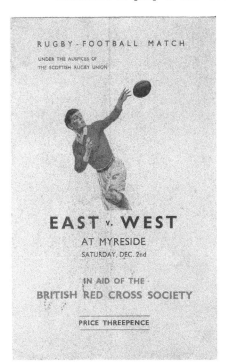

East v West, Edinburgh, 1939

On November 13th it was announced that, as in the previous War, Rugby League players were to be allowed to play in Rugby Union games, even though, as was ever their wont, the SRU disagreed. Within their own ranks, League's two matches with the NZ tourists before they returned home were: Sept 2nd – St Helen's 3 NZ 19; Sept 9th – Dewsbury 10 NZ 22. There was major League action just before the festive season, though, when on Dec 23rd at the vast stadium at Odsal, Bradford, England went down 16-3 to Wales.

The Red Cross had clearly decided not to reinvent the wheel – or programme cover – with that for the big Richmond clash very similar to (but twice the price of) the effort north of the border a fortnight earlier. That brought together East & West in Edinburgh (with SRU approval required, it goes without saying).

National Service Poster, 1939

The threat of dire days to come could rarely be ignored, though. As well as the mobilisation of military reservists, by early 1939 it is estimated that about half a million people also volunteered to join the ARP, the Territorial Army (TA) and the RAF Volunteer Reserve. But volunteers were not enough.

By April 1939 all British men aged 20 and 21 who were fit and able were required to take six months' military training: there'd be a lot of rugby and other sportsmen there. Even so, when war broke out the British Army could muster only 897,000 men, compared to France's five million.

The National Service Act made all able men between the ages of 18 and 41 liable for conscription; single men would be called to war before married men. Men aged 20 to 23 were registered in October 1939, with 40-year-olds eventually doing so in June 1941, and still older later in the war.

Wilf Wooller, star centre for Cambridge, Cardiff and Wales at rugby and later Glamorgan cricket legend, was typical in joining his local anti-aircraft battery on the outbreak and mixing periods of boredom with high jinks and time off for good quality fundraising rugby before the 'real stuff' began. 'The Skipper' and fellow Cardiff stalwart Les Spence (seated second left) were to experience seriously hard PoW times at Japanese hands before 1945.

Wooller and Military XV, Maindy Barrcks, Cardiff, 1939

By the end of 1939 more than 1.5 million men had been conscripted to join the British armed forces. Of those, just over 1.1 million went to the British Army and the rest were split between the Royal Navy and the RAF: quite a few were to play rugby for one or other of those services in the next five or six years.

3
1940

If the First World War had been (horribly optimistically) billed as being over by Christmas, what was to-date the largely European conflict of 1939 passed into 1940 with no great fanfare or change of mood. Britain and France somewhat belatedly rearmed, continued to recruit and were grateful for the pledges of assistance from 'empire' reminiscent of the 1914-18 conflict.

Australia, Canada, India, NZ and S Africa had rapidly declared war on Germany. What was missing so far, though, was real action on any western front, as Hitler's speedy success in the east with the temporary cooperation of Stalin's Soviet Union allowed no effective response from these parts.

The early air-raid false alarms and the gas-mask imperatives faded somewhat as people wondered what form this war would take 'when and if', and there was as yet no front line – of trenches or anything else – for which to cross the Channel in 1914 fashion.

Trenches were the last thing Hitler wanted. His own experience in WW1 had taught him that the answer to avoiding deadlock (as in rugby!) was speed and surprise, and that had worked in Poland. The other things which had changed were mechanical, and hugely aided his strategy: improved transport, tanks, weaponry and, above all, aircraft capable of bombing.

Before western Europe was to face that version of lightning strike, though, Mr. Chamberlain continued to lead His Majesty George VI's British government: and the Red Cross, knowing how much they were likely to be called upon ere long, redoubled their fundraising with the aid of, amongst many others, the rugby fraternity.

RED CROSS INTERNATIONALS:

In the spring Wales and England met in two Red Cross international matches, with many players capped pre-war taking part, along with several who had been playing Rugby League.

Wales v England, 1940

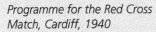

Programme for the Red Cross Match, Cardiff, 1940

March 9 – WALES 9 ENGLAND 18 (at Cardiff Arms Park) (42,000).

Twenty of the 30 players had won pre-war caps and five of them, plus Wilf Evans, went on to gain full caps after the war had ended. Wales full back Howard Davies and the entire front row played well, but England came from 3-6 down early in the second-half to finish with four tries and with skipper Tommy Kemp ruling the game at fly half.

Wales, playing with letters rather than numbers on their jerseys, were behind to a Kemp try before Davies levelled with a 45-yard penalty and in the second half, Ike Owens kicked ahead and gained a try. However, England regained the lead with a try by Jim Unwin that was started by Jack Heaton, who also converted.

Then, centre Francis Edwards beat his namesake Horace Edwards and Heaton's place-kick made it 13-6. Davies landed another penalty but Prince Alexander Obolensky's swift run saw Derek Teden, Rex Willsher and Kemp handle for the latter's second try that was goaled again by Heaton.

Wales – *+C. Howard Davies (Swansea); *Chris M. Matthews (Bridgend), *Wilfred Wooller (Cardiff, capt), Horace O. Edwards (Neath), E. Ronnie Knapp (Cambridge University); Willie E. Jones (Neath), *+Haydn Tanner (Swansea); *W.E.N. ('Wendy') Davis (Cardiff), *+ W. ('Bunner') Travers (Newport), +Wilf J. Evans (Pontypool), *Leslie Davies (Swansea), *E. Ron Price (Weston), Fred E. Dorning (Cross Keys), *+Leslie Manfield (Cardiff), Ike A. Owens (Maesteg/Leeds RL).

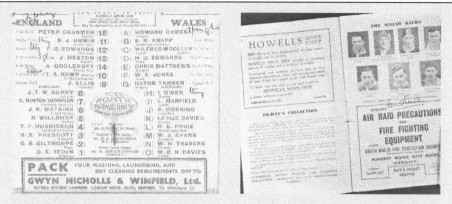

Team line-ups   Autographed programme inner

Touch-Judge: Robert Arthur Cornish (Cardiff, Wales, 10 caps, 1923-26).
Try: Owens. Pens: (CH) Davies 2.

England – *Peter Cranmer (Moseley); *E. Jim Unwin (Rosslyn Park), *+Jack Heaton (Waterloo), Francis G. Edwards (Gloucester), *Prince Alexander Obolensky (Rosslyn Park); *+Tommy A. Kemp (St Mary's Hosp, capt), *Jack Ellis (Wakefield); *Derek E. Teden (Richmond), C. George Gilthorpe (Wasps), *Robin E. Prescott (Harlequins), Rex Willsher (Bedford), *T. Fred Huskisson (OMT's), C.L. Newton-Thompson (Cambridge University), *J. Tom W. Berry (Leicerster), *John K. Watkins (US Portsmouth).

Touch-Judge: Capt. H.A. Haigh-Smith.

Tries: Kemp 2, Edwards, Unwin. Cons: Heaton 3.

Referee: Ivor David (Neath).

The return match came just five weeks later, with a similar result.

April 13 – ENGLAND 17 WALES 3 (at Kingsholm, Gloucester) (18,000).

A fine day brought a packed ground that saw a splendid match with Wales making too many mistakes and the England pack proving too experienced with prop Derek Teden totally unstoppable. He had played in the back row for England/Wales just five months earlier and was splendid in either role, but tragically he was killed in action six months after this game.

Wales, who were again well served by their front row, led after 18 minutes when Haydn Tanner found hooker 'Bunner' Travers in support to crash over. Then, from a careless drop-out, hooker George Gilthorpe collected and passed to prop Robin Prescott, who dropped an unexpected

IN AID OF THE RED CROSS & THE SERVICE SPORTS EQUIPMENT FUNDS

ENGLAND (White)			WALES (Red)	
15 P. CRANMER	Headley	Full Backs	(1) HOWARD DAVIES	Swansea
14 R. H. GUEST	Liverpool University	Three-quarters	(3) CHRIS MATTHEWS	Wellington
13 J. HEATON	Waterloo	2 Centre 4 Centre	(2) JACK MATTHEWS	Bridgend
12 H. G. EDWARDS		3 Centre 5 Centre	(7) WILFRED WOOLLER (Capt)	Cardiff
11 E. J. UNWIN	Blackheath Cared	4 Wing 6 Wing	(8) H. O. EDWARDS	Neath
10 T. A. KEMP (Capt)	St Mary's Hospital	Half Backs Stand off Stand off	(6) ROGER WADE	Newport
9 J. ELLIS	Wakefield	Scrum Halves	(5) HAYDN TANNER	Swansea
8 J. T. W. BERRY	Leicester		(3) J. OWEN	Mumbles
7 C. NEWTON-THOMPSON	Cambridge Univ.		(11) L. MANFIELD	Cardiff
6 J. K. WATKINS	United Services	Forwards	(6) STANLEY WILLIAMS	Llanelly
5 R. WILLSHER	Bedford		(1) E. KENIFIC	Aberavon
4 J. T. HUSKISSON	Old Merchant Taylors		(4) Rev. H. C. BOWEN	Llanelly
3 R. E. PRESCOTT	Harlequins		(5) W. J. EVANS	Pontypool
2 C. O. GILTHORPE	Maseley		(10) W. H. TRAVERS	Newport
1 D. E. TEDEN	Richmond		(1) W. E. N. DAVIES	Cardiff

Team line-ups

goal for a 4-3 lead. Teden soon charged through for Jack Heaton to convert and after a touchdown by Wilf Wooller was disallowed, Heaton scored and converted before Tommy Kemp and Francis Edwards combined to send wing Jim Unwin in at the corner.

The teams had stood for two-minutes silence as England wing Prince Alexander Obolensky had died in a plane crash on March 29. 'Obo' had been selected for this clash and his name was in the programme: 'Dickie' Guest came in to replace him.

Programme for the Red Cross Match, Gloucester, 1940

Manfield, right, in Wales action at Gloucester, 1940

England – *Cranmer; *Unwin, *+Heaton, Edwards, *+R.H. ('Dickie) Guest (Waterloo/Liverpool University); *+Kemp (capt), *Ellis; *Teden, Gilthorpe, *Prescott, Willsher, *Huskisson, Newton-Thompson, *Berry, *Watkins.

Tries: Heaton, Unwin, Teden. Cons: Heaton 2. DG: Prescott.

Wales – *+(C.H.) Davies; *(C.M.) Matthews, *Wooller (capt), +Jack Matthews (Bridgend), (H.O.) Edwards; Roger N. Wade (Newport/St Mary's Hospital), *+Tanner; *(W.E.N.) Davis, *+Travers, +(W.J.) Evans, Edwin Kenifick (Aberavon), Rev H.C.C. Bowen (Llanelli), +Stanley Williams (Llanelli), *+Manfield, Owens.

Touch-Judge: (R.A.) Cornish.

Try: Travers.

Referee: Alan S. Bean (Sunderland).

Perhaps the experiences of one of the Wales players, back-rower Les Manfield, may be taken as fairly typical of many fit young men of the time. Manfield had met his wife-to-be Mary, but volunteered for the RAF in 1940, being posted to Uxbridge, then Cosford on a PTI course, along with soccer caps Les Jones and George Male.

He was then posted to St Athan, near Cardiff, where Rugby League star Alan Edwards and Union cap Arthur Rees were based, and all three played in a charity game at Richmond organised by Air Commodore Ira Jones, the Welsh WW1 flying ace profiled in our *Kings Cup 1919* book. Next came training as an Air Observer at St Andrews in Scotland, followed by Harwell, eventual promotion and action: of which, more later.

WALES

Christmas HOWARD DAVIES – Full back. Born Llanelli 25/12/1916. Died Llanelli 5/11/1987. Burry Port/Llanelli/Swansea/Army. 6 caps (1939-47). A Steelworker/Power Station worker. Corporal and Sapper in the Army.

CHRIStopher Mansel MATTHEWS – Wing. Born Newton Nottage, near Bridgend September 1911. Died Cardiff 5/12/1965, aged 54. Bridgend/ Porthcawl/Maesteg/Cardiff. 1 cap (1939). A Commission agent.

WILFred WOOLLER – Centre. Born Rhos-on-Sea 20/11/1912. Died Cardiff 10/3/1997. Llandudno County School/Rydal School/Cambridge University/ Army/Cardiff/Sale/London Welsh/Barbarians. 18 caps (1922-1939). 77th Heavy Anti-Aircraft Regiment and Prisoner of War in Java 1943. Glamorgan cricket captain and secretary. Executive for coal business/Insurance broker/ Journalist/TV commentator.

HORACE O. EDWARDS – Centre/wing. Born Porthcawl 17/5/1916. Died Stroud January 2003. Llandovery College/Wales Senior Schools/St Luke's College Exeter/Cardiff/Neath/Barbarians. Chosen v. Ireland 1937, but snow intervened. Policeman/RAF PTI/Schoolteacher in Crypt School, Gloucester for 31 years. He played cricket for Bridgend/Old Cryptians/Woodpeckers. Farmworker at Porthcawl in 1939.

Edward Ronald (RONNIE) KNAPP, CBE – Wing. Born Cardiff 10/5/1919. Died 21/12/2005. Cardiff High School/Wales Senior Schools/Rosslyn Park/Cambridge University (captain 1940-41)/Penarth/Cardiff/Leicester/ Northampton. Radar Officer in RNVR/USA naval research station, later a managing director of Timken (Europe). He was awarded the CBE in 1979.

William Edward (WILLIE) JONES – Fly half. Born Carmarthen 31/10/1916. Died Gloucester 25/7/1996. Llanelli/Swansea/Neath/Gloucester. Glamorgan Cricketer with 340 appearances (1937-58). Corporal in the RAF. Cricket coach at Dean Close School, Cheltenham.

HAYDN TANNER – Scrum half. Born Gowerton 9/1/1917. Died Leicester 5/6/2009. Gowerton Grammar School/Wales Senior Schools/University College Swansea/Swansea/Cardiff/Army/Barbarians/London Welsh/Bristol/Penclawdd/Welsh Guards/Crawshays/Gloucestershire/GB 1938 tour to South Africa (one test). 25 caps (1935-1949). Schoolmaster at Bristol Grammar School/Industrial Chemist/Purchasing Director/Journalist for the 'News of the World'. Officer-Cadet/Sgt/Lieut in the Royal Corps of Signals.

William Edward Norman ('WENDY') DAVIES – Prop. Born Birmingham 7/9/1913. Died Cirencester January 2003. Cardiff High School/King's Edward School Birmingham/Cardiff HSOB/Penarth/Cardiff/Barbarians/Public School Wanderers/Rosslyn Park/North Midlands/South-East Command. 3 caps (1939). He owned a tannery and also was a Journalist, who served as a Gunner and Captain in the Royal Artillery.

William ('BUNNER') TRAVERS – Hooker. Born Newport 2/12/1913. Died Newport 4/6/1998. Newport/Pill Harriers/Cardiff/Barbarians/GB to South Africa 1938 (2 tests)/Army/Monmouthshire. 12 caps (1937-1949). Cpl/Gunner/Sgt in the Monmouthshire Regiment.

WILFred John EVANS – Prop. Born Griffithstown 12/5/1914. Died Pontypool 17/11/1992. Pontnewydd/Abergavenny/Panteg/Pontypool/Monmouthshire. 1 cap (1947). Chief Inspector of Police.

LESLIE ('Bychan') DAVIES – 2nd Row. Born Swansea 13/7/1913. Died Swansea 4/9/1984. Danygraig School/Bonymaen/Swansea. 2 caps (1939). A wagon repairer.

Edwin RONald PRICE – 2nd Row. Born Trealaw 16/9/1915. Died Weston November 1997. Porth County School/Merchant Ventures College (Bristol)/Penygraig/Porth/Weston/RAF/Somerset. 2 caps (1939). Electrician. He had a leg amputated in 1949. Cpl and Air Craftsman in RAF, mainly in South Africa.

FREDerick Ernest DORNING – Back Row. Born 9/7/1916, birth registered in Newport. Died Monmouth 3rd quarter, 1997. Cross Keys. Police Constable who in 1939 was living in the Police Station, Market Street, Ebbw Vale. It is believed that he lost a hand during WW2, whilst serving in the Navy.

LESlie MANFIELD DFC – Back Row. Born Mountain Ash 10/11/1915. Died Aberdare Hospital 2/11/2006. Mountain Ash County School/Wales Under-16s/Wales Senior Schools/Mountain Ash/University College Cardiff/Carnegie College Leeds/UAU/Penarth/London Welsh/Neath/Bridgend/RAF/Combined Services/Otley/Cardiff/Barbarians/Yorkshire. 7 caps (1939-1948). Schoolteacher/Navigator, F/O/Sqdn-Ldr in the RAF. Awarded the DFC in 1943.

Isaac Andrew (IKE) OWENS – Back Row. Born Pontycymmer 7/11/1918. Died Porthcawl 15/10/1998. Blaengarw/Maesteg/Aberavon. RL for Leeds (124 apps, 40 tries, 3 goals)/Castleford (7 apps, 2 tries)/Huddersfield

(127 apps, 20 tries, 1949-52)/York (25 apps, 1 try, 4 goals in 1954)/Wales/GB. Sgt. Parachute Instructor in the RAF. He was awarded the Air Force Flying Medal whilst in action as a parachutist during the war and became a publican in York. He played in two Red Cross (1940) and three Services Internationals (1943-44).

Dr. JACK MATTHEWS, OBE – Centre. Born Bridgend 21/6/1920. Died Porthcawl 18/7/2012. Bridgend County School/Wales Senior Schools/ University College Cardiff/Bridgend/Cardiff/Barbarians/Combined Services/ Harlequins/Army/Neath/Newport/1950 GB to NZ (4 tests) and Australia (2 tests). 17 caps (1947-1951). Army (RAMC) in 1946. A doctor who was awarded the OBE in 1981.

ROGER N. WADE – Fly Half. Born Risca 6/5/1918. Died Sydney (Aust) 20/6/2000. Richmond/Newport (65 apps 1936-37 to 1950-51)/St Mary's Hospital. Doctor, who emigrated to Western Australia in 1959.

EDWIN KENIFICK – 2nd Row. Swansea/Llanelli/Aberavon. Played for West v East at Swansea 24/2/1940. He was relatively unknown and was usually called Kenefig or Kenefick. Born Port Talbot 10/8/1914. Lived with his parents (William and Elizabeth) and elder brother (Cedric, 1908-74) at 41, Newbridge Road in Port Talbot and worked as a council plasterer. He married Betty Jacobs (died 1985) in 1944 and he died in the 3rd quarter of 1980 aged 66.

Rev HOWARD Charles Campbell BOWEN – 2nd Row. Born Llandeilofach, Carmarthenshire 30/3/1913. Died Bristol, 2nd quarter, 1995. Llanelli/Army/ South-East Command. Chaplain's Dept., Royal Artillery. He was later a vicar in the Tenby area. He played in Llanelli's final pre-war match against Felinfoel in 1939 and was married to Christine Gedin in Bournemouth 1947.

STANley WILLIAMS – Back Row. Born Llanelli 4/11/1914. Died Llanelli 21/11/1967. Felinfoel/Llanelli. 6 caps (1947-1948). A Steelworker/Council worker.

ENGLAND:

PETER CRANMER – Full back (but normally a centre). Born Acocks Green, Birmingham 10/9/1914. Died Peacehaven, Sussex 29/5/1994. St Edward's, Oxford/Oxford University/Moseley/Richmond/North Midlands/Barbarians/ Army. 16 caps (1934-1938). Stockbroker/Journalist. Warwickshire cricket captain. Served in the Army in Burma and Egypt.

Ernest James (JIM) UNWIN – Wing. Born Birdbrook 18/9/1912. Died Perth 23/11/2003. Haileybury & ISC/RMC Sandhurst/Army/Rosslyn Park/ Barbarians/GB to Argentine 1936 and to South Africa 1938 (2 tests). 4 caps (1937-38). Corn Merchant. Major and Lieut-Colonel in Middlesex Regiment. Cricket for Suffolk and Essex.

John (JACK) HEATON, JP – Centre. Born St Helen's 30/8/1912. Died Dwyfor, Pwllheli 25/10/1998. Cowley School, St Helen's/Liverpool University/ Notts/Waterloo/Lancashire/Barbarians. 9 caps (1935-1947). An architect.

FRANCIS G. EDWARDS – Centre. Born Dursley 1st quarter 1914. Wycliffe College/Gloucester/Gloucestershire/Birkenhead Park/Leicester/ Leicestershire/Barbarians. Played for GB against the Army in 1940.

Prince Alexander Sergeevich ('OBO') OBOLENSKY – Wing. Born St Petersburg, Russia 17/2/1916. Died Martlesham, Norfolk, 29/3/1940. Derby Prep School/Trent College/Oxford University/Rosslyn Park/Notts, Lincs and Derby/Chesterfield/Barbarians/Midland Counties/RAF/GB to Argentine 1936. 4 caps (1936). F/O in the RAF when died in a training accident.

Thomas (TOMMY) Arthur KEMP – Fly half. Born Bolton 12/8/1915. Died Hillingdon 26/11/2004. Denstone College/Cambridge University/St Mary's Hospital/Richmond/Manchester/Army/Barbarians/London Counties/ Middlesex/Lancashire. 5 caps (1937-48). An Honorary Consultant and Physician to the Army. Lieut-Colonel in the RAMC. RFU President (1971-72).

John (JACK) ELLIS – Scrum half. Born Rothwell Haigh, Leeds 28/10/1912. Died Northampton 27/12/2007. 1 cap (1939). Wakefield/Yorkshire/Army/ Barbarians/Rosslyn Park. Schoolmaster at Fettes College/Rossall/Scarborough. Major/Captain in the RAC.

DEREK Edmund TEDEN – Prop. Born Highgate 19/7/1916. Killed in action at the Fresian Islands 15/10/1940. Taunton School/Old Tauntonians/ Middlesex/Richmond/RAF/Barbarians. 3 caps (1939). P/O in the RAF.

Clarence GEORGE GILTHORPE – Hooker. Born 17/6/1910. Died Newcastle 5/10/1974. Chesterfield School/Brasenose College, Oxford University (1946-47)/Wasps/Coventry/Bedford/Notts, Lincs and Derby/RAF/Northern. Flt Lieut/Sqdn-Ldr/Wing-Cmdr in the RAF.

Robert Edward (ROBIN) PRESCOTT – Prop. Born Paddington 5/4/1913. Died Dartmouth 18/5/1975. Wells House Prep school/Marlborough College/ Oxford University/Harlequins/Army/Combined Services/Guildford/Middlesex/ Barbarians/Rosslyn Park/GB to Argentine 1936. 6 caps (1937-1939). Solicitor/ RFU secretary. Captain in the Army.

REX WILLSHER – 2nd Row. Born Northill, Biggleswade, Bedfordshire 9/3/1910. Died Ipswich 3rd quarter 1998. Bedford Modern School/Bedford/ Bedfordshire/Rosslyn Park. Chairman of Suffolk District Council. Also played for Sir Robert Webber's XV. Married, but divorced in 1949.

Thomas FREDerick HUSKISSON, MC, MBE – 2nd Row. Born Mortlake 1/7/1914. Died Stroud 25/4/2004. Merchant Taylors School/Old Merchant Taylors/Barbarians/London Counties/Eastern Counties/Lancashire/Army/ GB to Argentine 1936. 8 caps (1937-39). A meat company director. Captain, then Commanding Officer in 1st ATC Duke of Wellington's Regiment. He was awarded the MBE in 1947. Military Cross and bar in 1944.

Joseph Thomas (TOM) Wade BERRY – Back Row. Born Slawston, Leics 17/7/1907. Died Market Harborough 1/7/1993. Eastbourne College/Market Harborough/Leicester/Barbarians/Leicestershire/Army. 3 caps (1939). Farmer. Captain in the Army. RFU President (1968-1969).

CHRIStopher Lawton NEWTON-THOMPSON, MC – Back Row. Born Kensington 14/2/1919. Died Cape Town, South Africa 29/1/2003. Bishop's College, Cape Town/Cambridge University/Army. Lieut, then Major and Tank-Cmdr in the Duke of Wellington's Regiment, then the 145th Regiment Royal Armoured Corps. Severely wounded in Italy (1945). A politician in South Africa and an anti-apartheid campaigner. He was awarded the MC in 1945.

JOHN Kingdon WATKINS, OBE – Back Row. Born Taunton 24/2/1913. Died Marylebone 13/5/1970. Epsom College/Devonport Services/United Services, Portsmouth/Royal Navy/Combined Services/Barbarians. 3 caps (1939). A Company Director and a Rear Admiral in the Navy. He was awarded the OBE in 1945.

Richard Heaton ('DICKIE') GUEST – Wing. Born Prescot 12/3/1918. Cowley School, St Helen's/Waterloo/Liverpool University/Lancashire/UAU/Army/Barbarians. 13 caps – pre and post-war (1939-1949). Captain in the 128th Field Defence Regiment of the Royal Artillery. Played for Rhine Army XV and BAOR Combined Services in Germany 1946. He was believed to be possibly still alive in Australia in 2017, but sources now appear to confirm his death in May 2012.

Other matches of note in 1940 included:

Jan 13 – Ulster 9 Leinster 11 (at Ravenhill, Belfast).

Jan 20 – East Midlands v Barbarians at Leicester, for the Army Recreation Equipment Fund, was cancelled due to frost. The Barbarians had selected an all-international XV, including Louis Babrow (South Africa) and D.G. Cobden (NZ).

Jan 27 – Combined Universities of Ireland 5 The Rest of Ireland 0 (at Lansdowne Road, Dublin).

Feb 3 – Leinster 32 Connaught 7 (at Lansdowne Road, Dublin).

Feb 10 – British Army 27 Empire 9 (at Richmond).

Late changes saw M.M. Walker and John Megaw replace George Roberts (Scotland) and Derek Teden for the Empire. Earlier, the Australian internationals V.W. Wilson (unwell) and 'Weary' Dunlop (posted abroad)

THE ARMY v. THE EMPIRE
A. Obolensky (Empire) with the ball in an attacking movement by The Empire which led to a try in the match against The Army at Richmond on Saturday. The match, in aid of the Army Recreational Equipment Fund, resulted in a victory for The Army by 27 points to nine.

Obolensky attacking for the Empire, 1940

had dropped out. Teden was killed on October 15 and Roberts died as a Prisoner of War in Japan in 1943. Don Mackenzie died on June 12 when his plane crashed, as did Prince Obolensky, on March 29, just 47 days after this match, while NZ wing Donald Cobden crashed in a plane and died on August 11.

Army – (V.G.J.) Jenkins; Unwin, Cranmer, Wooller, Guest; F. Jeffrey Reynolds (Old Cranleighans/England), Ellis; (W.E.N.) Davis, Travers, Prescott, Horsburgh, Mayne, (A.W.B.) Buchanan, Duff, Sayers (capt).

Tries: Guest, Wooller, Ellis, Sayers, Reynolds, Unwin. 3 Cons/Pen: Jenkins.

Empire – M.M. Walker (St Mary's Hospital); Obolensky, Louis Babrow (Guy's Hospital/Western Province/South Africa, capt), R.E. Luyt (Oxford University), (D.G.) Cobden (Canterbury, NZ); (G.A, later Sir Augustus) Walker, Tanner; (J, later Sir John) Megaw, H. Muller (Pretoria University/ Oxford University), (R.W.F.) Sampson, Couchman, Huskisson, Watkins, Donald K.A. Mackenzie (Edinburgh Wdrs/Scotland), Arthur M. Rees (London Welsh/Cambridge University/Wales).

Tries: Couchman, Cobden. Pen: (M.M.) Walker.

Referee – (C.H.) Gadney.

Ralph William Fraser ('Sammy') Sampson, a prop in that match, was born in Chile on the 25 or 26/9/1913 and died at Bishopston on 31/1/2003, aged 89. His father was involved with the railway systems of Chile and Peru and sent Ralph to Rossall School, where he skippered the soccer

Pte. R. W. SAMPSON (London Scottish).—Capped last year for Scotland as a hooker, but is just as good as a front-row forward. Thick-set and strong, he should be a good binder for Teehan.

SPITFIRE OFFENSIVE

Sampson 1939, his personalised Spitfire and later Memoirs

team, but only played rugby for the 2nd XV, as a wing. However, he played for London Scottish and won a cap as a hooker for Scotland against Wales in 1939. He had joined the London Scottish Regiment in 1937 and by 1939 was in the 6th Battalion of the Queen's Own Cameroon Highlanders. However, he switched to the RAF as a trainee pilot, joining the 602 (City of Glasgow) Squadron and was then Flight-Cmdr. of 131 (County of Kent) Squadron, before commanding the Free French Wing. He was awarded the DFC and the Croix de Guerre, flying 189 operations. He came back to rugby and skippered London Scottish, Middlesex, London Counties and the Barbarians, gaining another cap for Scotland against Wales in 1947. He received an OBE after commanding the West of Scotland wing of the Air Training Corps, then became Deputy Lieutenant of Renfrewshire. He was a director of print suppliers Ault and Wiborg, being married for 54 years and living in Bridge of Weir, Renfrewshire.

Feb 17 – Cardiff 16 Barbarians 8 (at Arms Park, Cardiff): In aid of the Army Recreational Equipment Fund.

Cardiff – Duncan Brown; R.C. Gillard, Howell Loveluck, Graham Hale, Howard Roblin; Wooller, W. Guy Morgan; (W.E.N.) Davis, Emrys Jones, G. C. M. Fuller, L.G.S ('Jumbo') Thomas, Stanley Bowes, Leslie M. Spence, (L) Manfield, J. Selby Davies.

Tries: Hale, Gillard. Cons: Wooller 2. Pens: Wooller, Brown.

Howard Roblin died in the war while Hale, Wooller and Spence were all POW's.

Barbarians – Jenkins; Unwin, Davey (capt.), Babrow, Cobden; Kemp, Tanner; A. Russell Taylor (Cross Keys/Wales/GB 1938 to South Africa),

Travers, Prescott, G.F. Smith (Blackheath), Huskisson, (A.M.) Rees, Horsbrough, Watkins.

Late changes saw Jenkins, Taylor, Watkins and Smith replace (G) Roberts, M. E. Morgan (Wales), Sayers and Mayne.

Tries: Kemp, Unwin. Con: Jenkins.

Referee: T. Harold Phillips (Aberdare).

Feb 24 – West Wales 11 East Wales 9 (at St Helen's, Swansea).

West Wales – (C.H.) Davies; (C) Matthews, (J) Matthews, (H.O.) Edwards, W. Leslie T. Williams (Llanelli/Navy, later Cardiff/Wales then Hunslet/Wales RL); (W.E.) Jones, W. L. Thomas (Neath); (Leslie) Davies, Viv Eddy (Bridgend), Kenifick, J. D. Hunt (Swansea), (Stan) Williams (Llanelli/Wales), B.B. Jones (Neath), Walter Vickery (Aberavon/Wales), Owens.

Tries: Edwards, (Chris) Matthews. Con/Pen: (B.B.) Jones.

East Wales – D. Gordon Winstone (Cross Keys); Jack T. Knowles (Newport), T. Bacon (Ebbw Vale), Hale, Cpl. Marshall Harding (Newport); T.R. Davies (Cwmllynfell), (W. Guy) Morgan; W. Hall (Blackwood), Reg J. Flowers (Pontypool), (W.J.) Evans, (R.E.) Price, J. Jerman (Newport), (Selby) Davies, Manfield, Dorning.

The scorers of the try and two penalties are unknown.

Gordon Winstone began at Risca and played one season at Newport at the end of the war. J. Jerman, whose brother played scrum half for Newport against the 1927-28 Waratahs, appeared 161 times (4 tries) for Newport from 1936-37 to 1939-40. Marshall Harding scored 11 tries in 17 appearances for Newport from 1939-40 until 1945-46 and also played for Rosslyn Park and the RAF.

Referee: (Ivor) David.

Feb 24 – Oxford University 13 Cambridge University 14 (at Oxford). Blues were not awarded.

Oxford – Tries: (R.E.) Luyt, Hollis, S.D. Pearce. Cons: Scott (capt.) 2.

Cambridge – Tries: (E.R.) Knapp (capt.) 4. Con: Newton-Thompson.

Kenneth Arthur Noel Spray appeared at centre for Cambridge. He made 52 appearances for Newport (1946-1950) and also played at Oundle School, Blackheath and Wales Trials. He was born at Oundle, Northamptonshire 25/12/1920 and died in South Glamorgan during the second quarter of 1982.

Feb 25 – French Army 3 GB Army 36 (at Parc des Princes, Paris) (25,000).

GB Army – Jenkins (W); Unwin, Cranmer (both E), Wooller (W), Guest; (FJ) Reynolds, Ellis (all E); (W.E.N.) Davis, Travers (both W), Prescott (E), Horsburgh (S), Huskisson (E), Mayne, Sayers (capt.) (both I), Samuel (Sammy) Walker (Instonians/Ireland/Captain of GB to South Africa in 1938).

Tries: Wooller 3, Sayers, Cranmer, Walker, Guest, Prescott. Cons: Jenkins 6.

French Army – *Michel Bonnus (Toulon); Robert Tourte (St Girons), *George Libaros (Tarbes), *Edmond Ellissalde, *Maurice Celhay (both Bayonne); Henri Peyrelade (Tarbes/Montferrand), *Gilbert Lavail (Perpignan); *Pierre Dauloude (St Vincent de Tyrosse), J. Dutrey (Lourdes), F. Meret (Tarbes), Marcel Tucoo-Chalat (Paris Univ), Pierre Charton (Racing Paul/Montferrand), *Jean-Baptiste Lefort (Biarritz), *+Pierre M.B. Thiers (Montferrand), Lucien Ferrard (Chalon).

Pen: Thiers.

Referee: (CH) Gadney.

British Army XV v French Army, Paris, February 1940

Hat-trick star Wilf Wooller is said to have claimed that this was the best team in which he ever played. It was the first representative match between France and the home nations since their expulsion from the Five Nations in 1931, and French rugby union was at a low ebb.

For years there had been only an annual match against Germany – who had even beaten them at Frankfurt in 1938 – plus some games with Romania and Italy. Rugby league had grown in France since 1934, many clubs and players switching, and was almost as big as Union in numbers and big-game crowds by 1939, when the French XV hadn't played for a year.

France awarded full caps. Pierre Thiers, scrum half turned flanker, led the players called from their military units for the match, admitted they were less than finely-tuned. Nine of the team were international debutants, while of the six others, five had endured the loss in Frankfurt. Beyond the rugby field, there was worse to come from that direction very soon.

Francois Meret was killed in action on June 10, just 15 weeks after this game, and Joseph Dutrey was a PoW of the Germans from later in 1940 until 1945. Of the French, only Thiers was recapped after the war, while from their opponents Guest and hooker 'Bunner' Travers, played on for long enough to appear in post-war internationals.

As Huw Richards has commented, *'The 1949 reappearance of Travers so confounded the WRU that, believing he could not possibly be the same man who had played before the war, they gave him a new Wales cap!'*

Locks Tom Huskisson and Blair Mayne were to be decorated for their war services and fly-half Frank Reynolds was mentioned in despatches, while as mentioned, Sayers died on military service in 1943.

March 16 – Oxford University Past & Present 13 Cambridge University Past & Present 11 (at Richmond).

Oxford – Tries: Hollis 2, H.H. Pennington. Cons: (Viv) Jenkins 2.

Cambridge – Tries: William B. Young, (R.B.) Bruce-Lockhart. Con/Pen: Grahame W. Parker (Gloucester/England).

Oxford included Obolensky and Prescott. Harold Hammond Pennington of Upholland Grammar School and Oxford University (Blues 1937-38), died aged 23 on 28/3/1942 and is buried at Escoublac la Bault War Cemetery. He was a Captain in the Hampshire Regiment and No 4 Commando Unit. Cambridge included (A.M.) Rees, Kemp, (C.L.) Newton-Thompson (capt.) and Kenneth C. Fyfe (Sale/Scotland).

Referee: Captain L.S.H. Sanderson.

Mar 23 – Midlands XV 18 Barbarians 34 (at Welford Road, Leicester): In aid of the Army Recreational and Comfort Funds.

Midlands – Harry Pateman (Coventry); Ken H. Cooke (Leicester), R. Spiers (Stoneygate), (F.G.) Edwards (now Leicester), O.F. Wheatley (Coventry); Dr. Gordon Short S. Sturtidge (Victoria/Australia (9 caps and tour of South Africa 1933)/Melbourne University/Midlands XV/Rosslyn Park/Leicester (1 game)/Northampton (captain 1939-41), Jim Parsons (Leicester/Cambridge University and later Moseley); Harold Peter Jerwood (Leicester/Cambridge University), Gilthorpe, Denis Bolesworth (Leicester), W. Wheatley (Coventry), E.P.M. Bates (Rugby), (J.T.W.) Berry, Albert W. Seaton (Coventry), Maurice M. Henderson (Leicester).

One report stated that Berry did not play and that H. F. Wheatley (Coventry) did.

Tries: Edwards 2, Jerwood, Seaton. Cons: Gilthorpe 3.

Barbarians – R.T. Campbell (St Mary's Hospital); Hollis, Luyt, Babrow, Guest; Kemp, Ellis; Prescott, I.S. Jacklin (Cranleigh School/St Mary's Hospital), G.J. Reynolds (St Mary's Hospital), Huskisson, (S) Walker, Manfield, Newton-Thompson, (W.B.) Young.

Tries: Guest 3, Hollis 2, Babrow, Manfield. Cons: Walker 3, Prescott 2. Pen – Walker.

Hooker Ivan Jacklin was a South African-born doctor who was a Surgeon/Lieut in the RNVR. He died on the Murmansk convoys on 13/4/1943.

Referee: G. E. Beynon (London Society and Swansea).

Oscar Frank Wheatley was born in Coventry 4/3/1918 and died 20/6/1945, aged 27. He was a Lieut-Cmdr of 808 Flight-Squadron on the aircraft-carrier HMS Ameer, having already shot down a Japanese plane (being mentioned in despatches) when he was shot down and taken prisoner by the Japanese, dying at their hands in Dakar. He was buried in Jakarta Cemetery. It is believed that he had also been a POW in 1941 in French captivity. He played for Coventry and Warwickshire, as did the rest of this big rugby family. He lived at Sycamore Cottage, Greatworth, Banbury, Oxfordshire, leaving his widow, Hilda Rose Wheatley (nee Savage), whom he had married in 1940.

Apr 6 – Aldershot Command 8 'The New Zealand Contingent' 13 (at Aldershot Central Command Ground), in what was very probably the first game played by any NZ team in Britain during the war. Lieut. H.E. Blow (Auckland) was

'Substitute' Yorkshire Cup Final, 1940

the referee. Ronnie Morris and Haydn Tanner, who kicked five points, were at half-back for an Aldershot side captained by back-rower Lieut. R.J. Northcote-Green.

The NZ captain was a forward, Bombardier Francis (Canterbury). Full back, Bombardier Dennis Coombe (Wellington), was a 1937 NZ Davis Cup tennis player who lived in London and survived the war, becoming manager of the Davis Cup side. Watching the game was the NZ High Commissioner, W. J. Jordan.

Apr 13 – The Middlesex Sevens final was played on Richmond Athletic Ground and saw St Mary's Hospital defeat the Officer Cadets Training Unit (Sandhurst) by 14-10. The Cup was presented by Major J.J. Astor. The Cadets included two Cambridge University Rowing Blues.

Apr 14 – Perhaps Mussolini's rugby propaganda posters hadn't quite done the trick: Romania beat Italy 3- 0 at the Dinamo Stadium, Bucharest, with the clinching try by scrum half Eugen Marcelescu. Italy's fly half Valerio Vagneti and centre Arturo re Garbagnati were to be 1943 war deaths. Some said the referee was M. Ruffy (France), but *La Stampa* (honestly) criticized his only playing 70 mins, and called him the German, Krapp!

Apr 20 –Bradford beat Brighouse Rangers 22-3 in the Yorkshire RU 'Wartime Substitute' Cup Final at Odsal.

Apr 16 – Meanwhile, in Rugby League, it was England 5 Wales 8 at Oldham's Watersheddings.

Apr 20 – The Army 23 Great Britain XV 15 (at Richmond).

Army – Jenkins; Unwin, Cranmer, Wooller, A. F. Dawkins (Richmond); (F.J.) Reynolds, Tanner; (W.E.N.) Davis, Travers, Prescott, Mayne, Huskisson, Horsburgh, (S) Walker, Buchanan.

Tries: Wooller 2, Dawkins, Buchanan, Unwin. Cons: Jenkins 2. DG: Reynolds.

GB – (C.H.) Davies; Hollis, Heaton, (F. G.) Edwards, (C) Matthews; Kemp (capt.), (R.T.) Campbell; Sampson, Gilthorpe, Teden, Couchman, (Leslie) Davies, Berry, (C.L.) Newton-Thompson, (J.K.) Watkins.

Tries: Heaton 2, Hollis. Cons: Heaton 3.

Referee: (C.H.) Gadney.

Arthur Francis (Bill) Dawkins, from Little Baddow in Essex, became a Major of the Sierra Leone Regiment, Royal West African Frontier Force. He was educated at Marlborough and Balliol College, Oxford University. He later lived at Ramsden Heath in Essex. He was born at Madalay St Mary in Bengal on 26/10/1916 and died on 3/11/2009, aged 93.

As mentioned, Germany had been developing its rugby during the 1930s, and established itself as number two in continental Europe. The Germans played 14 tests against France before WW2, winning two of them, and did not lose to any team except their neighbour until 1937, when Italy beat them 9–7.

With war, rugby came to a halt after Germany had played only more game: May 5 – Germany 0 Italy 4 (at Stuttgart). This clash between the Axis allies was won by a drop goal from fly half Francesco Vinci, who had been born in New York. The referee was Mr. Erck (Romania).

Germany was to lose, in effect, a complete first XV in the war. RFU museum researchers found, to the surprise of many, that it was she who had most international rugby players

Army v Great Britain Programme, 1940

killed in action during WW2. They uncovered the identities of 16 capped German servicemen who lost their lives between 1939 and 1945.

The UK rugby season, such as it was, closed as ever at the end of April: whereupon, and doubtless through sheer coincidence, Hitler launched his assault in the west, into Scandinavia, then through Holland and Belgium, once again, into France. Churchill replaced Chamberlain on May 10th and battle was joined.

It was not long-lasting, the Germans' plans working shockingly well. The British Expeditionary Force, which had hoped to help defend France, retreated before the month's end to Dunkirk, where a mixture of bravery, stubbornness, luck and Nazi over-confidence in their Luftwaffe allowed over

Vichy French Rugby Poster, 1940

330,000 British and Allied troops to be evacuated by ships big and, famously, little. They had, vitally, lived to fight another day. To be precise, a D-Day, exactly four years later.....

In Britain, rationing of basic foods and meat had begun, while in the seas around her, U-boats were hitting shipping, including that bringing supplies. Italy joined Germany, while here, a mixture of old and young began to form the Home Guard. France surrendered on 25 June, for the north to become occupied. The Vichy south collaborationist: and very (and very unfairly), anti-Rugby League. Japan, Hitler's other friend, was meanwhile making strong progress in China and the Pacific, helping increase the 'isolationist' USA's fears and their aid to the Allies.

As Hitler planned the invasion of a Britain he hadn't expected to have to fight, he needed to ensure supremacy in the air. So, as the second season of war-time rugby began in September 1940, the skies above southern and eastern England saw the fighters and bombers of the Luftwaffe opposed by the 'Few': Churchill's lauded young RAF pilots, many of whom were to come from the Dominions, in the pivotal Battle of Britain.

Eventually and probably mistakenly, Hitler turned from the heavy airfield attack losses to blitzing London and other cities instead. (The rugby grounds at Cardiff Arms Park and Bath, amongst others, were to suffer from bomb damage in coming years). As Londoners proved 'they could take it', though, clubs outside London, including Gloucester, were organizing sides and following the example of clubs such as Rosslyn Park in encouraging fundraising games.

For instance, on Sept 21 at Clifton College, Bristol, a crowd of well over 3,000 paid one shilling each to see ex-English cap Rev. Peter W.P. Brook's XV beat an Empire XV 23-21 in a clash in aid of the Red Cross. It is uncertain as to who played, but many internationals were selected and the Empire side included New Zealander Eric W.T. Tindill as captain and the two Hook brothers (Bob and Bill) from Gloucester in the back division.

Oct 19 – Len Corbett's West of England XV 25 Empire XV 8 (at Bath).

Corbett's XV included Ronnie R. Morris (Swansea/Bristol/Wales) and the Empire XV included (W.E.) Jones, Travers, Maurice J. Daly (London Irish/Ireland), (C) Matthews, plus the NZ Services trio of Cyril S. Pepper, (Eric) Tindill and Sgt. T.G. Fowler, who gained the Military Medal and had played for Taranaki and the North Island). Pepper and Tindill had both toured GB with the 1935-36 All Blacks.

Nov 2 – Rev. Peter W.P. Brook's West of England XV 11 Welsh Army XV 16 (at Clifton College).

Welsh Army XV – Harold Westcombe Isaac (Newport); (C) Matthews (Bridgend), (D.A.) Brown (Cardiff), (R.R.) Morris, Lyn Williams (Cardiff); (W.E.) Jones (Neath), A. N. Other;

Rev Brook's XV v Welsh Army, 1940

W.G. Jones, Travers, W. Gough, Ernie Coleman (all Newport), Les Spence (Cardiff), Leslie Paul, P.T. Jones (both Newport), Samuel W.D. Seager (Chepstow).

Tries: (Chris) Matthews 3, Morris. Cons: Brown 2.

Nov 23 – Tommy Voyce's XV 18 Wavell Wakefield's XV 11 (at Kingsholm, Gloucester): the referee was Wakefield, 42, the former England captain. Over 4,000 watched the game. Also this day, the NZ Services side opened their account: a full listing follows below.

Dec 7 – Cambridge University 11 Oxford University 9 (at Oxford). Blues were not awarded.

Cambridge – Tries: (E.R.) Knapp (capt) 2, A.L. Evans. Con: G.T. Wright.

Oxford – Try/DG: P.L. Richards. Con: (E.K.) Scott (capt).

Dec 14 – Cardiff 17 Empire XV 3 (at Arms Park, Cardiff).

Dec 26 – Cardiff 16 Welsh Army XV 0 (at Arms Park, Cardiff).

NZEF: At the outbreak of war it had been decided that New Zealand should provide an Expeditionary Force of one division, under the then Major-General, former player and rugby supporter Bernard Freyburg. Their first echelon had landed in Egypt in February 1940, the third in September.

Lieutenant C. S. Pepper, of Auckland, awarded the Military Cross.

Eric Tindill   *Tindill in his 90s*   *Cyril Pepper*

The second was diverted to Britain on Italy's entry into the war and did not reach Egypt until the spring of the following year, ready for the move to northern Greece.

As in WW1, rugby organized or otherwise was a big part of NZ service life. As well as a local rugby competition for unit teams in 1940–41, before heading for the desert, there was soon a rash of fixtures against useful opposition. These regularly featured magnificent displays by that 1935 All Black tourist Eric Tindill at scrum half, though he had been capped at five eighth. Tindill died aged 99 in 2010 after a unique career as a NZ cap at both rugby and cricket, a Test cricket umpire and Test rugby referee.

In 1940 he played firstly for Aldershot Command. Also in the team was Cyril Pepper, the pre-war All Black prop mentioned earlier, who was wounded at Sidi Rezegh in 1941 where he earned the MC. However, he died in a fall in Wellington in 1943, aged 31.

The NZ side played in the following matches before they resumed their voyage to Egypt:

Nov 23 – Lost to Rosslyn Park 20-22 (at Old Deer Park, Richmond): Pepper and Tindill (capt.) both appeared in this opening match. Rosslyn Park led 22-0 with less than 20 minutes to go.

Nov 30 – Lost to St Mary's Hospital 3-15 (at the Command Ground, Aldershot).

Dec 11 – Beat Rosslyn Park 15-8 (at the Command Ground, Aldershot), in the presence of the Duke of Gloucester.

Dec 14 – Beat Aldershot Command 8-0 (at the Command Ground, Aldershot).

Dec 21 – Beat Rev. Peter Brook's West of England XV 13-8 (at the Memorial Ground, Bristol).

Dec 28 – Beat Guy's Hospital 33-3 (at Honor Oak Park). The try-count was 9-0.

On behalf of one of those venues and its teams, the British Journal of Nursing for December 1940 carried a plaintive and doubtless typical appeal:

'Aldershot Command: There is a big demand for football boots and footballs – both Association and Rugby – and for light novels and magazines. It is only necessary to hand in books at the nearest post office. Gifts of pianos, wireless sets, and indoor games will be welcomed by the Command Welfare Officer, Hut 26, Steeles Road, Stanhope Lines, Aldershot.'

Over 50 years on, a reunion booklet from NZ recalled, in detail that required only slight amendment, the Arms Park game above.... *During WW2 Maori Battalion teams fared very well against many of the Unit and international fifteens. In England, during the winter of 1940-41, the Maori Battalion team showed such superiority, that the Welsh Rugby Union invited it to play on the ground made famous by the 1905 All Blacks, when Deans' try was disallowed. After a long train ride in the cold, the team arrived at Cardiff at midnight. The next morning the team visited the ground and were shown the spot where Deans had 'scored.' The side included M. Delamere, M. Francis, T. Paraone, E. Howell, P. Kurupo, B. Jacobs, Bubu Matenga, G. Harrison (Capt.), A. Wanoa, N. Carroll, L. Harris, T. Timihou, P. Kutia, W. Cooper & G. Pitman. The game was played at a tremendous pace. Bunny Jacobs was caught offside and the hosts kicked a goal. Then came a repetition of the famous disputed Deans 'try'. In a melee on the Cardiff line, one of the Maori forwards dived over. The referee was unsighted and the try was disallowed. Many spectators booed the referee. Five certain points and the usual shot in the arm for the Maoris was lost. The Welsh scored soon scored a gem of a try. Stung by this reverse the Maori backs swung into action. Eddie Howell, playing magnificently, received from Bubu Matenga, drew Bunny Jacobs' man then unloaded to Bunny who sped through the gap to score. Thousands of hats flew into the air. Delamere missed an easy kick. Two more kicks by the Welsh clinched the game. The hosts presented ties to the Maoris later. Wilf Wooller, the famous international played in this game. Opposing Bunny Jacobs was a youngster who in 1950 toured New Zealand with the Lions team. (This would have been Bleddyn Williams, doubtless). He was a mere slip of a lad in 1940, but a very efficient one at that. Over 12,000 spectators watched, not only the game, but the skies above for German bombers.*

Haydn Tanner

Meanwhile, amongst the other miscellaneous pickings of that autumn,

Gloucester were captained by pre-war England full back Harold Boughton, while another full-back, W.G. (Bill) Hook, who was later to play for Gloucester and England, was with Sir Thomas Rich's School in Gloucester and playing for the South of England Public Schools.

Wales and 1930 GB fly half Harry Bowcott and Wales and GB 1938 scrum half Tanner both appeared for the Wasps. Tanner and E.J. Unwin (England) played for a London Area Army XV, while the 1929 Wales fly half 2nd Lieut. Bill Roberts (Cardiff) also turned out for an Army XV.

The Exeter ground was taken over by the military, mostly for Army transport and eventually for the American forces' preparation for D-Day.

In September it was reported that Lieut. John Walker Sinclair Irwin of the RAMC, the five-times capped Ireland back-rower of 1938 and 1939, was missing

IRFU President J W S Irwin with Tom Kiernan, 1970

after the evacuation of Dunkirk. However, it soon was known that he was a PoW in Germany. He was released in April 1943 and became IRFU President in 1969-70, dying on 13/8/2004, aged 91. His father was Sir Samuel Thompson Irwin, capped nine times in the Irish pack of 1900-01-02-03 and President of the IRFU in 1935-36, knighted in 1957 and died in 1961. The Ulster Hospital for Children where he was working was destroyed by German bombs in 1941.

With war truly under way – 'total' war, with civilians as well as servicemen and women under real threat and fear of enemy bombing and invasion; with retaliatory bombing of German cities and other targets; with fighting against the Italians in Africa and with the Battle of the Atlantic more than occupying the minds of the Royal and merchant navies, representative rugby was for some time less easy or viable to arrange or attend.

Aberavon's ground, allotments in 1914-18, became a barrage balloon site in 1939-45, but eventually clubs like Newbridge (reserved-occupation miners predominating), Newport and Cardiff (docks trade, mining and medicine) were to benefit from some continuity and growth in strength.

Although Swansea 'shut down' as a club, individuals there formed the less-than-snappily-titled Swansea and West Wales Rugby War Charities Effort, and with Nazi bombs mercifully avoiding the St. Helen's Ground, arranged a successful series of wartime 'internationals and semi-internationals' after 1940.

With leading professionals and amateurs in the services involved, good rugby and good crowds resulted, and over £15,000 was raised by 1945. Similar stories might be told elsewhere, with Gloucester's impressive Rugby Heritage website, for instance, one rich source of evidence of the kind of games – and lengths – gone to in order to raise sides and charity cash by the use of the Kingsholm ground, even if the club was out of action.

Similarly, J.E. Thorneloe, secretary of Leicester, was to organize impressive XVs in his name to play a series of fundraisers, especially involving Boxing Day and Easter games against the Barbarians at Welford Road: shades of the late Edgar Mobbs and his East Midlands efforts early in the First World War.

Deaths of internationals in 1940:

Mar 29 – Prince Alexander Obolensky (England, 4 caps – 1936, and GB to Argentine 1936) died in a training flight accident at Martlesham, Norfolk. He was the son of an officer in the Czar's Imperial Horse Guards and was buried in Ipswich Cemetery. Aged 24.
May 1 – Paul Cooke (England, 2 caps – 1939). He served as a 2nd Lieut. in the Oxford and Bucks Light Infantry and was killed in action at Calais. Aged 23.

Jun 12 – Donald Kenneth Andrew Mackenzie (Scotland, 2 caps – 1939) died when he crashed on a training flight near Edinburgh. He was a Pilot Officer in the RAF. Aged 23.

Jul 29 – Brian Henry Black (England, 10 caps – 1930-33 and GB 1930 v NZ (4 tests)/Australia (1 test)). He died when he crashed at Chilwark in Wiltshire, serving as an RAF Pilot Officer. He was born in South Africa and was a world champion in the two-man bobsleigh at Cortina and the four-man bob at St Moritz. Aged 33.

Aug 11 – Donald Gordon Cobden (NZ, 1 cap – 1937). He died on his 26th birthday while a Pilot Officer in RAF 74 Squadron. His body was washed ashore at Ostend after crashing in the English Channel during the Battle of Britain and he was buried by the Germans.

Oct 14 – Ernest Ian Parsons, DFC (England, 1 cap – 1939). He was a New Zealander who served as a Pilot Officer in Bomber Command, being awarded the DFC in 1940 and was reported missing after an air operation over Turin, Italy. Aged 27.

Oct 15 – Derek Edmund Teden (England, 3 caps – 1939). He was a Pilot Officer in the RAF and was killed in action in the Fresian Islands. Aged 24.

Dec 11 – Henry Rew (England, 10 caps – 1929-34 & GB to NZ and Australia in 1930 – 4 Tests). He was a Major in the Royal Tank Corps, killed in action near El Alamein, Tripolitania. Aged 34.

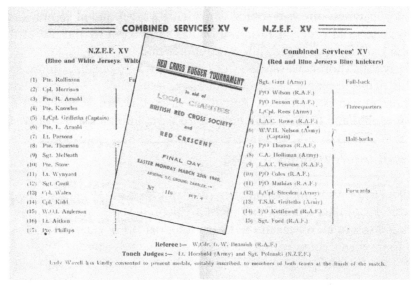

New Zealanders inevitably looked for games while awaiting orders and action in Egypt, Easter 1940

4
1941

The demands of the war at this juncture, though, meant that 1941 saw no international matches played in the UK. There were not many club games arranged, either: Richmond Athletic Ground (and indeed London generally) was the venue for the majority of those which did take place.

1941 literally started with a bang at Welsh rugby shrine, Cardiff Arms Park, the new North Stand of 1934 and West Terrace badly damaged by a parachute

Bomb-damaged Arms Park, six years on: terrace fixed, roof not yet

mine on the night of January 2nd, the city's worst bombing raid of the war. A month later Swansea town centre was almost obliterated by a three night blitz, and many other urban areas were to suffer in similar ways.

In the matches of note included below, clubs are generally identified alongside only those players who have not appeared in the 1939 or 1940 section, and 'E, S, I, or W' means the players concerned were either pre-war or post-war internationals from the home countries. Many players had to withdraw after selection as they were serving in the forces and liable to sudden postings or transport disruption.

Jan 11 – Bath 26 Ronnie R. Morris' XV 5.

Bath centre Air Craftsman Thomas Wooller, the brother of Wales cap Wilf Wooller, was unstoppable as he scored three tries and kicked four goals.

Jan 25 – Oxford University Past & Present 3 Cambridge University Past & Present 3.

For this clash at Richmond, Oxford included M.M. Walford, R. T. Campbell, Scott and Prescott (capt). Wing Ray W. Pennock (Billingham and Durham County) scored a try. Cambridge included (Wilf) Wooller (try), (T) Kemp (capt), Parsons, (W.B.) Young and Steeds.

Jan 25 – Combined Universities of Ireland 3 Rest of Ireland 16 (at Lansdowne Road, Dublin).

Feb 1 – Munster 9 Connaught 3 (at Limerick).

Feb 8 – Leinster 9 Munster 9 (at Lansdowne Road, Dublin).

Feb 22 – Connaught 9 Leinster 14 (at Galway).

Mar 1 – Cambridge University 13 Oxford University 0 (at Grange Road, Cambridge)

Cambridge – Tries: G.T. Wright, A.S. May, David G. Bratherton. Cons: Wright 2.

Captains: (E.R.) Knapp (Cambridge) and (E.K.) Scott (Oxford).

Referee: Captain L.H.F. Sanderson.

Mar 29 – Bath v Weston-super-Mare. The game was refereed by Len Corbett, the Bristol/England centre.

Apr 5 – South Wales 14 RAF XV 8 (at St Helen's, Swansea) (20,000).

South Wales – (C.H.) Davies; (E.J.H.).Williams, (J) Matthews, Sullivan, (K) Thomas; Ben Southway (Ebbw Vale), Tanner; (Bryn) Evans, Travers, (Will) Davies, Tamplin, (M.E.) Morgan, (Wilf) Harries, (A.R.) Taylor, Long.
Tries: Taylor 2, Matthews, (E.J.H.) Williams, Con: Taylor.
RAF – Cpl. J.J. Merritt (Ebbw Vale); A/C Robert E. (Bob) Hook (Gloucester), Sgt. D. Idwal Davies (Swansea/Wales/Leeds RL), Cpl. L.M.

RAF v S Wales and Programme, April 1941

Rees (Plymouth Albion/Devon), A/C Alan S. Edwards (Aberavon/Salford, Wales & GB RL); A/C Cliff Evans (Resolven/Neath/Wales Schools 1931/ Salford & Leeds RL), Cpl. Steve Morgan (Swansea/Hull KR RL); Cpl. Raymond J. Longland (Northampton/Bedford/England), Gilthorpe (capt.), Sgt. Roy Culver (London Counties), A/C Gerry T. Dancer (GB 1938 to SA/ Bedford), Sgt. Eddie V. Watkins (Cardiff/Wales/Wigan RL), A/C W. Elvet Jones (Swansea), Manfield, Cpl. A. Gordon Hudson (Gloucester).

Tries: Edwards, penalty try. Con: Longland.

John James Merritt was a Cpl., then Sgt. in the RAF and died on 3/4/1943 with two crewmates of 51st Squadron when their plane crashed en route to a raid on Essen (four lived). They had taken off from RAF Snaith, near Goole in Yorkshire, when a fire developed and they turned back to land, but crashed by Shortlands Farm, Carlton, seven miles from Selby in Yorkshire. Merrritt was buried at Beaufort Churchyard, near Ebbw Vale.

Apr 26 – Middlesex Sevens (Final) – Cambridge University 6 Welsh Guards 0.

(E.R.) Knapp skippered Cambridge. Tanner, P.R. Hastings (injured in Rd. 1), Harry Pimblett (RL), Gwyn Williams (Cardiff/Wigan RL – brother of Bleddyn) and Ossie Jones (RL) all played for the Welsh Guards.

A month later, an epic and costly pusuit in the Atlantic saw the German battleship Bismarck go down: hopes for more rugby were sunk, too, in more than one area. The 1941-42 season started in September with the news that

Gloucester would not be arranging any games due to lack of players, but the Kingsholm Ground was available to any Service teams. They were nor alone, as in Wales, for instance, Ebbw Vale soon followed by disbanding for the season.

SEMI-INTERNATIONAL RUGBY MATCH
IN AID OF
THE ROYAL AIR FORCE BENEVOLENT FUND AND
MAYOR OF SWANSEA'S AIR-RAID DISTRESS FUND

ROYAL AIR FORCE
v.
SOUTH WALES
At St. Helen's Ground, Swansea
On SATURDAY, OCTOBER 11th, 1941.   Kick-off 3.30

OFFICIAL SOUVENIR PROGRAMME - - 3d.
Total proceeds in aid of above Funds.

RAF v S Wales Programme, October 1941

Oct 11 – South Wales 16 RAF 11 (at St Helen's, Swansea) (15,000).

RAF – (J.J.) Merritt; A/C Vic J. Lyttle (Ireland), (D. Idwal) Davies, F/O H. Kenyon (Coventry), (AS) Edwards; Sgt. (W.T.H.) Davies (Swansea/Wales/Bradford Northern, Wales & GB RL), (S) Morgan; Dancer, Gilthorpe (capt), P/O P.L. Moxey (Pontypridd/Llanelli/Welsh Police/Wigan RL in 1938-39, 37 apps, 5 tries), (E.V.) Watkins, Cpl. Joe S. Mycock (Sale/Harlequins/England), LAC Stanley Paige (Wasps), Manfield, Officer Cadet, then P/O (A.M.) Rees.

Percy Leslie Moxey was born near Pontypridd on 1/1/1915 and died 7/8/1942 (aged 27) when his Wellington plane hit a barrage balloon near Birmingham. He had served in the Norwich Police in 1940 when living at Middlegate Street, Great Yarmouth and joined the RAF in 1941. He was buried at Southtown, near Gorleston.

Try: Kenyon. Con/2 Pens: Gilthorpe.

South Wales – (C.H.) Davies; (E.J.H.) Williams, (J) Matthews, Edward (Ted) Ward (Llanelli/Wigan RL), (T) Sullivan; William Benjamin (Billy) Cleaver (Cardiff/Wales/GB to NZ/Australia 1950), C (or P). Davies (Llanelli); (Bryn) Evans, Travers, (W.E.N.) Davis, (Will) Davies, (A.R.) Taylor, (Wilf) Harries, Tamplin, Long.

Tamplin broke a bone in his hand and (M. Edgar) Morgan was allowed to replace him.

Tries: Matthews 2, (E.J.H.) Williams 2. Cons: Taylor 2.

Nov 1 – Army 30 RAF 3 (at Richmond).

Army – Tries: (F.G.) Edwards 2, Wooller, (A.L.) Evans), Travers, Risman. Cons: Risman 4. DG: Wooller.

RAF – Try: (A.S.) Edwards.

Cpl. Howard Phillips Roblin (Cardiff) appeared at centre for the RAF. He was a Pilot Officer on a bombing raid to Essen on 25/3/1942, when he died (aged 22) and his body was not found. He had attended Pontypridd Grammar School and lived with his parents at nearby Church Village in Glamorgan.

In this game there was also a debut for prop forward LAC Ronald Vivian S. Tarrant (RAF Stormy Down, near Bridgend, born 1919 in Pontypridd, died 1995 in Abingdon).

Nov 15 – Oxford University 6 R.V. Stanley's XV 34 (at Oxford).

Nov 29 – Cambridge University 9 Oxford University 6 (at Grange Road, Cambridge).

Cambridge – Tries: H.E. Watts, J.R. Bridger. Pen: (G.T.) Wright.

Oxford – Try: H.T. Harvey. Pen: Howard Dickson Darcus.

The referee was Sqdn-Ldr. (C.H.) Gadney.

J.M. Blair captained Oxford. R.P. Sinclair captained Cambridge with H.J.C. Rees (Llandovery College) at centre.

Ronald Peter Sinclair was a captain in the Royal Engineers and played in six Varsity matches from 1939-40 until 1941-42, when the unofficial games were played 'home and away' at the two universities. He was killed in action in the Middle East during September 1943.

Dec 6 – British Army 21 The Army in Ireland 3 (at Richmond Athletic Ground).

British Army – (C.H.) Davies; (E.J.H.) Williams, (F.G.) Edwards, Pimblett, A.L. Evans (Rosslyn Park/Cambridge University/Worksop College); A.J.F. ('Gus') Risman (Salford, Wales & GB RL), Tanner; (W.E.N.) Davis, Ian N. Graham (Edinburgh Acads./Scotland), Lieut. G.F. Smith (Blackheath/Barbarians), A. Charteris (Scots Guards), W.G. Jones (Newport), E. Hodgson (RL), Newton-Thompson, (Gwyn) Williams.

Tries: (E.J.H.) Williams 2, (Gwyn) Williams, Pimblett. 3 Cons/Pen: Risman 3.

The Army in Ireland side included – W.H. (Bill) Clement (Llanelli/Wales/GB to South Africa 1938), J.L. Richards (Cardiff fly half), J.C.T. Wilson (an unknown Llanelli centre), George P.C. Vallance (Leicester) and the Ireland back row of Robert Alexander (GB to South Africa 1938), Sammy Walker and Mike Sayers.

Pen: Walker.

Both Alexander and Sayers, as mentioned, were killed in action in 1943. Richards, a relative unknown, played twice for Cardiff in 1938-39.

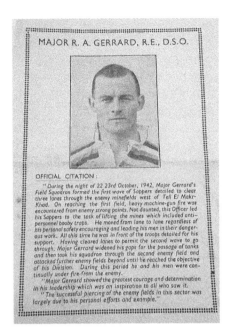

MAJOR R. A. GERRARD, R.E., D.S.O.

OFFICIAL CITATION :

" During the night of 22 23rd October, 1942, Major Gerrard's Field Squadron formed the first wave of Sappers detailed to clear three lanes through the enemy minefields west of Tell El Makr-Khad. On reaching the first field, heavy machine-gun fire was encountered from enemy strong points. Not daunted, this Officer led his Sappers to the task of lifting the mines which included anti-personnel booby traps. He moved from lane to lane regardless of his personal safety encouraging and leading his men in their danger-ous work. All this time he was in front of the troops detailed for his support. Having cleared lanes to permit the second wave to go through, Major Gerrard widened his gaps for the passage of tanks and then took his squadron through the second enemy field and attacked further enemy fields beyond until he reached the objective of his Division. During this period he and his men were con-tinually under fire from the enemy.

" Major Gerrard showed the greatest courage and determination in his leadership which was an inspiration to all who saw it.

" The successful piercing of the enemy fields in this sector was largely due to his personal efforts and example."

Major R A Gerrard

Dec 13 – West of England 6, Somerset Services 10 (at Bath). The West included Major Ronald Anderson Gerrard (the Bath/England centre) and David Dan Evans (Wales/Bridgend/ Cardiff University/New Brighton/Sale/ Birkenhead Park and later Gloucester scrum half).

Gerrard was awarded the DSO for clearing minefields at El Alamein, but was killed soon afterwards in Libya on 22/1/1943, aged 30. He played 14 times for England (1932-36) and after this game played a few more games for Bath before serving in Africa.

Dan Evans played further games for and against Bath during the war. Born in Barry, he served as a Flight-Lieut. and became a headmaster, dying at Bradford-on-Avon 7/9/1992, aged 82.

Dec 20 – South Wales 6 Army 13 (at St Helen's, Swansea) (Approx. 10,000): in aid of British Army Charities and the Mayor of Swansea's War Comforts Fund.

South Wales – S. Dowling (Llanelli); (Dennis) Madden, (J) Matthews, (B.L.) Williams, Sullivan; Cleaver, F.H. Wood (Bromsgrove); Bryn Evans (Llanelli), Eddie Morgan (Swansea/Wales/GB), Will Davies, (Les) Thomas, (John) Hopkins, Eddie Long (Swansea/Wales), Wilfred E. Harries (Swansea, capt.), Rees Williams (Swansea).

Pens: Harries 2.

Army – (C.H.) Davies; (E.J.H.) Williams, Pimblett, Risman, Cyril B. Holmes (Manchester/England); Lieut. O.J. Morris (Loughor/Furnace/ Pontypridd/Hunslet, Leeds & Wales RL), Tanner; Prescott, (W.E.N.) Davis, D.W. Malcolm (London Scottish), (E) Hodgson, P.J. McCarthy (Irish Trialist), (Gwyn) Williams, B.J.Flatcher (unknown).

Tries: Morris, Risman. 2 Cons/Pen: Risman.

Referee: Fred G. Phillips (Pontarddulais). Touch-Judges: Capt H.A. Haigh-Smith and Trevor Davies.

Late changes were made to both sides. 'Wendy' Davis was forced to play as a hooker.

Oliver James Morris, aged 28, was born in Pontypridd in 1916 and was killed in action on 27/9/1944 at Rimini, Italy and is honoured at the Gradara War Cemetery. He was in the Royal Artillery in Egypt, then was a Lieut. in the 1st Battalion Welch Regiment.

Dec 27 – J. Eric Thorneloe's XV 3 Barbarians 8 (at Welford Road, Leicester): in aid of Lord Wigram's Sportsmen's Committee of the Red Cross.

Barbarians – Major (G.W.) Parker; Lt. (E.J.H.) Williams, Lieut./Capt. John Graham-Jones (St Mary's Hospital/London Welsh/Newport/Rosslyn Park), A.W. Masters (Metropolitan Police), Sub-Lieut. Hollis; Cadet Logie Bruce-Lockhart (Cambridge University/Scotland), Sgt. Tanner; Capt. Prescott (capt), Sqdrn-Ldr. Gilthorpe, Capt. (W.E.N.) Davis, Pay-Lieut. H.C. Lyddon (Royal Navy), R.L. Hall (St Bart's Hospital), Pay-Lieut. (J.K.) Watkins, Lieut. (A.B.W.) Buchanan, M.R. Mullins (Guy's Hospital).

Tries: (E.J.H.) Williams, Tanner. Con: Parker.

Horace Collier Lyddon OBE, KB, CD (later Sir H.C. Lyddon) was a Captain, then Commander and finally Rear Admiral in the Navy. Born in 1912, he died in 1968. He was in charge of Navy rugby in 1958-59.

Richard Hall was a Surgeon-Lieut. in the RNVR. He died on 21/8/1944 when his ship was torpedoed. (See 1943 England Services game).

John Graham Jones, later known as Graham-Jones, was an occupational health physician in the steel industry in South Wales (1946-77). Born in Caerleon 30/6/1917, he died after a fall on 22/10/2005. He became assistant chief medical officer to the British Steel Corporation, but in 1978 set up an occupational health consultancy as an adviser to companies with overseas projects, spending retirement working at the Heinz factory in Harlesden.

In 1977 he received the Queen's Silver Jubilee Medal for interest in the employment of disabled people. The British Occupational Health Society awarded him the Bedford Prize, the Bedford Medal, and honorary membership. Educated at Newport High School and St Mary's Hospital he was mainly a fly half for London Welsh, St Mary's, Middlesex, Wales Trial and the Barbarians, playing in winning St Mary's sides in the Middlesex Sevens.

He was regimental medical officer to the First Battalion, The Border Regiment, part of the First Landing Brigade of the First Airborne Division, serving in North Africa and taking part in the first major Allied glider operation in Sicily and the Battle of Arnhem, when he chose to remain behind with his more wounded charges and thus became a Prisoner of War. In 1943 he was reported as being 'rescued from the sea' but in 1945 he played for Rosslyn Park.

J. Eric Thorneloe's XV included – (R) Rankin (RAF/Australia), (C.B.) Holmes, ('Gus') Walker, Parsons, Berry (capt), Bill Fallowfield (Northampton and later secretary of the Rugby League) and (J.H.) Steeds.

Try: Holmes.

Referee: Roy Francis Barradel (Leicester Society).

Other items of some note from the rugby of this year included:

Peter F. Cooper, later an International referee, played regularly at full back and centre for Rosslyn Park/Richmond/Middlesex.

Brigade of Guards teams included P.R. Hastings, Tanner, (Stan) Williams and RL players Pimblett, centre W. Ossie Jones (Resolven, Neath, St Helen's RL), scrum half Charlie Banfield (Briton Ferry, Neath, Wigan RL) and Bleddyn's brother, (Gwyn) Williams.

Lieut. H. R. M'KIBBIN (Instonians). — Another player who toured South Africa with the British team. First capped for Ireland against Wales in 1938. He is a good kick, and his strong point is defence. To-day renews his S. African partnership with Macrae.

Harry McKibbin

The Anti-Aircraft Division teams included (Viv) Jenkins, (W.C.W.) Murdoch, (M.J.) Daly, (R.R.) Morris, Viv J. Law (Newport/Wales), Thomas B. Dunn (NIFC/Ireland), H.R. (Harry) McKibbin (Queen's Univ. Belfast/Ireland/GB to South Africa 1938), G. Duncan Shaw (Sale/Scotland) and (E.O.) Coleman.

West of England teams included Nigel Gibbs (Clifton College/Harlequins/England), Wooller, (R.R.) Morris, (W.E.) Jones, Parsons, Arthur T. Payne (Bristol/England), (Keith) Scott and the Rev. Peter W.P. Brook (Cambridge University/Bristol/England).

John R.C. Matthews (Harlequins and, later, England) played for Guy's

Hospital in the second row and in 1951-52 was to skipper the London Counties to victory over South Africa – their only tour loss.

F. Philip Dunkley played for Aldershot Command, while Tom Dunn's grandson (Justin Bishop) was to play 25 times for Ireland. Dunn himself died in 1975. Arthur Payne became an aircraft engineer at Filton and died in 1968, aged 59. He made 163 appearances for Bristol. Nigel Gibbs, whose brother (George) was also capped, became a headmaster at Colston's School and died in 2014, aged 91.

On Mar 21 the British Police included Arthur Bassett (Aberavon/Cardiff/Wales/Halifax, Wales & GB RL) and (W.J.) Evans in a match against Len Corbett's XV at Taunton.

A Welsh Army XV was again skippered by Wales fly half Bill Roberts (Cardiff), and as well as Tindill, Aldershot Services teams included Robert G.M. Grieve (Gala/Scotland), (R.E.) Prescott, Capt. Antony L. Warr (Oxford University/England), Lieut-Col. B.E. Nicholson (Harlequins/England) and fly half Lyn Williams (Cardiff).

'Tim' Warr had been capped twice in 1934 and served in the South Gloucestershire Hussars, becoming a schoolmaster and died in Taunton in 1995, aged 81. Basil Ellard Nicholson died aged 72, at Oxsted, Surrey in 1985. He was involved in planning the Normandy invasion. He was capped twice in 1938 and was a GB tourist to South Africa (1 test) that year.

Other Army sides included (D.T.) Kemp, J. (Bernard) Gough (Newport/Wales Trials), Jackie E. Bowcott (Cardiff/Cambridge University scrum half), H. Burns (fly half from the Cardiff area), W.B. (or D) Evans (Penarth, 2nd row), Duff, Horsburgh, W.M. ('Joe') Inglis (Cambridge University/Scotland), R.H. Dryden (Army/Watsonians/Scotland), Couchman and 'Dai' Parker (Warrington RL half-back).

Robert Hunter Dryden, having won one cap in 1937 as a wing, became a solicitor and died in 1996 in Edinburgh, aged 78.

RAF sides included the promising Newport-born teenager Leonard Price-Stevens of Halton Apprentices at scrum half, plus Ron Rankin, Wally Reynolds (Bristol), (Marshall) Harding, Keith I. Geddes (Cambridge University/Scotland full back) and Swansea three-quarters Sgt. Haydn Walters and LAC Haydn M. Powell.

Powell scored 34 tries for Swansea in 1937-38 – a club pre-war record – and then 26 tries in 1938-39. He joined Swansea from Neath in 1933-34. It is believed that he survived the war.

Rosslyn Park selected wing Elvet L. Jones (Llanelli/Wales/GB to South Africa 1938), but he withdrew. However, they did include Harding, (A.M.) Rees and William H. Whittaker (Penarth/Old Penarthians prop). Bill Whittaker was player, secretary and finally president of Old Penarthians RFC and began the club's famous Sevens tournament in 1950.

A London District side included T.E. Bacon (Cross Keys/Ebbw Vale centre), A.G. Dyke (Cross Keys prop), W.H. Stead (Castleford RL), R.G. Forbes-Bassett (Richmond/Rosslyn Park/Acton & Willesden RL), Emyr Williams (Neath front row) and H. Roughledge (St Helen's RL). Reginald George Forbes-Bassett died in Chelsea in 1961, aged 56. He had been a good cricketer while at Sherborne School.

A South Wales XV included Bleddyn L. Williams (Cardiff/Wales/B Lions to NZ/Australia 1950), wing Dennis Madden (Aberavon/Acton & Willesden, Wigan, Wales RL), fly half A/C V.N. Taylor (Cardiff (1 game, 1940)/RAF), 2nd row John Hopkins (Bridgend/Leicester) and back-rower Rees Williams (Swansea).

Major Stanley's XV v. Oxford University included Hollis, Buchanan and (J.K.) Watkins, while Denys G.G. Coles, the Oxford University Blue of 1937 and 1938, was reported as having died in December 1941. Born in Bristol in December 1917, he was serving as a Flying/Officer in the RAF's 22nd Squadron.

L.-Cpl. A. B. W. BUCHANAN (London Scottish).—A regular member of the London Scottish XV. for the past few years. He is on the light side, but he makes up for it in speed and dash. He is never far from the ball. Many worse players have been capped for Scotland, and many good judges think that he should have been.

A B W Buchanan

Gwyn Bayliss turned out as full back for Wasps. He had played for Brynmawr Grammar School/Brynmawr/Llanelli/North Midlands/Ebbw Vale/London Welsh/Pontypool/Wolverhampton/Barbarians and Wales (v. Scotland 1933). He worked as a company secretary, schoolmaster and journalist and played for Llanelli against NZ in 1935. He was born in Brynmawr 7/5/1907 and died in Blaenau Gwent 10/3/1976, aged 68, having lived for many years in the Wolverhampton area.

Welsh internationals 'Bunner' Travers and Ronnie Morris both made an appearance for Bath, whose Somerset wing John Stuart Bartlett, DFC, a Wing Commander who died on 22/8/1941 from injuries received in a flying crash on active service, was regarded by many as one of the cleverest in the game. After seven years in the RAF, chiefly as a flying instructor, he joined the Imperial Airways administrative staff in London and played for Richmond. He rejoined the RAF on the outbreak of war and was awarded the DFC for gallantry in 1940.

One of Bath's finest wings, he was educated at Brighton College, where he learned his football under Ernie G. Hammett, the Newport/England/GB centre. He was the son of a former manager of Lloyds Bank, who moved to London when John joined Imperial's administrative staff. At the time of his death, aged 29, he was in 255 Squadron, and was buried at the Brookwood Military Cemetery in Woking.

In Egypt, too, as the 'Desert Rats', the Eighth Army and their Aussie and Kiwi comrades found themselves a worthy adversary in Rommel, the 'Desert Fox' and his Afrika Korps, behind the lines of action the men from the forces 'Down Under' managed some rugby.

Gunner W. H. TRAVERS (Newport).—Son of the famous G. Travers, who helped Wales to beat the "All Blacks" in 1905. Just as good in other departments of scrummaging as he is at hooking—and that's saying a lot. Ten Caps.

William 'Bunner' Travers

The Freyberg Cup

The 2nd NZ Division was largely stationed in Egypt from 1940 to 1942, with NZ base units encamped at Maadi right through to 1946. Their commander, Freyburg, recognised the value of sports for physical and mental fitness, morale and cohesion.

He presented a trophy, the Divisional Commander's Cup (always known as the Freyberg Cup), for unit rugby supremacy within the 2nd NZ Division. It was keenly contested from 1940 to 1944 (though not in 1942 because of the division's preoccupation with desert operations). 'Internationals' included hard-fought games with South African teams.

The Freyberg Cup was awarded on each occasion that a knock-out tournament could be completed by all units of 2NZEF. Winners of this trophy were:

1940 – 19th Wellington Infantry Battalion.
1941 – 32nd Training Battalion
1942 – Not competed for
1943 – 28th Maori Battalion (more on this later) and
1944 – 22nd Wellington Infantry-Battalion.

British Propaganda Postcard uses Desert Rugby

Back to 1941, though, and the New Zealand Middle East Army played some other matches.

On Dec 21 they overcame Combined Services 34-5 (at Alexandria):

Tries: WO/2 J. Wells 2, WO/2 A.J. McAneney 2, Pte W.P. McHugh 2, Pte K.A. Welsh. Cons: Gnr W.I. Perriam 4, Welsh. Pen: Perriam. They included All Black forwards 2nd Lieut. Jack Finlay, WO/2 John Wells, Lance-Bmdr. Arthur Lambourn, Sgt John J. Best and Pte. Athol Mahoney.

Dec 26 saw them enjoy the tastiest of antipodean festive gifts with a 16-0 with a win over the Australian Imperial Forces Ordnance, 16-0 (at Gezira, Cairo).

The sparse official New Zealand Services games during this period back in the UK were:

Nov 29 – Lost to Rosslyn Park 3-30 (at Richmond). (E.R.) Knapp scored two of six Park tries.

Dec 13 – Beat Guy's Hospital 17-6 (at Honor Oak Park),

Meanwhile, two major Rugby League clashes had been:

May 17 – RL Challenge Cup final – Leeds 19 Halifax 2 at Odsal, Bradford.

Oct 18 – England 9 Wales 9 at Odsal, Bradford.

The comparative paucity – in quantity, not quality – of rugby played bears witness to the demands and worries of the year. Britain still largely stood alone in the West, though Hitler's mid-1941 *volte-face*, in attacking his former ally of convenience the Soviet Union, did lessen fears of any German attack by sea and land, rather than from the air.

In December conscription in Britain was extended to men aged between 18 and 50, while women would now serve in fire brigades and in women's auxiliary groups. Others, friend or foe, had it worse. As the temperature on the Moscow front fell to −31 °F (−37 °C), the earlier rapid German advances were faltering and freezing, but Russians in the siege of Leningrad froze and starved too.

Jews were being rounded up, shipped, ghetto and camp-restricted, starved and massacred in several parts of Europe. German troops were assisting Italy's failing forces in North Africa, and in the Far East British possessions, current or former, were under threat from Japan. On Christmas Day 1941, on those respective fronts, Benghazi was retaken but Hong Kong fell.

As the year closed, though, it was from further east that the biggest news with the greatest consequences came. Japan attacked Pearl Harbour early in December. The 'sleeping giant' awoke, angered. The USA, Britain, Canada, New Zealand, Australia, India, the Netherlands and China (already deeply involved) declared war on Japan, and the might of the USA was also to be thrown against Germany and Italy in what was now truly a Second World War..

The causes and locations of the fatalities listed below tells that same tale of the stages and the state of the war at this stage: four at sea with the Royal Navy; three in the RAF; one in Hong Kong; one bombed in England. Of those, four were English, two Irish, with one Scot and a Welshman: and in addition, an Aussie in Libya and a New Zealander in Greece.

Deaths of international representatives during 1941:

Jan 10 – William George Ernest (Bill) Luddington (England, 13 caps – 1923-26). He was a Master at Arms in the Royal Navy and was killed in action in the Mediterranean. Aged 46.

Mar 5 – Thomas Fairgrieve (Tommy) Dorward (Scotland, 5 caps, 1938-39). Died at Bourne, Castle Bytham, Lincolnshire of wounds received serving in the RAF. His brother Arthur won 15 caps (1950-57). Aged 24.

Mar 21 – Charles Francis George Thomas Hallaran, AM (Ireland, 15 caps – 1921-26). He was awarded the Albert Medal, but was killed in action on HMS Springbok whilst a Lieut. in the Royal Navy. His father won a cap in 1934. Aged 43.

Apr 13 – Patrick Bernard Coote, DFC (Ireland, 1 cap – 1933). He served in the RAF as a Wing Cmdr. and Adjutant of Bomber Command, but was shot down over Greece near Lake Prespa and his body was never found,

---

being presumed dead by December 1940. He had been awarded the DFC in 1940. Aged 31.

Apr 23 – Frederick Raymond Kerr (Australia, 1 cap – 1938). He was killed in action near Athens, aged 22.

May 22 – Rev Christopher Champain ('Kit') Tanner, AM (England, 5 caps – 1930-32). He was awarded the Albert Medal posthumously for saving wounded men after HMS Fiji was hit and sinking off Crete. He died within minutes of dragging a wounded sailor aboard a rescue ship. Navy Chaplain. Aged 32. One survivor was Vice-Admiral Sir Peverill Barton Reibey Wallop William-Powlett, KCB, KCMG, CBE, DSO (England, 1 cap, 1922).

Sept 4 – Norman Atherton Wodehouse, CB (England, 14 caps – 1910-13). He served as a Lieutenant in the Royal Navy in WW1 and was awarded the Royal Humane Society Silver Medal for saving life in 1915, becoming an ADC to His Majesty King George VI. He was drowned when in command of an Atlantic convoy as Vice-Admiral in the RNVR. His body was never found. Aged 54.

Nov 23 – Arthur William ('Art') Wesney (All Blacks, no tests). He played in three matches on the 1938 tour of Australia. He was a Captain, who was killed in action at Sidi Resegh, Libya. Aged 26.

Dec 23 – Vivian Gordon ('Bobby') Davies (England, 2 caps – 1922-25). He served in the Duke of Cornwall's Light Infantry in WW1 and was a Captain in the Royal Artillery, being killed by a bomb in England. Aged 42.

Dec 20 – Edmund William Francis de Vere Hunt (Ireland, 5 caps – 1930-33). His death was not confirmed until June 1944. Lieut., then Major in the Royal Artillery, he was killed at Wing Nel Chang Gap, Hong Kong. Aged 33.

Dec 25 – Cecil Rhys Davies (Wales, 1 cap – 1934). Died on Christmas Day serving in the RAF as Sqdn-Ldr. of 22 Squadron.

5
1942

In a year which was to see dramatic developments - some advantageous for the Allies, some potentially disastrous - in several of the major theatres of conflict, a somewhat more settled pattern emerged, in the UK at least, for such Services-dominated rugby as was able to be played.

England's Services played their Welsh and Scottish counterparts in the first of an unbroken series of home and away clashes 1942-5. Programmes for those with the Scots - some facsimiles of originals, others mock-ups - were later bound into an attractive souvenir book.

The originals for both those and the Welsh games are rather harder to find, though not overly so because sport-starved crowds meant considerable attendances, with the players selected usually of a very high standard.

The morale-boosting effect of those matches (despite postings still sometimes causing late withdrawals for, as one report had it 'wholly honourable reasons') meant that considerable

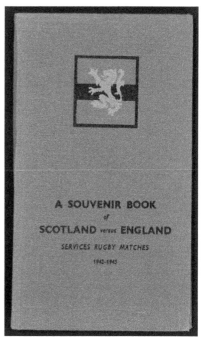

Wales v England Programme, Spring 1942

Souvenir Book of Programmes

lengths were gone to in ensuring that the likes of Welsh centre star Bleddyn Williams were available.

He and his boots were often rushed back from his RAF 'day job' home and abroad for what must sometimes have seemed an equally full time football field employment. His enjoyment of it, though, beams out from his host of team photographs, for the reproduction of some of which we are very grateful to his family.

Hitler's forces, meanwhile, advanced into the Soviet Union, and the battleship *Tirpitz* stalked the brave and frozen seamen on the Arctic convoys; Japan aimed at domination in and around the Pacific, bombed Darwin, Australia and stunningly took 'British' Singapore. Some 80,000, including Wilf Wooller, became prisoners of war, many failing to subsequently survive the privation and starvation inflicted in the Far East.

While the US sent General Douglas MacArthur and also eight fighter squadrons to Australia, the Phillipines fell; in the Mediterranean Malta continued to hold out against all odds; many from Down Under continued to vitally assist in the North African cause against the Italians and Germans, but Rommel and the Afrika Korps advanced across the desert, Tobruk falling; and the Dieppe Raid, with Canadians to the fore, sadly failed.

The spring, then, had brought four Services international matches, but club games were few and rugby was mainly confined to schoolboy and hospital games in the London area and service units' teams, though Cardiff, for instance, managed to play several home matches.

Wales Services v England, March 1942

SERVICES INTERNATIONALS:

The (non-capped) internationals were:

March 7 – WALES 17 ENGLAND 12 (at St Helen's, Swansea). (20,534).

The match had been postponed from February 28. Nearly £2,000 gate receipts were taken from a crowd that saw Gus Risman lead Wales back from 0-12 down at the interval.

A Gerry Hollis try had been followed by one from the New Zealander, Orton Knight, which George Gilthorpe converted. Then, Harry Kenyon's drop goal took England further ahead.

Wales hit back as Risman kicked a penalty, then he set up a try for Alan Edwards and he also converted Haydn Tanner's try to bring it to 11-12. Again Risman placed a long penalty and a try by fly half Willie Davies settled it for Wales.

Pre-war cap Harold Thomas (Neath/Salford RL/Army) withdrew and Leslie Thomas replaced him in the Welsh pack, while wing Edgar Williams was selected for both countries, but opted for England. Knight and Ron Rankin, a pre-war cap, were overseas players for England.

When Chris Newton-Thompson pulled out late, the newspapers listed a J. Jubb of the Royal Navy as playing, but it appears to be Ken Jubb of the Army and Leeds RL. England centre Francis Edwards and wing forward John Watkins also withdrew, with Kenyon and 'Ned' Hodgson coming in.

Wales - *+Cpl. (CH) Davies (now Army); A/C Alan S. Edwards (RAF/Salford RL), Sgt. A.J.F. ('Gus') Risman (Army/Salford RL, capt), L/Cpl. (formerly Driver) Tom Sullivan (Swansea/Army), *Cpl. Syd A. Williams (Army/Aberavon/Salford RL); *Sgt. W.T.H. (Willie) Davies (RAF/Swansea/Bradford Northern RL), *+O/Cadet (later Sgt.) (H) Tanner (now Army); *Capt. ('Wendy') Davis (now Army), *+Sgt. Travers (now Army), *Cpl. (E.R.) Price (now RAF), *Marine Harry Payne (Swansea/Navy), Lance-Cpl. Les M. Thomas (Llanelly/Army/later Oldham RL), Lance-Cpl. Gwyn Williams (Cardiff/Army/Wigan RL), *+F/O Manfield (now RAF), Sgt. Trevor J.F. Foster (Army/Bradford Northern RL).

Touch Judge: Vivian G.J. Jenkins (Wales/GB 1938).

Tries: Tanner, (WTH) Davies, Edwards. Con/2 Pens: Risman.

England - *Flight-Cadet Ron Rankin (NSW/Royal Australian Air Force); 2nd Lieut. E.J.H. Williams (Rosslyn Park/Army/Cambridge University), Sgt. Stan Brogden (Huddersfield/Army/Leeds RL), F/O C.G. Harry Kenyon

---

(Coventry/RAF), Lieut. Gerry A. Hollis (Oxford University/Navy); *Group-Ops. G.A. ('Gus') Walker (RAF/Blackheath), *Capt. (J) Ellis (now Army); *Cpl. Raymond J. Longland (RAF/Northampton), Sqdn-Ldr. Gilthorpe (now Coventry/RAF), *Capt. Prescott (now Army, captain), +Cpl. Joe S. Mycock (Harlequins/Sale/RAF), *Capt. Huskisson (now Army), F/O Orton W. Knight (Auckland/RNZAF), Sgt. E. ('Ned')

Hodgson (Army/Broughton Rangers RL), Cpl. Ken Jubb (Army/Leeds RL).

Tries: Knight, Hollis. Con: Gilthorpe. DG: Kenyon.

Referee: Fred G. Phillips (Pontarddulais, Wales). He was a builder, who became WRU President in 1958-59.

Allan McM. Buchanan (Ireland) was due to be the referee, but apparently did not get there.

ALLAN McMillan BUCHANAN was an Ireland prop forward who won six caps (1926-27). Born 21/5/1894. Died Barnet 24/11/1956 whilst a passenger in a car that was hit by a lorry. Portora High School/Trinity College, Dublin. He worked in medicine and later as a Schoolmaster and was Bursar at Leys School, Cambridge.

The following had appeared in the 1940 Red Cross Internationals:

Wales: (CH) Davies, Tanner, ('Wendy') Davis, Travers, Price and Manfield.

England: Ellis, Gilthorpe, Prescott and Huskisson.

WALES ('newcomers' only):

ALAN Spencer EDWARDS – Wing. Born Kenfig Hill 15/5/1916. Died December 1986. Kenfig Hill/Aberavon/RAF/Salford (from September 1935; 129 tries in 199 games), Dewsbury, Leeds, Bradford Northern (83 tries in 133 games; last game in September 1949), Wales (18 games) and GB (7 tests) RL. He was an Air Craftsman, then Cpl., then Sgt. in the RAF. Toured NZ/Aust with GB in 1936 when aged 19 (21 tries in 16 games).

Augustus John Ferdinand ('GUS') RISMAN – Centre/fly half. Born Cardiff 21/3/1911. Died Whitehaven 17/10/1994. His parents came from Latvia. Barry County School/South Church Street (Cardiff Docks)/Dinas Powys/Cardiff Scottish/Army/Salford, Dewsbury, Workington, Batley, Wales and GB RL. His son, Beverley, was capped for England/GB RU and GB RL. Gus was a Sgt., then Lieut. in the Army.

Thomas (TOM) SULLIVAN – Wing/Centre. Swansea (debut in 1936-37)/Army. He was a Driver, then a Lance-Cpl., then a Sgt. Instructor in the ATC.

Alan Edwards   *Gus Risman*

SYDney Arthur WILLIAMS – Wing. Born Aberavon 17/4/1918. Died in the Neath area 28/8/1976. Wales Under 16s/Aberavon Quins/Aberavon/Maesteg/ Army/Barbarians/Salford and Wales RL. 3 caps (1939). He became a café proprietor after serving as a Cpl. in the Army.

William Thomas Harcourt (WILLIE) DAVIES – Fly half. Born Penclawdd 23/8/1916. Died Rustington, West Sussex 26/9/2002. Gowerton Grammar School/Penclawdd/Swansea/Llanelli (1game)/RAF/Headingley/London Welsh. 6 Union caps (1936-39). Bradford Northern, Wales and GB RL. He was called 'Bill' in RL circles, then becoming a schoolmaster at Weston Grammar School and served as a Sgt. PTI in the RAF.

HARRY PAYNE – 2nd Row. Born Treboeth 10/12/1907. Died Swansea 22/12/2000. Morriston/Swansea/Royal Navy. 1 cap (1935). He served in the Royal Marines.

LESlie Morgan THOMAS – 2nd Row. Llangennech/Llanelli/Oldham (58 games, 91 points), Leeds, Cardiff, Wales and GB RL. He was a Lance-Cpl. in the Army.

GWYN WILLIAMS – Back Row. Born Taffs Well. Died Swanage 27/12/1996. Cardiff/Army/Wigan RL. Brother of caps Bleddyn and Lloyd. He was a Police

Willie Davies

Les Thomas

Trevor Foster

Officer, then a Lance-Cpl. in the Army and was shot in the head and lost an eye in North Africa while on duty with the Welsh Guards.

TREVOR John French FOSTER, MBE – Back Row. Born Newport 3/12/1914. Died Bradford 2/4/2005. Holy Cross Roman Catholic School (Newport)/ Pill Harriers/Newport/Army/Bradford Northern, Wales and GB RL. He was a Sgt-Instructor in the Army and later an Educational Welfare Officer in Bradford, being awarded the MBE in 2001 for his services to the Community.

ENGLAND

RONald RANKIN, DFC, Croix de Guerre – Full back. Born Majors Green (NSW)

Ron Rankin

3/11/1914 or 1915. Died 1991. Hurlstone High School/Sydney Tech College/ Randwick/Drummoyne/NSW/Australia/RAF/RAAF. 7 caps for Australia (1936-38). He was a Schoolmaster then a P/Officer and had come to GB in 1939 with the Australian team, who returned home without playing due to the outbreak of war. Believed to have taken part in the commando raid on St. Nazaire, destroyed many enemy planes in N Africa and survived a crash landing on a Pacific island.

EDGAR J.H. WILLIAMS – Wing. Born Birmingham 1918. Bromsgrove School/England Schools/Emmanuel College, Cambridge University/Army/ South Wales/Barbarians, later Moseley. Army (2nd Lieut., then Lieut.). He returned to Cambridge University in 1946 and was Discus champion there.

STANley BROGDEN – Centre. Born Holbeck 15/3/1910. Died Bradford 1981. Bradford Northern, Huddersfield, Leeds, Hull, Rochdale, Salford and GB RL/Army Sergeant).

C.G. Henry (HARRY) KENYON, DFC – Centre. Coventry/RAF/Birmingham. Born Coventry 22/4/1915. Died 2006 Redbridge. He was a Sgt., F/Officer, P/ Officer, then Squadron Ldr. in 550 Squadron and was awarded the DFC in 1943.

Gerard (GERRY) A. HOLLIS – Wing. Born Hull 16/5/1919. Died Salisbury 23/11/2005. St Edward's School (Oxford)/Christ Church College, Oxford University/Sale/Navy/Combined Services/Barbarians/Hull and East Riding. He was a PTI in the Navy at RNC, Dartmouth, but later was at Wells Theological

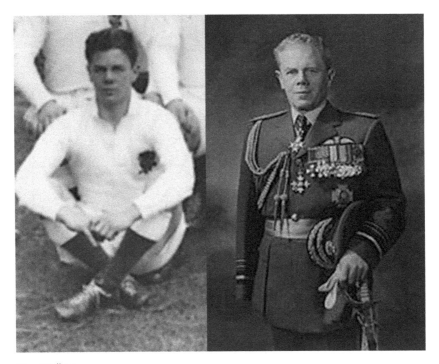

Gus Walker

College; then became a Curate at Stepney, then at Rossington (near Doncaster); Rector at Armthorpe; Vicar of Rotherham; Rural Dean and Honorary Canon of Sheffield Cathedral; Archdeacon of Birmingham; Honorary Canon of Birmingham Cathedral; General Synod (1975-84).

SIR George Augustus ('GUS') WALKER GCB, CBE, DSO, DFC, AFC– Fly half. Born Garforth 24/8/1912. Died King's Lynn 11/2/1986. St. Bees School/ RAF/Blackheath/St Catharine's College, Cambridge University (No Blue)/ Barbarians/Yorkshire/Eastern Counties. 2 caps (1939). He commanded bomber squadrons in WW2, but though he lost an arm in a bomb explosion, he stayed in the RAF to become an Air Chief Marshal. He later became an International referee and was RFU President in 1965-66.

RAYmond John ('Rastus') LONGLAND – Prop. Born 29/12/1908. Died Buckinghamshire 21/9/1975. Olney/Buckingham/Bedford/Northampton/RAF/ Combined Services/Barbarians/East Midlands. 19 caps (1932-38). He was a Carpenter, a Licensee and also a Schoolmaster, being a Cpl. and PTI in the RAF.

JOEseph Stephen MYCOCK – Second Row. Born 17/1/1914. Died 30/5/2004 Llanbedr-y-Cennin, Aberconwy, Wales. Moor Allerton Prep School (Didsbury)/Giggleswick School/Sale/Vale of Lune/Harlequins/Barbarians/

Scotland v England
Programme, March 1942

Fred Huskisson

'Robin' Prescott when later
Secretary of the RFU

Lancashire/RAF/Combined Services. 5 caps (1947-48). He was a Managing Director.

ORTON Wallace KNIGHT – Back Row. Born Auckland (NZ) 12/9/1912. Died Auckland (NZ) 23/3/1999. Beresford Street School/Auckland Grammar School/Auckland/Manawatu/Canterbury/NZ Services/RAF/RNZAF. He was a Flight-Lieut., P/Officer and Navigator in Malta, becoming a master butcher and senior executive with a meat company. His son, Michael, was a 1968 All Black.

Edward ('NED') HODGSON – Back Row. Army/Brookland, Oldham, Cumberland, Broughton Rangers, Bramley and Workington RL. He coached at Whitehaven RL and was an Army Sgt.

KENneth JUBB - Born 11/5/1912. Died 3rd quarter 1993 Bradford. Castleford, Leeds and GB RL. He was a Cpl., then a Sgt-Major and later became the landlord of the Red Lion public house and the Town Hall Hotel, Park Lane, Leeds.

March 21 – SCOTLAND 21 ENGLAND 6 (at Inverleith).
Scotland gained a deserved victory, being the better side both back and forward though it took them 26 minutes before they opened the scoring and the result was inflated by 'Copey' Murdoch's brace of drop goals, while Billy Munro had a fine game in the centre.

Scotland led 8-0 at the interval with tries by Duncan Shaw, after a 'Donny' Innes run, and then by scrum half M.R. Dewar that was converted by Murdoch. Though England full back Grahame Parker placed a penalty, Murdoch dropped a goal, but scrum half Jack Ellis fought his way over for a try to reduce Scotland's lead to 12-8.

Then, Scotland raced clear with fly half Tom Gray scoring a try and Murdoch not only converting, but followed by dropping his second goal.

This match was played at Inverleith as Murrayfield was being used by the RAMC as a supply depot. England centre Francis Edwards again withdrew and Harry Kenyon deputized, while Wally Reynolds came in the back row when Orton Knight could not play.

Scotland – *+Capt. W.C.W. ('Copey') Murdoch (Royal Artillery/Hillhead HSFP); *+Lieut. J.R.S. ('Donny') Innes (RAMC/Aberdeen GSFP), +Capt. W.H. (Billy) Munro (Commandos/Glasgow HSFP), Flt-Lieut. Eric G.C. Hunter (Watsonians/RAF), Cadet Ewan C.K. Douglas (Edinburgh University); +2nd Lieut. Tom Gray (Heriot's FP/KSOB), Ldg. Airman M.R. Dewar (Watsonians/Fleet Air Force); Cpl. J. Donald Maltman (Hawick/Cameronians), *2nd Lieut. Robert G.M. Grieve (Royal Engineers/Kelso/Edinburgh Acad-Wdrs), Lieut. Neil W. Ramsay (Army/Royal Engineers), Lieut. Stanley G.A. Harper (Watsonians/RNVR), *Major Christian L. Melville (London Scottish/Black Watch) (capt.), Lieut. Archibald W.B Buchanan (London Scottish), *Capt. P. Laurie Duff (Glasgow Acads./Highland Light Infantry), *Capt. G. Duncan Shaw (Sale/Gala/Royal Artillery).

Touch-Judge: Lieut-Col. David James MacMyn (11 caps, 1925-28). SRU President in 1958-59. GB to Argentine 1927, played for Cambridge University and served in the RAMC.

Tries: Shaw, Dewar, Gray. 2 Cons/2 DG: Murdoch.

England – *Major Grahame W. Parker (Army/Gloucester); 2nd Lieut. (E.J.H.) Williams, Sgt. Brogden, F/O Kenyon, Lieut. Hollis; *Grp/Ops (GA) Walker, *Capt. Ellis; *Capt. Longland, Sqdn- Ldr. Gilthorpe, *Capt. Prescott (capt.), +Cpl. Mycock, *Capt. Huskisson, *Rear-Admiral J.K. Watkins (United Services, Portsmouth/Navy), Lieut. C.L Newton-Thompson (Cambridge University/Army), P/O Wally T.W. Reynolds (Bristol/RAF).

Touch-Judge: Capt. H.A. Haigh-Smith.

Try: Ellis. Pen: Parker.

Referee: Allan McM. Buchanan (Ireland).

England's Newton-Thompson and Watkins had appeared in the 1940 Red-Cross internationals.

SCOTLAND

William Copeland Wood ('COPEY') MURDOCH – Full Back. Born Old Kilpatrick 3/10/1914. Died 12/10/1997 Helensburgh. Hillhead High School/Hillhead HSFP/ Barbarians/Army. 9 caps (1935-48). A Banker and a Captain in the Royal Artillery. He became an International referee and also controlled a Varsity match.

J. Robert Stephen ('DONNY') INNES – Wing/Centre. Born 16/9/1917 Aberdeen. Died 21/1/2012 Aberdeen. Aberdeen Grammar School/GSFP/Aberdeen Univ./Barbarians/ Army. A doctor and a Lieut., then Capt. in the RAMC. He became SRU President in 1973-74. 8 caps (1939-48).

William Hutton (BILLY) MUNRO – Centre. Born 28/9/1918. Died 12/9/1970. Glenalmond Acad/Scottish Public Schools/Glasgow High School/Glasgow HSFP/Army. He was a Capt. in the Commandos, and then the Royal Corps of Signals. 2 caps (1947).

'Copey' Murdoch

'Donny' Innes: v England (on the ground) 1939 and, later, as administrator.

ERIC George Campbell HUNTER – Centre. Born 6/10/1914. Died 3ʳᵈ quarter 1975 in Cheshire. George Watson's School/Watsonians/RAF. He was a Flight-Lieut. (later Lieut.) in the RAF and was the Lothian Boys Golf Champion in 1932.

EWAN Campbell Kennedy DOUGLAS – Wing/Centre. Born 14/11/1922. Died 29/12/1999, aged 77. Fettes College/Edinburgh University/Edinburgh Wdrs-Acads/RAF (Chessington). He was a Cadet, then a Flight-Lieut. in the RAF. Hammer thrower for GB in 1948/1952 Olympics and 1950/1954 European Championships and 1954/1958 Commonwealth Games (bronze in 1954). He competed 18 times for GB. A doctor, who was a GP in Penicuik, before emigrating to Geelong and St Kilda's (Australia) in 1962, retiring to France and later to Spain in the mid-1980s. 6'4" in height, he weighed 15 stones. He married three times, including a Lebanese-French countess, while his partner at the time of his death was an Irish opera singer.

Thomas (TOM) GRAY – Fly half. Born 20/1/1917. Died Edinburgh 31/3/2000. Heriot's College/Heriot's FP/Northampton/Army/Barbarians. He was a protective clothing salesman and served in the King's Own Scottish Borderers as a 2nd Lieut., then Lieut. Part of his left foot was blown off by an anti-tank shell, but he still played rugby after the war.

M.R. DEWAR – Scrum Half. George Watson's College (1936)/Watsonians/ Alleyn's School (Crescent House, 1938-41)/RAF. He was a Cadet in the Fleet Air Arm, then a Leading Naval Airman, but it is not known if he survived the war. He may have been Maurice R. Dewar (born 1924, died 2006).

John DONALD MALTMAN – Prop. Hawick/Army. He was a Cpl., then a Sgt. in the Cameronians.

ROBERT George Moir GRIEVE – Hooker/Prop. Born Maxton, St Boswell's 1/2/1911. Died Chiltern, Bucks 13/8/2000. Kelso High School/Edinburgh Acads/Edinburgh Wdrs/Kelso/Army. He worked in the family building business and served in the Royal Engineers as a 2nd Lieut., then Lieut. 7 caps (1935-36).

NEIL William RAMSAY, OBE – Prop. Army/Northern Command. He was a Lieutenant, then Captain (1945), then Lieutenant-Colonel in the Royal Engineers. In 1961 he was 'loaned' to the Government of Ghana and also in that year received an OBE. Born 7/1/1916. Died Surrey 2nd quarter 1989.

Stanley George Anthony HARPER – 2nd Row. Born 29/11/1912. Watsonians/Navy. Lieut in the RNVR. He was married in Bombay 1944. He may have died in Durban, South Africa after emigrating in 1957, being an hotelier.

CHRISTIAN Landale MELVILLE, DSO – 2nd Row. Born 9/12/1913. Died North Dorset 23/4/1984. Sedbergh School/London Scottish/Army/Barbarians. He was a Major in the Black Watch. 3 caps (1937).

Archibald W.B. BUCHANAN – Back Row. London Scottish/Barbarians/ Tonbridge Services XV. He was a Lieut. in the Army.

Peter Laurance (LAURIE) DUFF – Back Row. Born Bothwell, Lanark 12/11/1912. Died Stirling 31/10/2002. Glasgow Academy/Glasgow Acad's/Army/ Barbarians/B Lions 1938 (2 tests). He was a farmer and a captain in the Highland Light Infantry. 6 caps (1936-39). He was nicknamed 'The Laughing Cavalier'.

George DUNCAN SHAW – Back Row. Born Galashiels 29/5/1915. Died Galashiels 14/11/1999. Oundle School/Galashiels/ London Scottish/Sale/Cheshire/Tonbridge Services XV Barbarians/Army/ He was a textiles manufacturer and a captain in the Royal Artillery. 6 caps (1935-39).

ENGLAND

GRAHAMe Wilshaw PARKER, MBE, OBE, TD – Full back. Born Bristol 11/2/1912. Died Sidmouth 11/11/1995. The Crypt School/Cambridge Univ/Gloucester/Army/ Blackheath/Gloucestershire/Barbarians. 2 caps (1938). He was a schoolmaster at Dulwich College and Blundells School and a Gloucestershire County Cricketer, being a Major and later a Lieut-Colonel in the RASC. He became secretary of the MCC and Gloucestershire Cricket Club.

England v Wales programme, 1942

Walter Thomas Whitlock (WALLY, 'Foxy') REYNOLDS – Back Row. Born Bristol 21/11/1914. Died Bristol 1977. St George School/Cotham Park RFC/St Paul's College, Cheltenham/Bristol (debut 1934)/RAF. He was a schoolmaster at South-Bristol Central School and Cotham, serving in the RAF as a Cpl., then a P/Officer. He lived in the Bedminster area of Bristol.

March 28 - ENGLAND 3 WALES 9 (at Kingsholm, Gloucester). (12,000).
Though this game produced exciting moments there was very little top-class play behind a scrum that England generally dominated. The Welsh breakaway forwards stopped England's backs, though out wide there was a fine battle between the Williams wingers – one on either side, though unrelated.

Wales captain Gus Risman opening the scoring with a penalty but England wing forward Wally Reynolds levelled with a try before the break. Then, Wales pulled clear as Rugby League players Alan Edwards and Trevor Foster scored unconverted tries. In a frantic finish, England's centres had chances, but Harry Kenyon missed a drop at goal and the newcomer A.C. Simmonds dropped the ball on the line. It was said that 'Bunner' Travers had retired from rugby, but he was back playing a few weeks later, seemingly having regretted his hasty decision. For England, Ron Rankin had to withdraw and Grahame Parker was brought back to play on his home ground.

Action between England and Wales at Gloucester, 1942

England - *Major (G.W.) Parker; 2nd Lieut (E.J.H.) Williams, Sub-Lieut. A.C. Simmonds (RNE College, Dartmouth/Navy), F/O Kenyon, Sub-Lieut. A.L. Evans (Rosslyn Park/Cambridge University/Navy); *Group-Ops Walker, *Capt. Ellis; *Cpl. Longland, Sqdn-Ldr. Gilthorpe, *Capt Prescott (capt.), +Cpl Mycock, *Capt Huskisson, Lieut. Newton-Thompson, Sgt. Hodgson, P/O Reynolds.

Try: Reynolds.

Wales - *+Cpl. (C.H.) Davies; A/C Edwards, Sgt. Risman (capt.), L/Cpl. Sullivan, *Cpl. (S.A.) Williams; *+Sgt. (W.T.H.) Davies, *+O/Cadet (or Sgt.) Tanner; *Capt. ('Wendy') Davis, Pte. Jim Regan (Cardiff/Army/Huddersfield RL), *Cpl. (E.R.) Price (RAF), *Marine Payne, *O/Cadet Vivian J. Law (Newport/Army), Lance-Cpl. (Gwyn) Williams, *+F/O Manfield, Sgt. Foster.

Tries: Edwards, Foster. Pen: Risman.

Referee: Frank Mansell (Gloucester). (Also shown in the media as Mantell and Marshall!).

The England side, March 1942

The Wales side, March 1942

ENGLAND

A.C. SIMMONDS – Centre. RNE College, Dartmouth/RNE College, Keyham/ Navy. He was a Sub-Lieut. in the Navy and served on HMS Victory in 1949.

A.L. EVANS – Wing. Rosslyn Park/Cambridge University/Navy. He was a Sub-Lieut, then Lieut, then a Captain in the Navy (though the Programme said he was in the Army!).

WALES

James (JIM) REGAN – Hooker. Born 1st quarter 1909 at 13 North William Street, Cardiff. Died Cardiff 2nd quarter 1964. Cardiff/Army/Crawshay's Welsh/Huddersfield and Wales RL. He was a Private, then a Lance-Sgt. in the Army. His father was a docks labourer, while his mother came from Liverpool.

VIVian John LAW – 2nd Row. Born Cardiff 11/6/1910. Died Newport 22/4/1989. Newport High School/Newport HSOB/Newport/Army. Company Representative and served in the Army. He was an Officer-cadet in the Monmouthshire Regiment and the Royal Artillery and in 1934 had been selected for an Irish Trial, but did not play in it. 1 cap (1939) as a prop from Newport, whom he served as captain and later as a committeeman.

April 11 – ENGLAND 5 SCOTLAND 8 (at Wembley). (20,000).
Scotland again proved just too strong in the line-out and loose, though England held the edge in the set-scrums. England scrum half Jack Ellis scored the first try after 25 minutes with a solo effort from a scrum and the Australian Ron Rankin converted.

But, Scotland levelled before the interval when Tom Gray ran through superbly, handing on to centre Eric Hunter, who gave a pass that looked forward to the supporting back-rower Duncan Shaw, who crossed and 'Copey' Murdoch converted.

The only score of the second spell was a try by Scotland scrum half Dewar of the Fleet Air Arm, who raced over at the side of a post, though Murdoch failed to convert. Peter Hastings twice nearly scored but Gray was back to save on each occasion. Gray and Dewar played well at half back but England had their chances and did not take them.

Scotland had been forced to make late changes to their side as first, centre Billy Munro pulled out, having being injured playing for the Army against the RAF and 'Donny' Innes moved inside for the pre-war cap James Craig to take a place on the wing. An even later change saw Innes drop out and the almost unknown Cadet D.A. Roberts came in, while Stanley

---

Harper could not play in the pack and so another little-known player, Captain J.B. McNeill, played in the back row.

Programme and action from Wembley, 1942

For England, Peter Hastings replaced the selected Edgar Williams with Gerry Hollis moving from centre to wing. It was the first Rugby Union match at Wembley for 17 years, when the RAF had played against the Army in 1925.

England – *P/O Rankin; Lieut Hollis, Sub-Lieut. (A.C.) Simmonds, 2nd Lieut. Peter R.H. Hastings (Oxford University/Army), 2nd Lieut. (A.L.) Evans; P/O Kenyon, *Capt. Ellis; *Cpl. Longland, Sqdn-Ldr. Gilthorpe, *Capt. Prescott (capt.), +Cpl. Mycock, *Capt. Huskisson, Sgt. Hodgson, P/O W. (Bill) Fallowfield (Northampton), Cpl. Reynolds.

Touch-Judge: Capt. H.A. Haigh-Smith.

Try: Ellis. Con: Rankin.

Scotland – *+Capt. Murdoch; *Capt. John B. Craig (Heriot's FP), Flt-Lieut. Hunter, Cadet D.A. Roberts (Edinburgh Academy/Wdrs), Cadet Douglas; +2nd Lieut. Gray, Ldg. Airman Dewar; Cpl. Maltman, *2nd Lieut. (R.G.M.) Grieve, Lieut. Ramsay, *Capt. Duff, *Major Melville (capt), Lieut. Buchanan, Capt. J.B. McNeill (Glasgow HSFP), *Capt. (G.D.) Shaw.

Touch-Judge: Capt. T.C. Wilson.

Tries: Shaw, Dewar. Con: Murdoch.

Referee: Sqdn-Ldr. Cyril H.Gadney (Leicester).

ENGLAND

PETER Robin Hood HASTINGS (later became Captain P.R.H. Hastings-Bass) – Centre/Fly Half. Born Swindon 16/7/1920. Died Kingsclere, Hants 4/6/1964. Stowe School/England Schools/Oxford University/Army/Welsh Guards. He changed his name officially in 1954, having been a Lieut., then a Capt. in the Welsh Guards and he was later a successful Racehorse Trainer.

William (BILL) FALLOWFIELD, OBE – Back Row. Born Barrow 20/7/1914. Died 12/11/1985. Barrow Grammar School/Northampton/East Midlands/St Catherine's College,Cambridge University (1936)/Ulster/RAF. He became the RL secretary (1946-1974), having served in the RAF as an Education officer, Intelligence officer, P/Officer, then Flight-Lieut. He also became a TV commentator on Rugby League and was awarded the OBE in 1961.

SCOTLAND

JOHN Binnie CRAIG – Wing. Born 7/12/1918 Calcutta. Died Caithomgate, Edinburgh 1976. Gala Academy/Heriot's College/Heriot's FP/Army. 1 cap (1939). He was a sales manager and a Capt in the Army.

Programmes from Scottish wartime matches

D.A.ROBERTS – Centre. Edinburgh Academy-Wdrs. A Cadet, then a Flying-officer in the RNVR, little is known of him, though he survived the war and played in a Scotland trial in 1946.

J.B.McNEILL – Back row. Glasgow High School/Glasgow HSFP. He was a Captain in the Commandos. He survived the war.

February 7 - Ireland XV 6 British Army 9 (at Ravenhill, Belfast). (8,000).

Army - (CH) Davies; Unwin, Brogden, Risman, D.G. Bevis (Aldershot Services); (OJ) Morris, Tanner; (WEN) Davis, Travers, Prescott, Huskisson, P.J. McCarthy, Hudson, Newton-Thompson, (Gwyn) Williams.

Tries: Brogden, Morris. Pen: Risman.

Ireland XV - M.B. Williams (Clontarf/University College, Dublin); +Kevin Patrick O'Flanagan (University College, Dublin, 1 cap, 1947), S.D. Walsh (Dublin University), *J. Desmond Torrens (Bohemians, 4 caps, 1938-39), T. Chamberlain (Blackrock College); Hugh Greer (NIFC), +Hugh De Lacy (Dublin University, 2 caps, 1948); +Matthew Robert Neely (Queens University, Belfast/Navy, 4 caps, 1947), D. Riordan (University College, Cork), D. Ryan (University College Dublin), *2nd Lieut. Thomas Anthony Aloyisus (Tommy) Headon (University College, Dublin, 2 caps, 1939), +Ernest Keefe (Sunday's Well/6 caps, 1947-48), *Captain Robert A. Alexander (NIFC/11 caps (1936-39)/GB 1938 to South Africa – 3 tests), Jack J. Guiney (Clontarf), K. O'Brien (Bective Rangers).

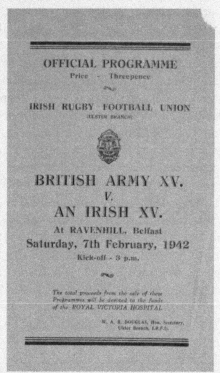

OFFICIAL PROGRAMME

Price - Threepence

IRISH RUGBY FOOTBALL UNION
(ULSTER BRANCH)

BRITISH ARMY XV.
V.
AN IRISH XV.

At RAVENHILL, Belfast

Saturday, 7th February, 1942
Kick-off - 3 p.m.

The total proceeds from the sale of these Programmes will be devoted to the funds of the ROYAL VICTORIA HOSPITAL

W. A. B. DOUGLAS, Hon. Secretary, Ulster Branch, I.R.F.U.

Programme from the match

Try: Walsh. Pen: (MB) Williams.

Robert Alexander was killed at the Battle of Lemon Bridge, Sicily during the Allied landings on 19/7/1943. He is buried at Catania War Cemetery. He was in the Royal Inniskilling Fusiliers.

> Dr. Kevin O'Flanagan was one of Ireland's greatest all-round sportsmen, playing, like his brother Mick, both rugby and soccer for his country; and representing Arsenal, UC Dublin and London Irish amongst others before building a notable career as physician and sporting and Olympic administrator.

In Scotland and in Ireland, as elsewhere, there was a variety of usually charity-related games held at all levels when possible during wartime, as the programme pictures show.

Other matches of note up to May 1942 included:

Jan 10 – Cardiff 26 NZ Naval Colts XV 14 (at Arms Park, Cardiff). Cardiff – Tries: T. Norton 2, T. Oppenshaw, Jim Hickey, (Bleddyn) Williams, A. Russell Taylor. Cons: (Bill) Tamplin 4. NZ Naval Colts – Tries: R. Ongley, A.G. Sutherland. Con/2 Pens: A. Stewart. Wales cap Russell Taylor, a 1938 GB tourist to South Africa, played probably his only game for Cardiff.

Jan 24 – D. Percival (Cardiff) scored five tries against RNE College, Dartmouth. He appeared only three times for the club in 1946-47.

Jan 31 – NZ Army 6 NZ Air Force 6 (at Chippenham).

March 12 – Oxford University 8 Cambridge University 17 (at Oxford). The game was postponed from February 28. The Oxford captain was Dudley A. Benjamin Garton-Sprenger and the side included 2nd Lieut. (later Lieut.) H.J.C. Rees (Llandovery School/Rosslyn Park/Army) at centre, who scored a try. The Cambridge captain was Ronald Peter Sinclair (see 1941 – who was killed in action during September 1943). The rival captains had previously attended Bedford School together. Oxford – Try: Rees, A.E. Murray. Con: H.D. Darcus. Cambridge – Tries: H.E. Watts 2, R.H. Whitworth. Con: C. McIver. Pens: McIver, Sinclair. Referee: (CH) Gadney.

Apr 4 – Army 3 RAF 14 (at Richmond). 'Bunner' Travers appeared for the Army – seven days after reports that he had retired. Edward H. (Ted) Sadler appeared in the RAF side.

> **Apr 6 – J.E. Thorneloe's XV 11 Barbarians 24 (at Leicester).**
> Mike Sayers was killed in an air crash in England on 6/12/1943, while it appears that L.G. Stevenson (Richmond), (E) Grant, (HJC) Rees, Hastings, Gilthorpe, H.L. Varnish (Rugby), R.A. Crouch (Felsted School/Rosslyn Park) and W.H. Richards (club unknown) all came in at the last minute to replace Parker, Innes, Murdoch, Munro, Toft, Prescott, Manfield and Duff.

> The Barbarians never recorded the newcomers as having played, while Stevenson had originally been selected for Thorneloe's XV.
>
> Tries: Evans 2, Sayers, Melville, Rees. Cons: Sayers 2, Gilthorpe. Pen: Sayers.
>
> J.E. Thorneloe's XV was to include – PTI Cyril B. Holmes (Manchester/Army/England 3 caps 1947-48), Haydn Walters (Swansea), A/C Victor J. Lyttle (Collegians/Bedford/Ireland 3 caps 1938-39), (Gus) Walker, (J) Regan, Harry F. Wheatley (Coventry/England 7 caps 1936-39), Longland, Fallowfield and (JTW) Berry (capt). It appears that Holmes, Lyttle, (Gus) Walker, Regan and Longland did not play.
>
> Try: K. James, K. Biggar. Con/Pen: (BWT) Ritchie.
>
> Referee: (RF) Barradell (Leicester Society).

Apr 25 – Middlesex Sevens (Final) - St Mary's Hospital 8 RAF 6.

Nim Hall and N.O. Bennett appeared for St Mary's while the RAF side was: (A.S.) Edwards, (E.C.) Hunter, (W.T.H.) Davies, Parsons; Sadler, Gilthorpe and (W.T.W.) Reynolds.

Norman Osborn ('Nobby', 'Billy') Bennett, formerly of Epsom College (1936-41), went on to play for Waterloo, Harlequins, United Services Portsmouth, Navy, Barbarians, Public School Wanderers, London Counties, Hampshire, Surrey and Lancashire. He was born in Putney 21/9/22 and died at Dinkley, Blackburn 7/7/2005, aged 82. He served in the Navy as a Surgeon-Lieut; played cricket for the Free Foresters, Navy, Worcestershire and the MCC; was a doctor in Wigan and gained 7 caps for England at rugby (1947-1948). He was an expert at Sevens with St Mary's Hospital, alongside England colleagues (E.K.) Scott and Hall.

A RNZAF side beat St Bart's Hospital 10-0 but then lost 3-8 to Guy's Hospital in Round 6 and a NZ Army side lost to St Mary's Hospital 0-16 in Round 5.

That weekend the city of Bath was badly bombed by the Germans, and amongst the damaged buildings was the West Stand of Barh RFC's Recreation Ground.

May 2 – Italy 22 Romania 3 (at Arena Civica, Milan). Referee: Mr. Hossenbach (Germany).

Bomb-damaged stand at Bath RFC

The New Zealand Middle East Army played the following matches in the first half of 1942:

Feb 1 – Beat Rest of Egypt 22-0 (at Alexandria).

Tries: Pte. W. Burgess, Cpl. L.R. Pye, 2nd Lieut. Jack Finlay, Cpl. T.F. Hegglun.

Cons: Gnr. W.I. Perriam, Sgt. J.W. Fleming. Pens: Perriam 2.

The side included All Blacks Finlay, Arthur Lambourn, Tom Morrison and Athol Mahoney and a future All Black in Pte. Fred. G. Hobbs (1947).

May 2 – Italy 22 Romania 3 (at Arena Civica, Milan). Referee: Mr. Hossenbach (Germany).

Feb 28 – Beat Rest of Cairo 44-6 (at Maadi).

Tries: Pte. W.P. McHugh 2, WO/2 J. Wells 2, Finlay, Morrison, Lambourn, Capt. D.J. Parsons, Fleming, Pte. R. Walker. Cons: Pte. K.A. Welsh 3, Fleming. Pens: Morrison, Welsh.

Other All Blacks in Jack L. Sullivan and John Wells joined Morrison, Lambourn and Finlay.

Official New Zealand Services games played in the UK were:

Feb 14 – Lost to Rosslyn Park 15-16 (at Old Deer Park, Richmond).

Mar 14 – Beat Wasps 6-3 (at Sudbury).

Mar 21 – Lost to Welsh Guards 6-9 (at Richmond).

The Welsh Guards included Lance-Cpl. (Harry) Pimblett, Sgt. (H) Tanner (try) and Guardsman Jefferies (one of several brothers who played).

Apr 11 – Lost to Metropolitan Police 3-12 (at Sudbury).

Apr 18 – Beat Rosslyn Park 18-5 (at Richmond).

The following NZ Services players died during this period:

Apr 16 – Pilot/Officer Alexander Leslie Ellis (fly half, Canterbury, RNZAF) killed in action in Belgium, aged 25.

May 19 – Pilot/Officer William John (Billy) Fulton (three-quarter, Wellington, RNZAF) killed in action in the North Sea off Vieland. His body was not found.

Meanwhile: June 6, Rugby League Challenge Cup Final: Leeds 15 Halifax 10 at Odsal.

There was only one 'international' match played in the UK in the remainder of 1942:

November 7 – WALES 11 ENGLAND 7 (at St Helen's, Swansea). (23,000).

Wales won more easily than the score suggested, spending most of the game on attack and inflicting England's fifth successive defeat in Services Internationals. Even though Wales were the better side, England defended well with full back Bob Campbell excelling and the young Welshman Leonard Price-Stevens playing splendidly in the white shirt.

The experienced Pontypool hooker Reg Flowers had a fine game and opened the scoring with a try that Gus Risman converted after five minutes and though New Zealander John Macdonald placed a penalty, wing forward Gwyn Williams, elder brother of Bleddyn, scored another Welsh try before the interval.

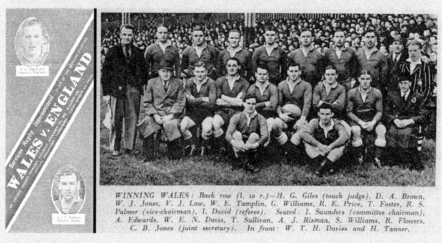

WINNING WALES: Back row (l. to r.)—H. G. Giles (touch judge), D. A. Brown, W. J. Jones, V. J. Law, W. E. Tamplin, G. Williams, R. E. Price, T. Foster, R. S. Palmer (vice-chairman), I. David (referee). Seated: I. Saunders (committee chairman), A. Edwards, W. E. N. Davis, T. Sullivan, A. J. Risman, S. Williams, R. Flowers, C. B. Jones (joint secretary). In front: W. T. H. Davies and H. Tanner.

Programme for Wales XV v England, November 1942

Then came the best try of the game as fly half Willie Davies received from his cousin, Haydn Tanner, and ran for 40 yards to touch down, though England replied when full back Duncan Brown missed touch and his opposite number, Campbell, put over a 40-yard drop goal to end the scoring.

Wales full back C. Howard Davies had not been available and Brown stepped in, while in the pack Les Manfield could not play and Bill Tamplin came in with (Gwyn) Williams filling a place left vacant.

England had left two places vacant and saw Peter Hastings and Henry Evington take them, while wing Surgeon-Lieut. R.F.Camp (Rosslyn Park/Navy) and 2nd Row Fred Huskisson were injured and replaced by Harry Pimblett and 'Ned' Hodgson.

Wales – Capt. Duncan A. Brown (Cardiff/Army); A/C Edwards, Sgt. Risman, Driver Sullivan, *Cpl. (SA) Williams; *Sgt. (WTH) Davies (capt), *+Sgt. Tanner; *O/Cadet Law, Cpl. Reg J. Flowers Pontypool/Army), Sgt. William G. Jones (Newport/Army), *Cpl. (RE) Price, +Pte. W.E. (Bill) Tamplin (Pontypool/Newport/Cardiff/Welsh Guards), Lance-Cpl. (G) Williams, *Capt. (WEN) Davis, Sgt. Foster.

Touch-Judge: (VGJ) Jenkins.

Tries: Flowers, (G) Williams, (WTH) Davies. Con: Risman.

England – Lieut. R.T. (Bob) Campbell (St Mary's Hospital/Army); 2nd Lieut. (EJH) Williams, Lance/Cpl. Ernest Ward (Bradford Northern RL/Army), Cpl. Harry Pimblett (St Helen's RL/Welsh Guards), Flt-Lieut. John H. Macdonald (Huddersfield RL/NZ Services/RAF); 2nd Lieut. Hastings, Cpl. Len Price-Stevens (RAF); *Cpl. Longland, Sub-Lieut. Henry O. Evington (Navy), *Capt. (RE) Prescott (capt), +Cpl. Mycock, Hodgson, *Cpl. E.H. (Ted) Sadler (Castleford, Oldham RL/RAF), P/O Fallowfield, P/O Reynolds.

Pen: Macdonald. DG: Campbell.

Referee: Ivor David (Neath).

WALES:

DUNCAN Alexander BROWN – Full Back. Born Cardiff 23/12/1912. Died Cardiff 2nd quarter 1994. St Illtyd's Grammar School/Old Illtydians/Cardiff/Army. He was a Corporal, then a Captain in the Royal Artillery and was a Schoolmaster.

REGinald John FLOWERS – Hooker. Born Pontypool 25/3/1915. Died Pontypool first quarter 1992. Pontypool/Army. He was a Corporal in the Gloucestershire Regiment.

William George (BILL) JONES – Prop. Born Newport 24/6/1918. Tredegar Park/Newport/Bath (in a war-time game)/Army/Combined Services/NZ 'Kiwis' (one Sevens game as a guest). He was a Sgt. in the Army. (NB: He was NOT the prop W.G. Jones who played for Cardiff before joining Hull Kingston Rovers RL).

William Ewart (BILL) TAMPLIN – 2nd Row. Born Risca 10/5/1917. Died Pontypool 20/10/1989. Abergavenny/Pontypool/Newport/Cardiff/Barbarians/Army. He was a Pte., then a Lieut. in the Royal Welch Fusiliers, then a Policeman and a Solicitors Clerk. 7 caps (1947-48).

ENGLAND

Robert (BOB) T.CAMPBELL – Full back. St Mary's Hospital/Rosslyn Park/ Richmond/Army/Middlesex/Barbarians. He was a Lieutenant in the Army and later a Doctor in Bramwell, Amersham. Played for GB vs Army in 1940 and was often a scrum half.

ERNEST WARD – Centre. Born 30/7/1920. Died Bradford 1987, aged 66. Bradford Northern (captain, 391 apps, 1,427 pts), Castleford & GB (captain, 20 apps) RL/Army. He served in the Fusiliers, then the Yorkshire and Lancashire Regiment as a Lance-Cpl. He captained GB RL to Australia/NZ 1950.

HARRY PIMBLETT – Centre. Born Gerard's Bridge 1920. Died November 2013, aged 93. Windle School/St Helen's (104 apps, 22 tries), Dewsbury (loan), Wigan (loan), Belle Vue Rangers RL/Army. Also guested at RU in war-time for Wasps/Sandown Park/Metropolitan Police. He was a Corporal in the Welsh Guards and a Prisoner of War, being captured at Cassino in 1944 then held at Perugia and a camp near Dachau. He had a leg amputated in 2005. Worked at BICC, the Corporation Transport Dept, and United Glass Bottlers (St Helen's). His son (aged 27 in 1971) died playing for Pilkington Rec. RL.

Jack (JOHN) Hoani MACDONALD – Wing. Born Blenheim, NZ 26/10/1907. Died Picton, NZ 31/12/1982. Streatham-Mitcham and Huddersfield RL/RNZAF/ NZ Services/South Island/Marlborough/Maoris. He became a restaurant owner in London, having served in the RAF-Transport Command as a Leading A/C and Flight-Lieut. He was an oarsman in both the 1930 Empire Games and the 1932 Olympic Games and toured GB with the Maoris rugby team of 1926.

Leonard (LEN) PRICE-STEVENS – (real name PRICE-STEPHENS). Scrum Half. Born Newport (Gwent) 25/5/1921. Died Alicante 13/5/1983. He had lived at 'The Garlands', Scarborough, having served at RAF Halton Apprentices as a Corporal, then becoming a bookmaker in Scarborough where he bought a public house, 'The Copper Horse', in 1968.

HENRY Ollis EVINGTON – Hooker. Born Weymouth 4th quarter, 1920. Died Saltburn 3/4/2013, aged 92. Oundle School/Navy/RNE College, Keyham. He was a Sub-Lieut., Lieut. and later a Lieut-Commander in the Navy and last played for the Navy in 1946. He married a naval commander's daughter (who predeceased him) and he was the son of Engineer-Captain C.B. Evington RN, from Salisbury.

Edward Harry (TED) SADLER – Back Row. Born Chichester 8/5/1910. Died Surbiton 26/12/1992. Royal Signals/Hampshire/RAF/Aldershot Services/ Castleford, Oldham and England RL. 2 caps (1933). He was a Cpl. in the RAF and then a Wireless Instructor in Blackpool.

> **Oct 17 – South Wales 12 Army 16 (at Swansea), (12,000)**
>
> South Wales – Wyndham Lewis (Llandybie/Llanelli/RAF/Wigan RL); (Jack) Matthews, A/C Bleddyn L. Williams, (T) Sullivan, (SA) Williams; (WTH) Davies, W.L. Thomas (Neath); Will Davies (Neath), Bryn Evans (Llanelli), Law, (LM) Thomas, (ER) Price, (AR) Taylor, Wilf Harris (Swansea), Tamplin.
> Tries: (BL) Williams 2, (SA) Williams. Pen: Tamplin.
> Army – (CH) Davies; Unwin, (HJC) Rees (Oxford University), Munro, (CB) Holmes; Risman, Tanner; Prescott, Captain Ian Nicoll Graham (Edinburgh Acads/Royal Artillery/Scotland - 2 caps 1939), Captain C.M.A. Bathurst (Cambridge University/Anti-Aircraft Command), Guardsman John Stoddart (Swinton RL), (CL) Newton-Thompson, Sayers, Hodgson, Foster.
> Tries: Risman, Tanner, Foster. 2 Cons/Pen: Risman.
> Bathurst became the captain of the Golfing Society of Southern India in 1954.

The Services stars cartooned

Nov 21 – Army 18 RAF 0 (at the Athletic Ground, Richmond).

'Gus' Walker was concussed and sidelined in what was to prove his last match as a player, before losing an arm in a military explosion.

Nov 28 – Oxford University 0 Cambridge University 9 (at Iffley Road, Oxford) (3,000).

Cambridge could not make the planned 2.30 pm kick-off and just arrived in time for 3.15pm.

The captains were (DAB) Garton-Sprenger (Oxford) and (GT) Wright (Cambridge).

Referee: Lieut-Col. L.H.F. Sanderson (England). (Born 1915, Died 1975).

Dec 12 – South Wales 19 Anti-Aircraft Command 3 (at Swansea).

South Wales – Alban Davies (Newport - per programme!); Dennis Madden (Aberavon/Salford RL), (J) Matthews, (D. Idwal) Davies, S. Finch (Bridgend); (BL)

The South Wales side v Anti-Aircraft, December 1942 (Courtesy Bleddyn Williams' family)

The Anti-Aircraft side v South Wales, December 1942

Programme—Price 3d.

Recreation Ground, Camborne
Boxing Day, 1942

Official Programme
— OF THE —
Grand Charity
Football Match

R. Parnell's County XV.
VERSUS
H. Curnow's County XV.

Referee : Mr. T. BRYANT
(Cornwall Referees' Union)

Kick-off at 3.15 p.m. by J. G. YOUNG, Esq.

ADMISSION: 1/- Stand 1/- extra
H.M. Forces 6d. Stand 1/-

Match Organised by the Joint Team Secs.—Mr. R. E. Parnell
and Mr. H. Curnow—in conjunction with the A.E.U.
Social Committtee. Hon. Sec. : Mr. W. H. Verran.

ENTIRE PROCEEDS FOR THE RED CROSS, REDRUTH HOSPITAL
AND REDRUTH HOSTEL.

E. ST. GEORGE PRINTING WORKS, CAMBORNE

Camborne Boxing Day programme, 1942

Williams, Ivor Davies (Bridgend); (Will) Davies, C. Brererton (Keighley RL), Law, John Hopkins (Bridgend/Leicester), J. Richards (Llanelli), (AR) Taylor, Tamplin, J. Scott (Pontypridd or Pontypool).

The Anti-Aircraft side included – (DA) Brown and Howell Loveluck (both Cardiff), Travers, (WG) Jones, Coleman and C.R. Paul (2nd row) (all Newport), (RR) Morris, J.T. Thomas (London Welsh s/half), (EJH) Williams and (GD) Shaw.

At Camborne on that same Boxing Day, at an altogether less-exalted level but pleasantly and revealingly typical of what was managed when it could be, two local Cornwall worthies raised sides from the County and, fittingly, charged those in uniform half price for ground and stand (see picture).

Dec 26 – J.E. Thorneloe's XV 17 Barbarians 21 (at Leicester)
Barbarians – (WM) Penman; Unwin, Murdoch, Peter R.G. Graham (St Mary's Hospital), Captain J.C. Swanson (Cambridge University (Blue 1938)/ Middlesex Hospital/United Hospitals/RAMC/Barbarians); Kemp, C.S.M. Stephen (St Bart's Hospital/Civil Defence/Army); Prescott (capt), Surgeon-Lieut. John H. Steeds (RNVR/Saracens/Cambridge University/England 5 caps 1949-50), (WEN) Davis, R.L. Hall (St Bart's Hospital), Major G.P.C. Vallance (Army/Leicester), Lieut-Col. Henry Arthur Fry, TD (Waterloo/ Rosslyn Park/England 3 caps 1934), Peter N. Walker (Gloucester), Capt. M.R. Mullins (Guy's Hospital/United Hospitals/Oxford University (no Blue)/South African Medical Corps).
Tries: Steeds 2, Vallance, Swanson. Con/DG: Murdoch. Pen: Penman.
Reports varied for the two tries by Steeds, Fry possibly being credited with one of them.

J.C. Swanson was a Londoner who died of his wounds in Western Europe during January 1945.

Michael Robert Mullins was a South African from Grahamstown University who died of pneumonia in Italy on 26/12/1944. His father and his grandfather also captained Guy's Hospital.

Charles Stephen became a Lieutenant in the RAMC before working as a doctor and living at Wallington in Surrey.

Major George Philip Colles Vallance TD, JP, died aged 88 on 20/2/2008 at Widermerpool, Nottingham. He was commissioned in July 1939 to the 8th Btn. of the Sherwood Foresters and took part in the Norwegian campaign of April 1940, escaping to Sweden where he was interned before rejoining his battalion in Northern Ireland. He took up staff appointments in North Africa, Italy, Malta and Greece. He had been picked for a full cap for England against Wales in 1933 at Twickenham, but withdrew due to a bout of influenza and was never again selected.

Thorneloe's XV included Eric Grant (RNZAF) and a back row of (JTW) Berry (capt), (GD) Shaw and Wing Cmdr. Arthur M. Rees, CBE, OBE (Cambridge University/London Welsh/Wales 13 caps, 1934-38). (J) Parsons, (BWT) Ritchie and (AE) Murray also played.

Tries: H. Webber (Metropolitan Police), G.J. Humphrey (Loughborough), (E) Grant.

Con/2 Pens: Keith H. Chapman (Harlequins).

Referee: (RF) Barradell (Leicester Society).

Official NZ Services games played in the latter part of 1942 were:

Oct 3 – Lost to Wasps 3-5 (at Sudbury).

Oct 17 – Beat Guy's Hospital 11-0 (at Honor Oak Park).

Oct 31 – Beat Welsh Guards Training Battalion 8-6 (at the Athletic Ground, Richmond).

Nov 14 – Beat St Bart's Hospital 13-3.

Nov 28 – Beat Rosslyn Park 23-5 (at Richmond).

Dec 12 – Lost to Wasps 0-3 (at Sudbury).

The following NZ Services players died during this period:

Jul 16 – Sgt. Malcolm V. Cato (three-quarter) RNZAF, aged 24. Buried in Suffolk (GB).

Oct 28 – Flt/Lieut. Eric Clarence Cox, DFC (forward) Hawke's Bay/ RNZAF, aged 28. Killed in action at Suda Bay, Crete.

> Nov 3 – Pilot/Officer Patrick Joseph Farren. RNZAF. Played for a star-studded RAF XV v Midlands XV 3/1/1942. Killed in action in Egypt.
>
> Also: Sgt. H. George (wing, RNZAF); Sgt H.T. Hataland (full back RNZAF); Sgt Stuart D. Wells (forward, Tauranga/RNZAF) and Sgt. Jack Tanner (forward, RNZAF).
>
> Flt/Lieut. James Himiona (Jimmy) Wetere, DFC (back, Taranaki/RNZAF) was reported as dead in 'Five Seasons of Services Rugby', but actually he did survive the war and was an ace pilot. He was named as being aged 24 on 16/8/1942.

Miscellaneous:

RAF teams included Wing-Cdr. William Mitchell (Bill) Penman, AFC, DFC at full back. He was capped for Scotland against Ireland in 1939 and played for Royal High School/United Services Portsmouth/Barbarians. He was killed in action on October 3, 1943. Also in RAF teams were Cpl. A. Gordon Hudson (Gloucester), A/C Johnny Lawrenson (Wigan RL), an Australian, F/O Brian J. McMaster (Bedford), and the New Zealander F/O Eric Grant, who went on to play for Scotland Services. Llanelli centre A/C Gordon Lewis was selected, but withdrew.

Army sides included Vallance, (HA) Fry, (E) Ward, Lieut. Thomas Graham H. Jackson (Royal Corps of Signals/Scotland 12 caps 1947-49), forwards H. Roughledge (Broughton Rangers & St. Helen's RL) and Castleford and England RL's F.Smith in the London District, Bombardier Freddie Miller (full back, Hull RL), backrower J. Stoddart (Swinton RL) and John Raymond Evans, a back-row forward with Newport who was both hooker and captain on his debut for Wales against England in 1934. Serving as a Lieutenant in the 3rd Battalion Parachute Regiment, he was killed in action in North Africa on March 8, 1943.

Rosslyn Park sides included England caps Prescott, Jimmy L. Giles (Coventry, 6 caps 1935-38 and 1 test on GB tour of South Africa 1938) and Major (HA) Fry as well as (Mike) Sayers.

It was in December 1942 that the brilliant England and Barbarians fly half ('Gus') Walker lost that arm on service with the RAF. He returned, as mentioned, to become an International referee and Air Chief Marshal.

(AR) Taylor (Cross Keys/Wales/GB to South Africa 1938), a Police Sergeant, appeared for R.V. Stanley's XV v Oxford University.

Thomas L. Turner, an Oxford University Blue of 1931, was reported as missing, 'presumed lost at sea', in December 1942. He appeared to be a civilian and not in the Forces.

'The Palestine Post' newspaper referred to an England-Wales game played at Mount Scopus there, to raise money for the Malta Relief Fund. The report

Tom Holley: as Trainer, as MBE, and at 99

said that: "All Welshmen are urged to meet here to create a Cardiff Arms Park or St Helen's atmosphere and cheer the red jerseys on in their struggle for supremacy."

The match report then stated that supporters hung leeks on the posts and sang to create a real international atmosphere. Wales won by 5-3 with the Red-Cross 'International' centre, Horace Edwards (Cardiff/Neath), being the key player and scoring a try and conversion against an England penalty.

The try came when forwards Ellis (Cross Keys) and Tom Holley (Cardiff) opened the way with Holley selling a perfect dummy to send Edwards between the posts. Thomas Holley, MBE, had lived to the age of 99 years and nine months when he died Cardiff in 2016, having long been the club's trainer/masseur and, as the Club's website put it 'the lifeblood of Cardiff rugby'.

Lifeblood aplenty was being spilt elsewhere in 1942, but as late summer became autumn and winter in the northern hemisphere, the tide of the war - as it eventually turned out - began to turn. With the USA and its huge potential resources and reinforcements having joined the Allies, with Germany overextended in the Soviet Union and North Africa, and further afield Japan finding it harder going in the Pacific, reports came of those battles whose names were to have a happier ring to them.

'Monty' and the Eighth Army, the 'Desert Rats', and their allies from Down Under and S Africa were successful at El Alamein and began the process of trapping the Axis forces; the Russians turned the tables on their surrounded and

Rugby 'Dust-Up' in the Desert

Les Manfield in action

frozen foe at Stalingrad; and the Japanese began to withdraw from Guadalcanal as the year ended.

No-one could have predicted the longer term with any certainty at the time, though, and while there were now many troops abroad, the UK remained in many ways a huge holding camp for British and Dominion forces, for many of whom sport proved a welcome release.

It did so, too, behind the lines, amongst those waiting to see more dangerous and often fatal action. Dominion troops played amongst themselves and against British forces, sometimes seriously, sometimes less so: with the caption for this makeshift desert clash typical of the atmosphere of the latter – 'Aussies against some RAF bods'! It all helped influence for the better what Montgomery himself called the most important single factor in war – morale.

Squadron Leader Les Manfield's name has been missing from these later match accounts because in 1942 he went via Gibraltar and Malta to Cairo and was to spend three years in the Middle East, flying Wellingtons with 104 Squadron. He was twice hit by flak over Tobruk and on the second occasion, he was navigator when his plane was shot down in the Mediterranean Sea off Crete.

He went back into the plane attempting to bring out the rear-gunner, and spent two days afloat in a dinghy with three other crewmen before a motor torpedo Boat picked them up. Despite the heat, no food and little water, they – and he – had survived for further action off and on the pitch (see 1945 and after).

Manfield's 104 Squadron had 126 men killed or missing in action in one six-week period but on April 4, 1943 he was awarded the Distinguished Flying Cross (DFC) for his work in a Special Operations Unit.

Deaths of internationals in 1942:

Jan 27 – Eric Ebsworth Hutchinson (Australia, 2 caps, 1937). RAAF. He was killed when landing at Brisbane, aged 25. He was the brother of Frank Hutchinson (4 caps, 1936-38), who was killed a year later.

Mar 4 – Clifford William Patrick ('Haggis') Lang (Australia, 2 caps 1938). Born in India, but raised in England. He was a Lieutenant in an Infantry Regiment. Killed in action at Tjiberunam, Java, aged 32.

March 10 – Hubert Dainton ('Trilby') Freakes (England, 3 caps, 1938-39). Born in Natal, South-Africa. He was a Flying-Officer in the RAF and crashed in a bomber at Honeybourne Airfield in Worcestershire and died in Weston-super-Mare of his injuries. Aged 28.

May 3 - Patrick Munro (Scotland, 13 caps, 1905-11) died aged 58 whilst on a Home Guard exercise in the Houses of Parliament in Westminster. He was a Member of Parliament for the Llandaff area of Cardiff and the Barry area in South Wales and had skippered both Scotland and Oxford University.

June 25 – Lewis Alfred ('Lu') Booth (England, 7 caps, 1933-35). Born Horsforth, Leeds 1909. He was a Pilot-Officer in the RAF and was killed in action. Aged 32. He is remembered on the Runnymede Memorial in Surrey.

Jul 1 – Kenelm Mackenzie ('Mac') Ramsay (Australia, 4 caps, 1936-38). Died at sea when a Japanese POW ship was torpedoed by a United States submarine off Luzon in Phillipines. He had been taken prisoner near Rabaul. Aged 27.

Jul 6 – James McPhail Ritchie (Scotland, 6 caps, 1933-34). Died of enteric fever at Rawalpindi. He was a Water Polo international. Aged 34.

Sept 12 – John Joseph Clune (Ireland, 6 caps, 1912-14). He was on a POW ship HMS Laconia returning either in Mediterranean or off West Africa when it was torpedoed. He had been a veterinary surgeon and also a 2nd Lieut. in the RAVC in WW1. He was aged 49, though some records stated he was 52. Sept 14 – John Gordon Scott Forrest (Scotland, 3 caps, 1938). He was a Lieut. in the Navy based on HMS Blackcap. Aged 25.

Sept 22 – Roy Muir Kinnear (Scotland, 3 caps, 1926). Died during a Rugby Union game at RAF Uxbridge. He toured with the GB team to South Africa in 1924 and joined Wigan RL in 1927. He was a Corporal in the RAF. Aged 38.

Sept 28 – William Alexander (Willie) Ross (Scotland, 3 caps, 1937). He was a pilot in the RAF, who was shot down by Anti-Aircraft fire at a Libyan airport of Bardia. Aged 28.

Oct 9 – Michael (Mick) Clifford (Australia, 1 cap, 1938). He was in the Royal Australian Air Force and was killed whilst on a training flight off Terrigal, NSW. Aged 26.

Nov 2 – James Gladwyn Wynyard (All Blacks, no tests, but played 1935-36-38). He played in 13 matches including the 1935-36 tour of GB/France/America and the 1938 tour of Australia. He was a Captain in the Divisional Cavalry when killed in action at the Battle of El Alamein in Egypt. Aged 27.

Nov 8 – John Berchmans Minch (Ireland, 5 caps, 1912-14). He was a Lieut., then a Major in WW1 and a doctor and Lieut-Col. in the RAMC in WWar2. He died of a liver infection in Delhi, India. Aged 52.

Dec 12 – Drummond J. St Clair Ford (Scotland, 5 caps, 1930-32). He was killed in action in the Mediterranean whilst serving as a Lieut-Cmdr. on the submarine HMS Traveller in the Navy. The submarine struck a mine and all hands were lost. He was aged 34 and his son, who died in 2016, was knighted.

Also, not in action: Jul 31 – John Dewar Dallas (Scotland, 1 cap vs England 1903, scoring a try). He refereed eight International matches, the first being, to eternal controversy, Wales' 3-0 win against New Zealand at Cardiff in 1905). He was SRU president in 1912-13. He died in Aberdeen, aged 64.

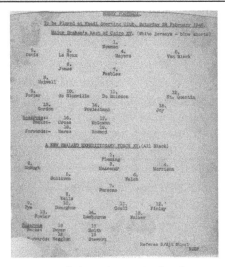

*More morale-boosting rugby for the
NZEF and their desert allies in early 1942*

6
1943

The war had now already lasted nearly three and a half years, and while the news – even if usually heavily filtered and boosted for propaganda purposes – was better for the Allies than it had been for some time, there was absolutely no prospect of an early end to the conflict, the sacrifices and the sad news for families worldwide.

With 'total war', the targeting of civilians from the air, German U-boat successes, evacuation (though never as widespread as intended), rationing, substitute foods, the blackout (and the black market), air raid shelters, government information posters ('Keep Calm and...'), cinema newsreels, the Home Guard, Land Girls, a huge growth in the scale and scope of jobs done by women and the appetite for escapist entertainment, including sport, all became familiar features of life in Britain: and many of them, of course, elsewhere.

Only fruit grown in these islands was available, and with home-grown vegetables not only free but unrationed, all were urged to Dig for Victory. There was a huge growth in allotments, including many former rugby grounds – and, of course, one of Twickenham's car parks: for once it really was Billy Williams' 'Cabbage Patch'! The other car park became a coal dump.

Many thousands of the troops who had flown or sailed away on service were still alive but not at liberty, of course, as in Europe, the Middle East and Far East prisoners of war, including many rugby men, were taken and treated across a wide spectrum of humaneness and inhumanity, with many never to return. Increasingly, though, Britain became used to the sight of GIs and the men of the USAF, those

Sport 'rationed', too!

The Americans try rugby in NZ

American troops sarkily summarised by some as 'overpaid, oversexed, and over here'!

They also brought Spam, Gum, and the helmets, pads and smaller oval ball of American Football - and not only to these shores. The rugby-religious New Zealanders tried a little cross cultural instruction when the Yanks were there readying for the Pacific theatre of war, and an interesting picture shows the padded US boys preparing for a match (described as carnage) against their hosts Down Under in Wellington.

Other than for Services matches, rugby travel was not made easier by petrol being available only for business or essential purposes. Further, with civilian clothing becoming plain and utilitarian – pleats and turn-ups disappeared, and women painted gravy browning and eyebrow pencil on bare legs as a replacement for silk stockings and their seams – there was a constant struggle to try to mock up, make do and mend one's inevitably-rippable rugby kit. Restaurant food was curtailed by price (a maximum of five shillings per meal), if you could eat out, and even just after the war, new England cap Micky Steele-Bodger, who passed away in 2019 aged 93, commented on the coldness and discomfort of trains, the restricted (if healthy) diet and the inability to offer opponents the hospitality one might have wished. Still, a considerable number of fixtures continued, if more sporadic than settled, and amongst the more 'fixed', three internationals took place in the first half of the year:

February 27 – SCOTLAND 6 ENGLAND 29 (at Inverleith).

England's forwards were well on top and gave their backs plenty of room to run in, while also helping to stifle any room that Scotland could have had when they gained rare possession.

Tries in the first half came from back-row forward Chris Newton-Thompson and centre Micky Walford and five more, three converted by full back Ernest Ward, came after the interval, including a hat-trick by centre Johnny Lawrenson, while wing Roy Francis and back-rower Ted Sadler added the others.

Both Scotland tries by centre Billy Munro were scored in the first half when England only led 8-6, but they added 21 more points without reply in a very convincing performance.

For England, full back R.T. Campbell withdrew with Ward moving from centre and Walford from fly half to bring in Frank Reynolds. Second row Fred Huskisson also dropped out with Richard Hall replacing him.

Scotland – *+Capt. Murdoch; +Capt. Tom G.H. Jackson (Cheltenham/Army), Cadet Douglas, +Capt. Munro, *+Lieut. (JRS) Innes; +Lieut. (T) Gray, Lieut. James M. Blair (Edinburgh Acads/Oxford University/Army); *Wing Cmdr. W.F. ('Jock') Blackadder (West of Scotland/Cambridge University/RAF), *Capt. Ian N. Graham (Edinburgh Acads/Army), Capt. Ramsay, Sgt. Maltman, Cpl. Robert Cowe (Melrose/Army), Lieut. Colin McLay (Edinburgh Acads), *Major Melville (capt), *Capt. (GD) Shaw.

Touch-Judge: Lieut-Col. D.J. MacMyn.

Tries: Munro 2.

England – Lance-Cpl. (E) Ward; *(EJ) Unwin, Sgt. Johnny Lawrenson (Wigan RL/RAF), Capt. Micky M. Walford (Oxford University/Royal Corps of Signals), Sgt/Inst. Roy L. Francis (Dewsbury RL); *Major Frank J.C. Reynolds (Old Cranleighans/Army), *Capt Ellis; *Cpl. Longland, Flt/Lieut. Brian J. McMaster (RAF/Bedford), *Capt. Prescott (capt.), +Cpl. Mycock, Surgeon/Lieut. Richard L. Hall (St Bart's Hospital), *Cpl. Sadler, Capt. Newton-Thompson, Cpl. A. Gordon Hudson (Gloucester/RAF).

Touch-Judge: Capt H.A. Haigh-Smith.

Tries: Lawrenson 3, Newton-Thompson, Francis, Walford, Sadler. Cons: Ward 4.

Referee: Allan McM. Buchanan (Ireland).

Scotland v England programme

SCOTLAND

Thomas (TOM) Graham H. JACKSON, OBE, MBE – Wing. Born Sidcup, Kent 15/10/1921. Died Newport Pagnall 21/5/2010. Cheltenham College/Cheltenham/Army/Barbarians/Wasps/London Scottish. He was a Lieut., then Capt. in the Royal Corps of Signals and was stationed at Royal Signals Catterick.

JAMES Michael BLAIR – Scrum Half. Born Darjeeling, Bengal, India 2/8/1922. Edinburgh Academy/Edinburgh Acads/Corpus Christi College, Oxford University (Blues 1940-41). He was a Lieut. in the Army Reconnaisance Corps and died of his wounds in Normandy, 16/7/1944, aged 21. He was at Oxford for only four terms, but he played three times for the University against Cambridge, being Secretary the third time and was also an editor of the Pelican Record.

William Francis ('JOCK') BLACKADDER, OBE, DSO – Prop. Born Edinburgh 23/1/1913. Died 27/11/1997. Merchiston Castle School/Edinburgh University/Caius College, Cambridge University (no Blue)/Northumberland/West of Scotland/Edinburgh Wdrs./RAF. 1 cap (1938). He was a Wing Commander in the RAF and was later in shipping business.

IAN Nicoll GRAHAM – Hooker – Born Forfar 8/5/1918. Died Forfar 2/3/1982. Edinburgh Academy/Edinburgh Acads/Army/Barbarians. 2 caps (1939). He was a Gunner, then a Capt. in the Royal Artillery and was mentioned in despatches during 1945.

Robert (BOB) COWE – 2nd Row. Melrose/Scotland Trials 1934. He was a Cpl. in the King's Own Scottish Borderers.

COLIN McLAY – Back Row. Edinburgh Academy (1933-39)/St Andrew's University (1939)/Edinburgh Academicals. He was a Lieut. in Recce Regiment, then a Major and had been a Medical Student in 1939. Both Cowe's and McLay's birth and death details cannot be traced.

ENGLAND

John (JOHNNY) LAWRENSON – Centre. Born Wigan 29/3/1921. Died 28/3/2010. RAF/Wigan Old Boys, Wigan, Workington and GB RL. He was a Leading Air Craftsman, then a Sgt. in the RAF, later being a Lottery agent, Wigan RL coach and physiotherapist.

England v Scotland, February 1943.

Michael Moore (MICKY) WALFORD – Centre. Born Norton-on-Tees 27/11/1915, Died Sherborne 16/11/2002, Rugby School/Somerset/Co. Durham/Harlequins/Oxford University. He was a Capt. in the Royal Corps of Signals. Played hockey for England (17 caps) and GB in the 1948 Olympics (5 caps and a silver medal). Played Cricket for Somerset/Oxford University/ Durham/MCC/Dorset and was a Schoolmaster at Shelborne.

ROY L. FRANCIS – Wing. Born Cardiff or Brynmawr 1919. Brynmawr Elementary School/Abertillery RU/Wigan (from 1936, aged 17-19), Dewsbury, Barrow, Warrington, Hull, GB & Wales RL. He was a Sgt-Instructor and is thought to be the first black professional coach in any British sport. Hull/ Leeds/Bradford Northern/North Sydney Bears. He scored 229 tries in 356 RL games. Died 1989.

FRANK Jeffrey C. REYNOLDS – Fly half. Born Canton, China 2/1/1916. Died Somerset West, South Africa 1/8/1996. Cranleigh School/England Schools (captain)/Old Cranleighans/RMC Sandhurst/Army/Blackheath/Kent/ Barbarians/GB to South Africa 1938 (two tests). 3 caps (1937-38). He was a Major in the Duke of Wellington's Regiment and the Royal Armoured Corps, being twice mentioned in despatches and ended as an Adjutant-General in the War Office. He later became a manager of a hotel in Cape Town and in country clubs in Johannesburg and Rhodesia. His left leg was amputated in the 1990's.

BRIAN John McMASTER, DFC – Hooker. Born in South Africa, 1916. Died 30/3/1943 (aged 27). Bedford/RAF/East Midlands. He was a Flt/Lieut. in 542 Squadron (RAF) and was killed in action. He had been awarded the

Two different covers for England v Wales at Gloucester, 1943.

DFC in January 1943 and was the ninth Bedford player killed in the War, having already been picked for the return game against Scotland. He was educated at King Henry VII School, Johannesburg and is remembered on the War Memorial in St Ippolyts, near Hitchin, Hertfordshire, near where he lived with his wife, Mary (married 1940), and his son.

Richard Leslie ('DICKIE') HALL – 2nd Row. St Bart's Hospital/Barbarians. Born 1st quarter 1916 Croydon, Surrey. He was a Surg-Lieut. in the RNVR who was killed in the HM Sloop 'Kite' on 21/8/1944 when it was torpedoed by a U-Boat while on a North Sea convoy. Of the 217 crew, 60 got into the sea, but only 14 were picked up alive, of whom five died on board HMS Keppel and only nine lived. He died on the ship, aged 28.

Arthur GORDON HUDSON – Back Row. Born Gloucester 29/11/1915. Died Gloucester December 1993. Gloucester/Gloucestershire/RAF/Barbarians. In 1939 he was a Sports Outfitter from 'The Chestnuts', Longford Road, Gloucester: then a Cpl. and PTI in the RAF and he later became secretary, chairman and vice-president of Gloucester RFC. His father was an England international.

March 20 – ENGLAND 7 WALES 34 (at Kingsholm, Gloucester). (18,000).

Bleddyn Williams was an exciting new face in the Wales team and celebrated his call-up with three tries before leaving for pilot training in the USA. His brother Gwyn was selected in the back row, but was posted overseas a week before the match only to be hit by a sniper's bullet that ended his playing career. England's South African-born forward Brian McMaster was killed in action just ten days after this match.

F.M. (Peter) McRae (St Mary's Hospital) was selected as centre for England, but had to withdraw and never represented his country (*see below) while scrum half Jack Ellis alsoithdrew and England was further handicapped when centre Ernest Ward was injured and departed early, full back Bob Campbell coming up to fly half as Micky Walford moved back.

Bleddyn Williams side-stepped over to open the scoring and Bill Tamplin converted, but Jim Unwin dropped a splendid goal from the touchline to make 5-4 to Wales at half-time. Then, Wales opened up, Tamplin, wing Syd Williams and centre Tom Sullivan scoring tries, one converted by Tamplin, while wing Roy Francis, also a Welshman, scored for England at 16-7.

Wales left their best for the final quarter as Bleddyn scored two more tries and both Tamplin and Syd Williams crossed for their second touchdowns with full back Alban Davies goaling on three occasions.

It was the fourth successive win for Wales over England and in second rower Tamplin they had the best forward on the field as the pack helped half backs and cousins, Willie Davies and Haydn Tanner, control the match.

Frank Reynolds and Chris Newton-Thompson had also dropped out of England's original selection with Campbell and pre-war cap and back-rower Dermot Milman coming in. The latter was to

A 'Leeked' photograph? Gloucester, 1943.

become Sir D.L.K. Milman when he succeeded his father in 1962. For Wales, Rees Williams took the place of Gwyn Williams and Viv Law came in for 'Bunner' Travers, so that Reg Flowers hooked. Gus Risman was abroad.

*F.M. (Peter) McRae, the adopted son of a vicar, was a talented rugby and cricket player, studying at Christ's Hospital and working at St Mary's Hospital, playing for them and for Taunton, gaining an England trial. He was a fine cricketer for Somerset and skippered Scotland at squash rackets.

He became a Surgeon-Lieutenant and in February 1944 his ship HMS Mahratta was torpedoed north of Norway on a convoy to Russia. He joined an overcrowded raft of 17 wounded soldiers but went over the side saying: "I seem to be in the way." He was never seen again. He was aged 28.

England – Lieut. Campbell; *Major Unwin, Sgt. Lawrenson, Lance-Cpl. Ward, Sgt/Instructor Francis; Capt. Walford, Sub-Lieut. Bernard L. Cunningham (Navy/United Services); *Cpl. Longland, Flight/Lieut. McMaster, *Capt. Prescott (capt), +Cpl. Mycock, Surgeon/Lt. (RL) Hall, *Cpl. Sadler, *Capt. Dermot L.K. Milman (Cambridge University/Bedford/Edinburgh Wdrs/Army), Cpl. Hudson.

Try: Francis. DG: Unwin.

Wales – Private Alban A. Davies (Cardiff/Army/Huddersfield RL); A/C Edwards, +F/O Bleddyn L. Williams (Cardiff/RAF), Lance-Cpl. Sullivan, *Cpl (SA) Williams; *Sgt (WTH) Davies, *+Sgt Tanner (capt); *O/Cadet Law, Cpl. Flowers, Sgt. (WG) Jones (Newport), *Cpl. (RE) Price, Lance-Cpl. (LM) Thomas, Gunner Rees Williams (Swansea/Navy), +Pte. Tamplin, Sgt. Foster.

Tries: (BL) Williams 3, Tamplin 2, (SA) Williams 2, Sullivan.

Cons: (A) Davies 3, Tamplin 2.

Referee: Stanley H. Budd (Knowle, Bristol).

Action from the 1943 clash.

ENGLAND

BERNARD L. CUNNINGHAM – Scrum Half. Navy/United Services. He was a Sub-Lieut. in the Navy. No records can be found of his birth or death, but he came from Sunderland and played for Sunderland/Durham County (1949-51)/Royal Navy/United Services/RNE College, Plymouth/Devonport Command. Educated at Rock Lodge Preparatory School, Sunderland.

The England team v Wales, 1943.

DERMOT (later Sir Dermot) Lionel Kennedy MILMAN – Back Row. Born 24/10/1912. Died Warlingham 13/1/1990. Uppingham School/Corpus Christi College, Cambridge University (No Blue)/Army/Bedford/Edinburgh Wanderers/Army/East Midlands/Barbarians. 4 caps (1937-38). He was a Schoolmaster at Epsom College and Fettes College. He served as an Army capt. in the RASC and was mentioned in despatches. He later became a British Council officer in South America, Italy and Pakistan and was knighted in 1962.

WALES
ALBAN Aubrey DAVIES – Full Back. Born Machen 14/1/1914. Died Newport area March 1993. Risca/Cross Keys/Cardiff (16 apps, 1938-39)/Newport/Army/Huddersfield and Cardiff RL (1949-50). He was a Private, then a Sgt in the Army.

BLEDDYN Llewellyn WILLIAMS, MBE – Centre. Born Taff's Well 22/2/1923. Died Penarth 6/7/2009. Rydal School/Wales Schools/Neath/Taff's Well/Newbridge/once for Pontypool!/Cardiff/RAF/Rosslyn Park/Llanelli/Barbarians/GB to NZ (3 tests)/Australia (2 tests) 1950. 22 caps (1947-1955). He was a F/Officer in the RAF, then became a Journalist, director of a Bus Company and a Regional Marketing Manager for Wimpey Construction.

REES WILLIAMS – 2nd Row. Swansea/Navy. Played for Swansea until 1948. He was a Gunner, then a Lance-Bombardier in the Navy.

The Wales team v England, 1943.

April 10 – ENGLAND 24 SCOTLAND 19 (at Welford Road, Leicester). (18,000).

England completed the double over Scotland, but not quite as easily as they did in Inverleith, while this game was marred by both sides being reduced to 14 players.

Scotland lost second row forward J.B. McNeill in the first minute and England centre Johnny Lawrenson followed with a cracked rib after 25 minutes and in addition wing Gerry Hollis carried on though limping badly throughout the second half.

England, forced to use prop forward Ray Longland as their hooker, led 8-0 : Hollis and Lawrenson both crossing, Jimmy Stott converting one before Scotland scored eight points themselves, with tries by 'Donny' Innes (converted by Duncan Shaw) and Russell Bruce.

Then came a master stroke from England skipper Robin Prescott as he pulled back-rower Ted Sadler out onto the wing as Lawrenson departed with Francis moving in to his favourite position of centre.

Sadler was outstanding and was very instrumental in England racing away to 21-8 as Peter Hastings, Jim Parsons and Stott all crossed with the latter adding a drop goal, despite missing the conversions.

However, Scotland rallied, with fly half Tom Gray outstanding as they closed the gap to just two points at 19-21 after tries by Innes (his second), Shaw (who also converted) and Matthew Kennedy, their new prop forward.

Then England had the final say as Francis raced away for their sixth try, and the fifth to be unconverted, to clinch it.

Gerry Dancer had come in when Brian McMaster died after selection and Joe Mycock was picked in the middle of the back row, but it was Dermot Milman who played. Billy Munro had dropped out of the Scotland side with New Zealander Eric Grant coming in.

England – Lieut. Campbell; Lieut. Hollis, A/C Lawrenson, Pte. Jim Stott (St Helen's RL/Army), Sgt/Inst. Francis; Capt. Hastings, Flight-Lt. Jim Parsons (Leicester/Cambridge University/RAF); Sgt. Gerry T. Dancer (Bedford/RAF), *Cpl. Longland, *Capt. Prescott (capt), Capt. George P.C. Vallance (Leicester/Army), Surg-Lieut. Hall, *Cpl. Sadler, *Capt. Milman, Cpl. Hudson.

Touch-Judge: Capt H.A. Haigh-Smith.

Tries: Hollis, Lawrenson, Hastings, Parsons, Stott, Francis. Con/DG: Stott.

Scotland – Capt. W. Gibson Biggart (Glasgow Acads/Army); F/O Eric Grant (RNZAF), Cadet Douglas, +Major C. Russell Bruce (Gala Acads/ Army), *+Capt. Innes; +Lieut. Gray, Lieut. Blair; Sgt. Maltman, *Capt. Graham, Lieut. Matthew D. Kennedy (Edinburgh Wdrs/Army), *Major Melville (capt), Capt. McNeill, *Capt. Duff, *Lieut. Jack A.Waters (Selkirk/ Army), *Capt. (GD) Shaw.

Touch-Judge: Major Andrew ('Jock') Wemyss.

Tries: Innes 2, Bruce, Shaw, Kennedy. Cons: Shaw 2.

Referee: Ivor David (Neath).

Andrew ('Jock') Wemyss: Gala/Edinburgh Wanderers/Leicester/Army/ Barbarians forward, 14 caps for Scotland 1914-1922, the last ten were won despite losing an eye in World War 1 when he was a Major in the Army. Born Galashiels 22/5/1893, died Edinburgh 21/1/1974. He was a great Barbarians committeeman and much loved banker, journalist and broadcaster.

ENGLAND

James (JIMMY) STOTT – Centre. Born Prescot 15/11/1919. Died 6/7/1944 Liverpool. St Helen's and GB RL/Army. He was a Private and a Craftsman in the Army and served in the 4th Welch Regiment. He played for the Rhine Army XV and BAOR Combined Services in Germany 1946.

JIM PARSONS – Scrum Half. Born 1917. Died 7/5/2013 at his house in Lapworth, aged 96. Rydal School/Leicester/Cambridge University/RAF/ Wasps/Moseley (Captain 1947-48). He went from Flight-Lieut. to Sqdn-Ldr.

in the RAF and became president of Moseley RFC in 1984. He was a teacher at Wellington College, then a director of Guest Keen and Nettleford for many years. He was listed in one report as Met. Police before joining the RAF.

Gerald Thomas (GERRY, 'BEEF') DANCER – Prop. Born Bedford 15/1/1911. Died Huntingdon 29/8/1991. Queen's Park School/Bedford Modern School/ Bedford (317 apps, 25 tries)/East Midlands/Barbarians/RAF/England Trials/ GB to South Africa 1938 (3 tests). He was an Aircraftsman, then a Sgt. in the RAF and later became a Landlord of the Seven Wives public house in St Ives, Cambridgeshire.

GEORGE Philip Colles VALLANCE, TD, JP – 2nd Row. Born Barton upon Irwell. 1909. Died Widermerpool, Nottingham 20/2/2008 (aged 99). Army/ Leicester. He was a Lieut., Capt., then Major in the 8th Battalion of the Sherwood Foresters. He escaped capture by going from Norway to Sweden and eventually to Northern Ireland and later held staff appointments in North Africa, Italy, Malta and Greece.

SCOTLAND

William GIBSON BIGGART – Full Back. Glasgow Academy (1928-32)/ Merchiston/Glasgow University/Glasgow Academicals/Army. Capt. and Temp. Major (1945) in the Royal Regiment of Artillery. Mentioned in dispatches. Born 27/8/1918. Died Gargunnock 13/2/1999, aged 80. He was the Chairman of Clyde Petroleum.

ERIC GRANT – Wing (but normally a centre). Born Paeroa, NZ 21/10/1914. Died 2/6/1999 in New Zealand. Gisborne High School/Auckland University/ NZ Univs/Whangarei Old Boys/Poverty Bay/Auckland/RNZAF/Wasps (GB). He was a Flying/Officer, then Flight-Lieut. in the NZ Air Force and had toured Japan in 1936 with the NZ Universities. He became headmaster of Owairoa School (Howick) from 1970 and coached Auckland Primary Schools and was still alive in 2010, aged 95, but it is thought may since have died, in 2013.

Charles RUSSELL BRUCE – Centre. Born 25/4/1918. Died Glasgow 17/4/2009. Gala Academy/Gala Academicals/Barbarians/Army. 8 caps (1947-49). He was a Major in the Royal Artillery and also was a Surveyor. He died at Gartnavel General Hospital.

MATThew Durreen KENNEDY – Prop. Edinburgh Academy-Wanderers/ Army. Lieut, then Capt, then Major in the Argyll and Sutherland Highlanders and was attached to No 9 Commando. He may have died at Monte Cassino in 1943-45. He also fought in North Africa.

John Alexander (JACK) WATERS – Back Row. Born Musselburgh 11/11/1908. Died Selkirk 29/9/1990. Selkirk High School/Selkirk/Barbarians/ Army/GB to Argentina 1936/GB to South Africa 1938 (1 test). 16 caps (1933-37). He was a Lieut. in the Army and a Master Butcher.

Other matches of note in the early months of 1943 included:

Jan 9 – East Wales 21 Army 21 (at Arms Park, Cardiff).

East Wales – (DA) Brown; Graham Jones (St Mary's Hospital/Newport), (J) Matthews, Sgt. Marshall Harding (Newport/RAF), Lt. George Watkin Myrddin-Evans (Rugby School/Rosslyn Park/Oxford University (Christ Church College)/Coldstream Guards – died 4/3/2002); (BL) Williams, Tony L. Rees (Abertillery); Pte. C.J. Green (Pontypool), C. Parker (Crumlin), Petty Officer A. Stanley H. Bowes (Cardiff/Navy), E.L. Bevan (Cardiff), (WEN) Davis, Eddie V. Watkins, Tamplin, (AR) Taylor.

Tries: Matthews 2, (BL) Williams 2, Watkins. Cons: Tamplin 3.

Army – Sgt (AA) Davies; Jackson, Ward, Logie Bruce-Lockhart, Unwin; Lieut. (HJC) Rees, Ellis; Prescott, Guardsman G. Jefferies (Welsh Guards), Guardsman Reg Rowland (Welsh Guards/Newport), Sgt. Fred Jeffcoat (Northampton), Lieut. Peter N. Walker (Gloucester/Oxford University), Foster, (HA) Fry, (Gwyn) Williams.

Tries: Ward, Foster, Ellis, Unwin. Con/Pen: Ward. DG: (A) Davies.

Referee: Vernon Parfitt (Newport).

NB: Brothers Bleddyn and Gwyn Williams opposed each other.

Jan 16 – South Wales 15 RAF 16 (at St Helen's, Swansea).

South Wales – (AA) Davies (listed now as Newport); Dennis Madden, (J) Matthews, Sullivan, (SA) Williams; W.B. (Billy) Cleaver (Cardiff, later Wales/GB 1950), Ivor Davies (listed now as Cardiff); (Will) Davies (capt.), (Bryn) Evans, (WG) Jones (Newport), Bombardier (Rees) Williams, John Hopkins (Bridgend/Leicester), (LM) Thomas, Tamplin, (AR) Taylor.

RAF – Penman (capt); (HM) Powell, (BL) Williams, Lawrenson, (AS) Edwards; (WTH) Davies, Parsons; Longland, McMaster, (RE) Price, (EV) Watkins, Chris Brereton (Halifax RL), Sadler, (AM) Rees, Hudson.

Referee: F.G. Phillips.

The RAF finally beat S Wales, 1943.

As mentioned, the often-thorny issue of Union teams involving professional players was largely and effectively sidestepped by the Services during the war: and on January 23 1943 a then-unique meeting of Rugby League v Rugby Union sides was played under Union rules, as Northern Command organized the historic clash.

January 23 – Rugby Union XV 11 Rugby League XV 18 (at Headingley, Leeds). (8,000).

The sides were from the Army's Northern Command. The Scottish Rugby Union were still against the inclusion of Rugby League players, but it seems that the nine Scots in the RU side had other ideas!

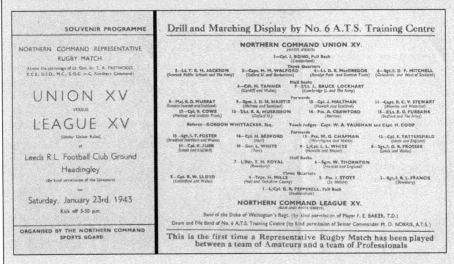

League v Union programme, 1943.

Rugby League – Lance/Cpl. G.R. Pepperell (Huddersfield/England RL); Sgt-Inst. (RL) Francis, Trooper H. Mills (Hull), Pte. (J) Stott, Cpl R.G. Lloyd (Castleford/Wales RL); Lance-Bdr. T.H. Royal (Huddersfield/Dewsbury/Wales RL), Signalman William (Billy) Thornton (Hunslet/England RL); *Sgt-Inst. David Rees Prosser (York/Leeds/Wales/GB RL/Glynneath, Neath, Swansea and Wales 2 caps 1934), Lance-Cpl. Les L. White (Pontypridd/Hunslet/Wales RL), Gunner Leslie White (York/Wigan/Halifax/GB), Cpl. (K) Jubb, Cpl. Edward (Ted) Tattersfield (Leeds, later Hull/England RL), Pte. W.G. Chapman (Warrington/Hull/Wales RL), Cpl. H. Bedford (Hull), Sgt-Inst. (TJF) Foster.

Tries: Jubb 2, Mills 2, Tattersfield, Chapman.

George Russell ('Russ') Pepperell played 350 times for Huddersfield and died in Bundaberg (Australia) in 2003, aged 84.

Reginald G. ('Wolla') Lloyd played for Resolven and Neath before joining Keighley in 1938 at the age of 18. He moved to Castleford and in 1946 and 1947 played seven times for Wales RL. He scored 59 tries in 248 games for Castleford, ending in 1951.

Thomas Henry (Harry) Royal was born in the Bridgend area 19/2/1914 and after playing for Blaengarw and Bridgend he joined he joined Huddersfield in 1938 for £500, then moving to Dewsbury and being capped by Wales RL. He died in Dewsbury in 1995, aged 81. He was a Weftman in a mill and married in 1939 in Huddersfield. He served in the Royal Artillery.

William George (Bill) Chapman was born in 1912 and moved from Bridgend to Warrington in 1935, playing 179 times and scoring 27 tries until 1947. He died in Newcastle in September 2003, aged 91 after 61 years married to Ethel, who reached 100 years of age in 2015.

Rugby Union – Cpl. J. Bond (Cumberland); +Lieut. (TGH) Jackson, Capt. (MM) Walford, Lieut. D.R. McGregor (Rosslyn Pk/Scotland Trials), Sgt-Inst. D.F. Mitchell (Galashiels/West of Scotland); +2nd Lieut. Logie Bruce-Lockhart (Scotland), *+Officer/Cadet Tanner; *Major R.O. Murray, MBE (London Scottish/RAMC/Scotland 1935), *Signalman John Dickson Hart Hastie (Melrose/Scotland 1938), Cpl. (JD) Maltman, Cpl. (R) Cowe, Capt. R.C.V. Stewart (Moseley/Waterloo), 2nd Lieut. R.A. Huskisson (Oxford University), Pte. A. Crawford (Melrose), 2nd Lieut. R.G. Furbank (Worksop College/Bedford/Army).

Try: Walford. Pens: Cowe 2.

Referee: J. Gordon R. Whittacker.

Touch-Judges: Capt W.A. Vaughan and Capt H. Coop.

Ronald Ormiston Murray was born 14/11/1912 in Glasgow and died on 5/3/1995 in Basingstoke, Hampshire, aged 82. He was a Consulting Radiologist at Royal National Orthopaedic Hospital; Lord Mayor Treloar's Orthopaedic Hospital, Alton, and Heatherwood Hospital, Ascot. He was awarded the MBE in 1945. He was educated at Glasgow Academy, Loretto School, St John's College Cambridge (Rugby Blues 1933-34) and St Thomas's Hospital and gained a rugby cap for Scotland in 1935 against Wales and England, playing also for London Scottish. He qualified in 1938 and was a Lieut. in the RAMC in May 1939 ending up as a Lieutenant

Colonel and was involved in the assaults on Sicily, Anzio and Salerno and also served in Normandy. He helped free prisoners from the Sandbortel concentration camp and after the war he trained in radiology and spent two years as Associate Professor of Radiology at the American University Hospital in Beirut. He was the Baker travelling Professor in Australia in 1974 and President of the Radiology Section of the Royal Society of Medicine 1978-79. In 1940 he married Dr. Suzette Gauvain, who died in 1980, and in 1981 married Jane Mathewson, who survived him. His elder brother, George, won two caps between 1921 and 1926.

January 30 – Irish XV 11 GB Army 12 (at Ravenhill, Belfast). (12,000).

Ireland XV – *+Cornelius Joseph (Con) Murphy (Lansdowne, capt); W.J.B. Higson (Queen's University, Belfast), (SD) Walsh, Greer, T. Chamberlain (Blackrock College); E. Austin Carry (Old Wesley), S.G. McCombe (Malone); F. Cromey (Collegians), E.G. Ryan (Dolphin/Blackrock College), J. Griffen (Galway Corinthians), James J. (Jimmy) Joyce (Galwegians), +Keeffe, *David B. O'Loughlin (Dolphin, University College, Cork/Garryowen/Ireland, 6 caps, 1938-39), Guiney, (K) O'Brien.

Irish XV v British Army, 1943.

Tries: Higson, O'Brien, Carry. Con: Carry.

GB Army – (AA) Davies; Jackson, Murdoch, (T) Sullivan, (SA) Williams; Gray, Ellis; Prescott, Graham, (WEN) Davis, Melville, Maltman, Foster, (HA) Fry, Tamplin.

Tries: Maltman, Williams. Con/DG: Murdoch.

Feb 13 – Welsh Guards 8 Bridgend 3 (at Richmond).

This was billed as the first visit by a Welsh club to London in war-time, and they included several 'guest' players.

Bridgend (with 'guests') – J. Bell (capt); Stanley J.R. Walter (Aberavon/ Cheltenham), V. Marsden Howells, J. Russell, J. Morgan; W.B. (Billy) Cleaver (Cardiff), B. Jones; Sedley Davies, Cyril Eddy, R. Tarrant (Army), John Hopkins (Leicester/Swansea/Glamorgan Police), William Ernie (Will) Hopper (Maesteg/Warrington (1948-49), Leeds (1950-58), Wales RL 1 cap-1953), George Tomkins (Cardiff), Verdun (Viv) Eddy, Clifton (Cliff) Davies (Cardiff/ Kenfig Hill/Wales/1950 Lions).

Bridgend captain Jack Bell played for Kenfig Hill/Welsh Guards/London Welsh/Wasps/London Districts/Surrey/BAOR (Germany).

Feb 13 – RAF 11 Army 3 (at Leicester).

RAF v Army, Leicester, 1943.

Feb 13 - Bath 6 A NZ XV 3. Prior to the start, the crowd stood with bowed heads, for a minute's silence, observed in memory of the late Major Ron A. Gerrard (see death in Jan 1943). A Liberator bomber swept across the sky.

Feb 27 – Cambridge University 16 Oxford University 3 (at Grange Road, Cambridge).

The captains were Garton-Sprenger (Oxford) and (GT) Wright (Cambridge), and in the latter's pack was John Forsyth Bance, who was to win one cap for England in 1954. Educated at Radley College, he played for Bedford/Barbarians. He became a farmer and owned a herd of pedigree cattle and two National Hunt horses. He died in 2009, aged 84.

The Oxford pack included Flight/Lieut. Arthur Bryan Curtis, DFC, who was to win three caps for Ireland in 1950 and a full Blue in 1949. Born 27/3/1924 in Shanghai, he was educated at Eastbourne College, became a headmaster and emigrated to Rhodesia in 1954, dying on 17/4/1989, having been awarded the DFC in the RAF's 35 Squadron in 1945. His son was capped for Ireland in 1991.

(GW) Myrddin-Evans played for Oxford on the wing. He became a Lieutenant in the Coldstream Guards, who seemed not alone in having difficulties with part of his surname. The Welsh 'dd' was often reduced to one 'd', with 'rr' substituted, as Myrrdin. The Guards' own records have him down by those different names in successive years, including 1944, when he went ashore after D-Day, wrote to his mother asking her to copy the letter to all platoon members' families in case they had not received news, and commented on the good quality of the French food and wine. A Rugby School boy, he also played for Rosslyn Park and died in Brecon on 4th March 2002.

Cambridge – Tries: D.G. England (wing) 3, Wright. Cons: Bance 2.

Oxford – Try: A.E. Murray.

Referee: Wing/Cmdr. (CH) Gadney.

Also that day, amongst the many wartime games played amongst the Irish provinces, Munster & Ulster met Connacht & Leinster.

Mar 21 – French Championship final – Aviron Bayonnais 3 Agen 0 (at Parc des Princes, Paris).

Irish Provincial clash, 1943.

Apr 24 – Middlesex Sevens Final - St Mary's Hospital 8 Middlesex Hospital 3 (at Richmond Athletic Ground). St Mary's included N.O. Bennett and (TA) Kemp in the backs. Oxford University scratched but they did field a Greyhounds Seven. RAF Jurby (Isle of Man) reached the semi-finals.

Apr 26 – J.E. Thorneloe's XV 0 Barbarians 32.

Barbarians – B.W.T. Ritchie (St Thomas Hospital); D.G. England (Eltham School/ Cambridge University (Christ's College)/ Public School Wdrs), R.W. Watson (St Mary's Hospital), Heaton, (JC) Swanson; Kemp, Tanner; Longland, M. Shirley (Cambridge University/Middlesex Hospital), (WEN) Davis, K.H. Chapman (Harlequins), (JA) Waters, Sayers, A.W. Young (St Mary's Hospital), L.L. Bromley (St Mary's Hospital/ Cambridge University).

Tries: Swanson 3, Watson, Tanner, Young, Kemp. Cons: Heaton 3, Watson. Pen: Heaton.

Referee: Roy Francis Barradell (Leicestershire Society).

Lancelot (Lance) Lee Bromley was a consultant cardiothoracic surgeon at St Mary's Hospital. Born 16/2/1920 Bermonsey, London. Died in 2013 at Barcombe. He was educated at St Paul's and Caius College, Cambridge (1938). He joined the RAMC and was based at the 40th West African General Hospital as a Captain, becoming director of health services in Gibraltar for three years.

Kenneth W. Chapman (born 1902, died 1989), was the son of Herbert Chapman, the great Huddersfield Town and Arsenal soccer manager, and he was to become President of the RFU in 1974-75.

A.W. Young was an Old Cranleighan, who served as a Lieut. in the Dorset Regiment.

J. E. Thorneloe's XV programmes.

F/O. A. T. Dance, of Omaka, Blenheim, missing on operations.

Alfred Dance

Brian William Thomas (Tommy) Ritchie was a New Zealander. Born 1915 in South Canterbury. Timaru Boys HS/St John's College, Cambridge University/St Thomas's Hospital/North of England XV/Northumberland. Anaesthetist. Died in NZ in 1992.

J.E. Thorneloe's XV selected full back Flying/Officer A.T. Dance and wing (Eric) Grant, both of the RNZAF, but they had to withdraw. (AM) Rees (Wales) was selected in the back row, but may not have played, though (NO) Bennett, (J) Parsons, (JTW) Berry (capt) and (AE) Murray all appeared.

Alfred Thomas (Bill) Dance, aged 25 from Omaka in Blenheim (NZ), was to be killed in action on 4 November 1943. The plane, in which he was an Air Bomber, was from the 75th (RNZAF) Squadron and all seven crew died in the Baltic Sea.

Miscellaneous:

New Zealander (Eric) Grant captained a Public School Wanderers team that included (WEN) Davis, N.O. Bennett and full back J.M.H. Roberts of the Welsh Guards. Roberts also played for Bromsgrove School and later for the Army and Harlequins.

Rosslyn Park sides included Leo F.L. Oakley (Bedford, later England), Capt. (later Lieut-Col.) Roy Leyland OBE (England 1935/GB to South Africa 1938), Rex Willsher (Bedford/England Services/Rosslyn Park) and Rev Peter W.P. Brook (Harlequins/England 1930 cap).

Pat Sykes (later Wasps/England) played for St John's Leatherhead and Eastern Counties School teams.

Anti-Aircraft Command sides included (VGJ) Jenkins, (CR) Bruce, 2nd Lieut (RR) Morris, Lance-Sgt Jim Regan (Cardiff/Wales Services/Huddersfield and Wales RL), Gunner (EO) Coleman and Capt (DA) Brown.

Wasps included (VGJ) Jenkins, (TGH) Jackson and Desmond J. O'Brien (later London Irish/Cardiff/Ireland and manager of the 1966 British Lions). Skipper Neville Compton missed his first game for 16 seasons on Feb 23 after being involved in a motor accident.

South-East Command included Rev H.C.C. Bowen (Llanelli/Wales Services).

In February, HMS Daedalus, a Fleet Air Arm base and one of the best Navy sides, won eight matches in a row, scoring 169 points and conceding only 17.

Mar 27 – Coventry gained their 24th successive win, scoring over 600 points and conceding less than 100. The backs included Harry Pateman, Harold

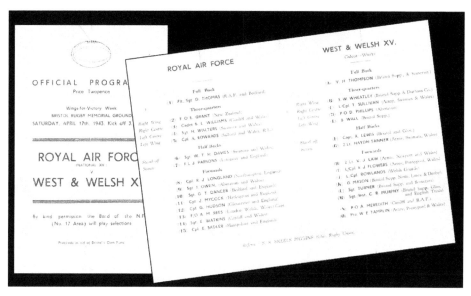

West & Wales XV v RAF

Greasley, Ivor Preece (later England/B Lions to NZ/Australia 1950) and Nigel Stock; Harry Walker (later England) was at prop, Capt H.F. Gilbert a back rower and three Wheatley brothers (H, A and H.F) in the pack.

Apr 7 – Harlequins played their first war-time match when they beat Rosslyn Park 8-6. Harlequins included Major M.J. Daly (Ireland), R. Edgar Bibby, Prescott, Rev Brook, (JRC) Matthews, (RT) Campbell, (Logie) Bruce-Lockhart and Willsher, but (EK) Scott (later England), (PRH) Hastings and Walford all had to withdraw. (KH) Chapman was captain.

The same day the RAF beat a West & Welsh XV 24-8 at Bristol's Memorial Ground, Ike Owens filling the fliers' hooking role, though by then better known as a fine back row operator.

Official NZ Services games played in 1943's early months were:

Jan 2 – Lost to RAF 19-25 (at Bedford). Eric Grant scored three of the five NZ Services tries.

RAF included (BL) Williams, Edwards, Lawrenson, Dancer, Longland, Parsons, (WTH) Davies,

Leyland, McMaster, (AM) Rees, (E) Watkins, Horsfall and Hudson.

Jan 30 – Lost to Guy's Hospital 0-23 (at Honor Oak Park).

Feb 6 – Beat Royal Australian Air Force 8-5 (at Old Deer Park, Richmond).

NZ – Try: Sgt T. Blomfield. Con/Pen: P/O A.T. Dance.

RAAF – Try: F/O J.R.W. Redman. Con: Sgt G.S. Hotchkiss.

Feb 20 – Beat Middlesex Hospital 6-5 (at Chislehurst).

Mar 13 – Beat Rosslyn Park 9-6 (at Richmond).

Apr 10 – Lost to Metropolitan Police 8-16 (at Hendon).

Sergeant **Hawea Tomo-ana**, of Hastings, missing on operations.

Flt/Sgt. Tomoana

Apr 16 – Lost in Round 5 of the Middlesex Sevens to the eventual runners-up, Middlesex Hospital, by 5-0 at Richmond Athletic Ground.

The following NZ Services players died during this period: -

May 25 – Flt/Sgt. Charles Little Saundercock of Waikari (scrum half, RNZAF). Killed in action off the Dutch Coast. All eight in crew died.

Jun 23 – Flt/Sgt. (Navigator) George KIng Samson (forward, RNZAF 75 Squadron), aged 27. Killed during raid over Mulheim. Crashed over town of Gelsenkirchen and all seven in crew died.

Jun 29 – Flt/Sgt. Tamaturanga Te Rakai-a-Hawea Tomoana (fly half, RNZAF 149 Squadron), aged 29 of Hastings (NZ). Killed in action in the North Sea. He had married Joyce Butler in Epsom (GB) on 24/11/1942.

Deaths of international representatives in the first half of 1943 included:

Jan 4 – Francis Ebsworth Hutchinson (Australia, 4 caps, 1936-38). RAAF. He was killed in action over Liben in Holland, aged 25. His brother Eric (2 caps 1937) was killed in 1942.

Jan 12 – Edward Sautelle ('Dooney') Hayes (Australia, 5 caps, 1934-38). RAAF. He was killed in action at El Alamein. Aged 31.

Jan 22 – Ronald Anderson Gerrard, DSO (England, 14 caps, 1932-36). He was killed in action in Libya clearing mines as a major with Royal Engineers. Aged 30.

January 27 – William Henry ('Taffy') Townsend (South Africa, 1 cap, 1921). He died as a Prisoner of War in Sicily as a Cpl. in the South African Infantry. Aged 46-47. He had played in the 1919 King's Cup. Born in Newport (Wales), he had also fought in WW1.

Mar 8 – John Raymond Evans (Wales, 1 cap; Capt. on 1934 debut) He was killed in action in Tunisia whilst a Lieut. in the 3rd Battalion, Parachute Regiment. Aged 31.

Mar 30 - Brian John McMaster, DFC (England Services 1943). Born in South Africa. He was in the RAF as a Flt-Lieut. in 542 Squadron when he was killed when the aircraft he was in crashed on take-off. He had been awarded the DFC in January 1943. Aged 27.

'Taffy' Townsend

May 4 – Georges Yvan ('Le Bison') Andre (France, 7 caps 1913-14). A WW1 fighter ace who escaped six times when a Prisoner of War. He won the high jump silver medal at 1908 Olympics (aged 18) and competed in the 1912 Olympics at decathlon, high jump, standing jump, standing long jump and 110 metres hurdles. In the 1920 Olympics he won a bronze medal in the 4 x 400metres relay and was fourth in the 400 metres hurdles. In the 1924 Olympics he took the Athletes Oath and was fourth again in the 400 metres hurdles. He joined the French Infantry and was killed near Tunis, aged 53.

Home to Serve

THE former Welsh Rugby and Newport Rugby captain, Mr. John R. Evans, returned to Newport on Saturday. He has left his business appointment on the Gold Coast, West Africa, in order to offer himself for War service. He has been in West Africa for nearly three years, and last year was home on leave. An old boy of Newport High School, he

John R. Evans

May 31 – Cyril Stennart Pepper, MC (All Blacks, no tests, but played in 17 matches 1935-36). He died of wounds received when earning the Military Cross at Sidi Rezegh, Libya. He was invalided home and died soon afterwards in Wellington, NZ, aged 31.

Meanwhile in Rugby League:

Feb 27 – England 15 Wales 9 at Central Park, Wigan.

Apr 24 – RL Challenge Cup final (1st leg) Dewsbury 16 Leeds 9 at Crown Flatt, Dewsbury.

Apr 26 – RL Challenge Cup final (2nd leg) Leeds 6 Dewsbury 0 at Headingley. Dewsbury won 16-15 on aggregate.

With the resumption after the summer, only one international was played in the second half of the year:

ST. HELEN'S GROUND, SWANSEA
SATURDAY, NOV. 20th, 1943
KICK-OFF — 3.15 P.M.

GREAT SERVICES
RUGBY INTERNATIONAL

WALES
v.
ENGLAND

IN AID OF
THE NAVY · THE ARMY
AND R.A.F. CHARITIES

Official Programme: 3d.

The Wales v England programme, 1943.

November 20 – WALES 11 ENGLAND 9 (at St Helen's, Swansea). (25,000).

Despite a sixth successive Wales win over them, England put up a great challenge, winning the scrums, even though Ray Longland had to play again as a hooker when Bert Toft withdrew because of Service duties, while for Wales, Haydn Tanner broke his nose during the match, but bravely stayed on the field.

Sergeant Bevan had replaced the injured Ernie Coleman in the Wales pack and Bob Weighill replaced Officer-Cadet Jimmy ('Pongo') Wareing (Army/Silloth) in the England eight, when the latter was forced to withdraw.

Several thousand American servicemen were present at the match and they waited for 25 minutes before the first score came when full back Ernest Ward put England in front with a penalty.

Wales hit back with a run by wing Alan Edwards that saw the new forward

Bevan in support to send fly half Willie Davies over, but another Ward penalty gave England a half-time lead of 6-3. Full back Alban Davies placed a penalty to level the scores before another Edwards run led to a try for fellow wing Syd Williams that Davies converted.

England came back at the finish as centre Johnny Lawrenson ran over near to the posts, but somehow a tired Ward failed to level the scores by missing the conversion. He then had a chance to win it but failed again, this time with a penalty effort.

Ernest Ward, RL star.

Wales – Sgt. (AA) Davies; Cpl. Edwards, Cpl. Randall D. Lewis (Aberavon/ Swinton, Huddersfield RL), Lance-Cpl. Sullivan, *Cpl. (SA) Williams; *Sgt. (WTH) Davies (capt.), *+Lieut. Tanner; Sgt. (WG) Jones (Newport), Cpl. Flowers, Leading-Sgt. Reg F. Rowland (Newport/Army), Gunner (Rees) Williams, Sgt. E.L. Bevan (Pontypool/Army), Owens, +Lieut. Tamplin, Sgt. Foster.

Tries: (WTH) Davies, (SA) Williams. Con/Pen: (A) Davies.

England – Lance-Cpl. (E) Ward; Lieut. Hollis, Sgt. Lawrenson, Private/ Cfn. Stott, Sgt/Inst. Francis; Lieut. Hastings, *Capt. Ellis; *Capt. Prescott (capt), *Cpl. Longland, P/O Ian H. Dustin (NZ Services/RNZAF/RAF), +Cpl. Mycock, Sub-Lieut. J.B. (Jim) Doherty (Sale/Manchester/Navy) Capt. Frank W. Gilbert (Army/Coventry), +Flight-Lieut. R.H.G. (Bob) Weighill (Harlequins/Waterloo/RAF), Cpl. Hudson.

Try: Lawrenson. Pens: Ward 2.

Referee: George Goldsworthy, Newport (99 apps at centre), later Penarth.

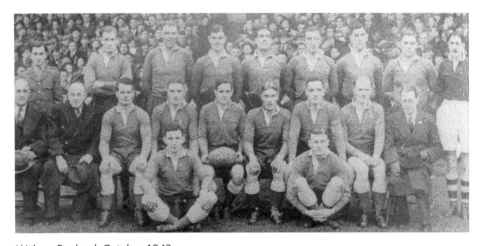

Wales v England, October 1943.

WALES

RANDALL D. LEWIS – Centre. Died Tanygroes Place, Port Talbot 6/9/2009, aged 95. Neath/Aberavon/RAF/Swinton (1936), Huddersfield (loan) and Wales RL. Cpl. in the RAF.

REGinald Frank ROWLAND – Prop. Born 18/2/1924 Newport. Died 1982 Newport. Newport/Welsh Guards/Army. Sgt. in the Welsh Guards, then later employed by Newport Council Parks Department.

E.L. BEVAN – 2nd Row. Pontypool/Cardiff/Army. Sgt. in the Army. 31 games for Cardiff (1937-38 to 1948-49). Cardiff Athletic cap 1938; Cardiff 1st XV cap 1939.

ENGLAND

IAN Henry DUSTIN – Prop. Born 1918 in NZ. Killed in action over Norway 11/4/45, aged 26. He is remembered on the Runnymede Memorial in Surrey. His plane was shot down but there was no trace of the plane or the eight

England v Wales, October 1943.

airmen on board. Manawatu/RNZAF/NZ Services. He was a Pilot/Officer in the RNZAF and in 502 Squadron (RAF Coastal Command out of Storoway).

James (JIM) B. DOHERTY – 2nd Row. Sale/Manchester/Lancashire/ Barbarians/Navy. A Sub-Lieut., then Lieut. in the Navy. Also a Schoolmaster on HMS Gosling. He is known to have survived the war.

FRANK William GILBERT, MC – Back Row. Coventry/Army/Southern Command. Born in France. A Lieut., then Capt. in the Queen's Royal Regiment, then the 7th Battalion of the 8th South Staffordshire Regiment. He was made a temporary major, but was killed in action on 7/8/1944 and was posthumously awarded a Military Cross on 19/10/1944. His body was not found, but he is remembered at the Bayeux War Cemetery.

Robert Harold George (BOB) WEIGHILL, DFC, CBE – Back Row. Born King's Norton 9/9/1920. Died Halton 27/10/2000. Wirral Grammar School/ Birkenhead Park/Waterloo/RAF/Harlequins/Leicester/Cheshire/Barbarians/ Notts, Lincs and Derby. 4 caps (1947-48). In the RAF Fighter Command as a Flying-Officer and Flight-Lieut., and rose to Air Commodore. He was awarded the DFC in 1944 and the CBE in 1970. Secretary of the RFU and Five Nations and ADC to HM the Queen in 1968.

Jimmy ('Pongo') Wareing was forced to withdraw after selection as he had been evacuated from Dunkirk. He was a Lieut. and tank commander in the Army. In 1946 he played for North-Eastern Counties against the 'Kiwis', then played 189 times for Workington RL, including their 1952 RL Cup final victory. He also worked for Carr's Biscuits and became a foundry manager in Distington Engineering, before his death in Distington in December 2005, aged 88.

Other later 1943 matches of note included:

In Tripoli the 28th Maori Batt. had triumphed in the Freyburg Cup for 1943, but back at home:

Aug 14 – South Island 17 North Island 16 (NZ Inter-Island match, at Athletic Park, Wellington)

South's tries came from J.E.B. Kerr and A.T. Smeaton, 2 cons., 1 pen by P.R. Callanan and a drop by D.H. Murdoch. Pre-war cap John Dick and post-war cap Ron Elvidge played.

North's were by Cpl. J.B. Smith, R.G. Sorensen, A.D. Pike, and P. Stanaway, with two Sorensen cons., and Smith and Eric Boggs went on to be post-war caps and 'Kiwis' tourists.

Referee: E.J.B. Matthews (Wellington).

Sept 4 – Auckland 25 A NZEF XV 10 (at Auckland)

Auckland – Tries: Jack McLean 3, G.M. Sellars 2, R.G. Sorensen. 2 Cons/Pen: L.J. Gilmour 2.

NZEF – Tries: J.B. Coull, A.C. Glen. DG: E.W.T. Tindill.

All Blacks Eric Tindill and Morrie McHugh (1946-49) played for the NZEF side while Auckland included Fred Vorrath and John M. Dunn (1947). Back in the northern hemisphere:

Maori Battalion, Freyburg Cup winners.

While back in the northern hemisphere:

Sept 25 – South Wales 9 RAF 9 (at St Helen's, Swansea).

South Wales – (AA) Davies; Jack Knowles (Newport), Sullivan, Cpl. B. Treharne (Llanelli), K. Thomas (Swansea); +Cleaver, Sgt. Ivor Davies (Bridgend/Army); *Law, Flowers, (Will) Davies, D.R. Goronwy Williams (Pontarddulais/Llanelli), (Rees) Williams, +Tamplin, *(AR) Taylor, G. Scott (Pontypool).

Try: Knowles. Pens: Tamplin 2.

RAF - *Penman; (E) Grant, +(R) Rankin, (Haydn) Walters (Swansea), Edwards; *(WTH) Davies, Parsons; Dancer, *Longland, *(EV) Watkins, *(RE) Price, Hudson, Owens, Fallowfield, *(AM) Rees.

Tries: Edwards, Price, Owens.

Oct 9 – South Wales 10 Army 31 (at St Helen's, Swansea). (14,000).

South Wales – (AA) Davies; (K) Thomas, Treharne, (RD) Lewis, Knowles; +Cleaver, (I) Davies; (Will) Davies, *Law, (WG) Jones (Newport), John Hopkins (Bridgend/Leicester), (DRG) Williams, (Rees) Williams, O/Cadet J. Williams (Fleet Air Arm/Llanelli), *(AR) Taylor (capt).

Touch-Judge: Ivor Jones (Llanelli), the pre-war Wales forward and 1930 GB tourist to NZ/Australia.

St. Helen's Ground, Swansea
SATURDAY, OCT. 9th, 1943

Grand Rugby Match
SOUTH WALES
v.
BRITISH ARMY

OFFICIAL PROGRAMME - 2d.

The Army XV which beat South Wales by 31-10 at Swansea.

The Army XV, and S. Wales v Army programme.

Tries: Lewis, Taylor. Cons: Taylor 2.

Wings Edwards and (SA) Williams withdrew after selection.

Army – Lance/Cpl. W. Belshaw (Royal Engineers/Liverpool Stanley, Wigan (as guest), Warrington, England & GB RL); +Jackson, (E) Ward (now in the York and Lancaster Regiment), Walford, Francis; Lieut. (HJC) Rees (now South Wales Borderers), *+Tanner (now Lieut. in Royal Corps of Signals); Sgt. (R) Rowland, Flowers (now Gloucestershire Regt.), +Prescott (capt.), Lieut. Peter N. Walker (Royal Welch Fusiliers), (Rev) Bowen (now Royal Artillery Chaplain's Dept), Foster, +Tamplin (now Royal Welch Fusiliers), Capt. R.G. Furbank (Royal Artillery/Bedford/East Midlands/Worksop College/Airborne Division).

William (Billy) Belshaw played 11 times for England and eight for GB at RL. He toured Australia and NZ in 1946.

Tries: Jackson 2, Ward 2, Prescott, Francis, Rowland. Cons: Belshaw 5.

Referee: George Goldsworthy (Penarth/Newport).

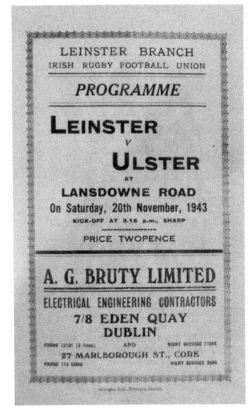

Irish programme, 1943.

Oct 20 – RAF 30 Army 14 (at Gloucester). (7,000).

The RAF brought pre-war England forward H.A. (Bert) Toft (Waterloo) out of retirement and included New Zealander (IH) Dustin (RNZAF) in the front row.

RAF – Tries: Lawrenson 3, Remlinger 2, (AS) Edwards, Walters, (Eddie) Watkins. Cons: Lawrenson, (Ike) Owens, Edwards.

Army – Tries: Francis, (TGH) Jackson, Oakley. Con/Pen: Tamplin.

Nov 20 – Another Irish provincial clash saw Leinster host Ulster at Lansdowne Road.

Nov 27 – Cambridge University 13 Oxford University 4 (at Cambridge).

Cambridge, captained by J.M. Langham (Bedford), included Welshmen in full back R.H. Lloyd-Davies (Ammanford) and centre C.D. Phillips (Newport High School), while fly half G.W. Kettlewell came from Rydal School. Massey University, NZ's front rower J.R. Wallace played while forwards J.F. Bance and D. Brian Vaughan (later

England selector and 1962 British Lions' manager) and scrum half Pat W. Sykes all later played for England. It was their eighth successive win over Oxford.

The Oxford XV was captained by Garton-Sprenger and included back-row forward J.C. Dawson (Strathallan/Queen's), who later won Scottish caps in the front row.

Cambridge – Tries: W.D. Morton 2, Bole. Cons: Bance 2.

Oxford – DG: P. Blandy.

Dec 11 – RAF 8 Dominions Air Force 0 (at Richmond Athletic Ground).

RAF – Tries: J. Lawrenson, P.K. Waterkyn (see 1944 Chapter). Con: Lawrenson. Two strong sides were skippered by (WTH) Davies and (E) Grant.

Dec 11 – East Wales 6 Army 35 (at Rodney Parade, Newport).

Among the East Wales side were the Cardiff players Graham Hale (centre), T. Oppenshaw (wing) and Ray Bale (prop). Others included the halves – Lieut. J. L. Richards and G. Meredith (Newbridge); D. Glyn Jones (Cardiff Medicals) at wing and the second row of W. Talbot (Ebbw Vale/Newport (1 game)) and Leslie Smith (Newport). Cleaver was at centre.

Jack L. Richards (Monmouth School (Head boy)/Selwyn College, Cambridge University/Wasps/Cardiff (2 games in 1938-39)/Newport (1 game in 1939-40)/Cross Keys) of the 240th Field Company, Royal Engineers was to be killed in action in Normandy on 2/11/1944, but his death was not announced until June 1945. In this match he retired injured at half-time.

East Wales – Try: (G) Jones. Pen: (G) Bayliss.

Army – Tries: (Sid) Williams 3, Munro, Oakley, Foster, (GD) Shaw, Ellis, Smith. Cons: H.J. Roberts (Welsh Guards) 2, (Alban) Davies, R.J.F. Avery (Anti-Aircraft Command).

Dec 26 – London 9 Dominions 13 (at Richmond Athletic Ground).

Dec 26 – J.E. Thorneloe's XV 16 Barbarians 42 (at Welford Road, Leicester).

Barbarians – (BWT) Ritchie; (RW) Watson, +Munro, *+Heaton, Hollis; *+Kemp, *+Tanner; Dancer, A.B. Lee (Guy's Hospital), *Longland, Doherty, D.J.B. Johnston (St Mary's Hospital), *(GD) Shaw, *(JA) Waters, Willsher.
Tries: Munro 2, Heaton 2, Hollis 2, Johnston, Kemp, Watson, Willsher.
Cons: Heaton 3, Ritchie. DG: Heaton.
Another report gave Hollis three tries and Shaw one, with Heaton reduced to one and Johnston not scoring.
J.E. Thorneloe's XV – Tries: (JC) Swanson (now Middlesex Hospital), (J) Parsons, D.M. Strathie (Rugby School/Guy's Hospital), D. Ballard (Leicester Harlequins), Capt J. Gilbert (Coventry).
Cons: Gilbert, (KH) Chapman.

Referee: (CH) Gadney.
Ivor Preece (Coventry) was at fly half for Thorneloe's. He played for England post-war, was a British Lions tourist to NZ/Australia in 1950 and the father of later England cap Peter Preece. (JTW) Berry (capt.) and Harry Walker (Coventry, later England, died 05/06/2018 aged 103) were in the pack.

Miscellaneous:

Rugby had been scheduled to resume after the summer on September 25, but games were played before that and Public School Wanderers, Sutton and Richmond, in particular, arranged many games with Richmond looking to run three sides. Guy's Hospital celebrated their centenary with a Past vs Present game on the opening day at Honor Oak Park, watched by Guy's skipper from 1886.

Anti-Aircraft Command included a Pontypool second-rower, Staff-Sgt. L. Davies, Cardiff centre Lieut A.H. Loveluck, Major (MJ) Daly, Major (CR) Bruce, Lieutenant (JB) Craig and Captain (GD) Shaw (as the captain of the side).

Arthur Howell Loveluck (born Cornelly, Pyle 23/3/1919; died June 1992 Bridgend, aged 73) played 36 games for Cardiff (72 points) from 1945-1950, having previously played for Bridgend Grammar School and Bridgend. He captained Cardiff Athletic in 1949-50, then became the vicar of St Oswald's in Gloucester for many years and was a Chaplain with the British Forces in Africa for the Mau Mau Uprising in 1955.

A South Wales XV included Pontypool back-rower A. Gardner.

Bath were able to include the Cardiff forward Sqdn-Ldr. Hubert Johnson on several occasions. He was to become the chairman of Cardiff RFC and one of the club's greatest administrators. He was stationed at RAF Colerne in Wiltshire. Bath also had guest appearances by (MJ) Daly (Ireland) and W.G. Jones (Newport/Wales Services).

A Civil Defence XV began playing for the first time and their players included Cleaver, (Jack) Matthews, K. Thomas (Swansea wing), Will Davies (Neath prop), (EK) Scott, (AR) Taylor, (Harry) Wheatley and (Tommy) Kemp (captain).

Major W.H. (Bill) Clement, the pre-war wing for Llanelli/Wales/GB 1938 to South Africa, was selected for Rosslyn Park, S-E Command and R.V. Stanley's XV, but withdrew from the latter. Later, as WRU Secretary, his signature became very familiar on international tickets.

Wasps selected a young lock, Lieut. John A. Gwilliam, who was to go on to skipper Wales to Triple Crown wins in 1950 and 1952. In 2016 he became the oldest surviving Wales cap and captain. Gwilliam played against the Guards Brigade in the same Wasps pack as Des O'Brien and J.R. McClure with Neville Compton as captain and the fine New Zealander, Eric Grant, at centre with Sergeant J.J. Remlinger, the 'French Englishman', outside him.

Peter D. Young (later an England lock) played for Clifton College against Downside, who were skippered by centre Michael D. Corbett, son of the former England centre, Len Corbett.

Rosslyn Park included Tanner (as a centre) and (VGJ) Jenkins at full back.

A Midlands XV included the pre-war Wales wing Arthur Bassett (Aberavon/Cardiff/Kenfig Hill then Halifax, York, Wales and GB RL).

Micky Steele-Bodger (Rugby School) was classed as the 'best forward on the field' when he played for the North v South in a Schoolboys match at Richmond on December 30. The South won 17-3.

Bill Clement

Aussies with a 'Sunderland', and a different Pembroke's programme.

— RUGBY UNION —
R.A.A.F. v SUTTON   SAT. 6ᵗʰ DEC. 1943.   WON BY R.A.A.F. 8-5

RAAF XV v Sutton, December 1943.

On Sept 25th, Bath full back H. David Rees, while serving in the 6th Battalion of the Home Guard, won the British Empire Medal for bravery in the Bath Blitz. He pulled 30 people from a burning hotel, with at least five found to be alive.

In September former Cambridge University captain, Ronald Peter Sinclair of Whitton in Middlesex was killed in action in the Middle East while serving as a Captain in the Royal Engineers. He was educated at Bedford and Trinity Hall, Cambridge. He played in six games against Oxford University, being skipper in two and a winner in five.

Wherever troops were stationed, sport was attempted. In the far south west of Wales, at the RAF's leading flying-boat station, Australians practised their rugby, and in the far Atlantic, on Bermuda's BAA Field, a Royal Navy XV met a Britsh Army XV. Both venues were called Pembroke!

The Royal Australian Air Force appeared quite regularly, too, and the picture notes that in their particular guise for that December day, they overcame Sutton 8-5. Harder games (see below) had gone before.

Official NZ Services games played were:

Oct 2 – Drew with Wasps 3-3 (at Sudbury).

Oct 16 – Beat London Hospital 33-5 (at Walthamstow).

Oct 23 – Beat Royal Australian Air Force 15-3 (at Richmond).

Wing (E) Grant skippered the New Zealanders, Flight-Lieut. J.B. Nicholls was the Australian captain and had F/O Edmund George (Eddie) Broad at fly half, who was to be capped for Australia in 1949 and who toured GB in 1947-48.

Several of the players in this match were soon killed in action. They included 24-years-old F/O Leonard Alfred Arthur Kilgour of 190 Squadron, who died in a Lancaster over France

Wasps v NZ Services programme

on 23/7/1944. He was from Palmerston North (NZ).

In January 1944, the fine full back Flying/Officer Alfred Thomas Dance was reported as missing after operations in Europe. It transpired that, as mentioned, he had died on 4/11/1943, aged 23. His name is included on the Runnymede Memorial in Surrey.

Nov 6 – Beat Public School Wanderers 8-0 (at Sudbury).

Nov 13 – Drew with Welsh Guards 3-3 (at Richmond). Included in the NZ pack was Sub-Lieut. Robert C. (Bob) Stuart (RNZ Navy), who went on to skipper NZ on tour to GB/France in 1953-54 and later be an IRB member.

Further afield, and in more straitened circumstances, prisoners still tried to keep a semblance of normality with the devising, recording, improvising and playing of all sorts of sports and games: not least, where possible, rugby. In the Far East and in Japanese hands, Wilf Wooller, his Cardiff RRC teammate and 77th Heavy Anti-Aircraft Regiment colleague Les Spence and so many others did their best to sustain both physical and mental health against the odds.

By 1943 they had already spent a year in captivity. After the fall of Singapore their group of Welsh soldiers were captured in Java and spent more than three years as POWs in Java and Japan. 70 years on Greg Lewis edited the camp diary kept at great risk (and later lost then re-found) by Sgt-Major Les Spence, who survived to be chair of the WRU in the 1970s.

Many of the 77th were sportsmen, with several of Cardiff 's rugby team, whom Spence had captained in 1936-37, Glamorgan cricketers and footballers, too, including Ernie Curtis, a veteran of Cardiff City's 1927 FA Cup win. As Les feared from the start, many died from starvation, dysentery, accidents and cruelty, but others learned to survive through luck, bargaining for food, playing rugby and football, and maintaining a sense of discipline.

Spence and Wooller were to spend a lot of time at the coal-mining Camp 8 Kamo talking about the old days. At one point in his journal, Spence remembers that April 22, 1939: a 'big day in the history of Cardiff Rugby Club', when they had been in the team which won the Middlesex Sevens at Twickenham.

Liberation for the prisoners came following the dropping of the atomic bomb on Nagasaki, a city less than 100 miles from Spence's camp. 'We went down [the air-raid shelter] no fewer than four times,' he wrote on August 9, 1945. Only four planes flew on the raid that destroyed Nagasaki, and the Japanese guards and prisoners were in a state of confusion for days. Les thought the huge cloud seen must have been big oil wells catching fire.

Les Spence: serving country and club.

Later they saw the result of the bomb: 'It was simply astounding, nothing left standing for miles, everything flat and burnt out. We were taken by sea to San Francisco, east by train and on boarding the Queen Mary in New York received letters from home. I received five letters. Lovely day, beautiful sunshine. Pleased to see that Babs is still waiting. I hope that she will accept my proposal..'

She did: the two were married. Wilf Wooller was the best man. Les was to become chairman of Cardiff Rugby Club and joint secretary of Glamorgan County Cricket Club. Later, in perhaps his greatest role, as WRU President, he helped take a small step to heal the wounds opened between the UK and Japan during the war.

In 1973 he had formed a firm friendship with 'Shiggy Konno', manager of the visiting Japanese rugby side and the epitome of Japanese rugby. As he told everyone, 'I was due to be the next kamikaze pilot, but the war ended just in time'! in 1975 Les led the Welsh rugby team on a tour of Japan. As the South Wales Echo reported: 'He learned to forgive, if not forget, the tragedy of war."

Deaths of internationals in this latter part of 1943 included:

Jul 18 – Reginald Vere Massey Odebert (Ireland, 1 cap, 1928). He was killed in action over Scunthorpe (GB). A Squadron-Ldr. in the RAF, then Wing-Commander and then Grp-Capt. He was previously in the Middle East Command. Aged 39.

Jul 19 – Robert Alexander (Ireland, 11 caps, 1936-39 and GB tour to South Africa 1938 – 3 tests). He was killed in action during the Allied landings at the Battle of Lemon Bridge in Sicily. A Capt. in the Royal Inniskilling Fusiliers and formerly in the Royal Ulster Constabulary. An Ireland cricketer, he also played rugby for RBAI/NIFC/Queen's University, Belfast/Army/Barbarians. He is buried at Catania Wall Cemetery. Aged 32.

Robert Alexander

Aug 2 – George Roberts (Scotland, 5 caps, 1938-39). Died in Kanchanabun, a Japanese Prisoner of War camp. Aged 29. He was a Lieut. in the Gordon Highlanders who was captured in the fall of Singapore and forced to work on the Burma-Thailand railway.

Oct 3 - William Mitchell (Bill) Penman, DFC, AFC (Scotland, 1 cap, 1939). A Wing-Cmdr. in the RAF. He was awarded the AFC in 1942 and the

DFC in 1943, but was killed when shot down over Hanover. He was classed as missing in action until his death was verified in April 1944. Aged 26.

Dec 6 – News came of the death of Herbert James Michael (Mike) Sayers (Ireland, 10 caps, 1935-39). He was the only son of Sir Frederick and Lady Sayers. A Major in the Royal Artillery, he was killed when the plane he was travelling in crashed into a tree at Potsgrove in Bedfordshire. Aged 32.

Mike Sayers

Dec 25 – Russell Lindsay Frederick Kelly (Australia, 7 caps, 1936-38). He died in Sydney on Christmas Day of wounds received at Tobruk, where he was captured, but following a prisoner exchange with Germany he returned to Australia in earlier 1943 but died at Concord Repatriation Hospital, aged 34.

Those lists underline the fact that rugby and all sport was only a distraction, albeit welcome, from the grim realities of the war. Gradual progress was being made by the Allies throughout 1943: in the Pacific; in Russia; across North Africa and up into Sicily and Italy (the South African Armoured Division amongst those taking their rugby balls and competitive edge with them).

Mussolini fell but was restored by his German backers; Warsaw 'rose' but was brutally repressed; the Soviets continued to push Germany back across eastern Europe – but all of this at a huge cost. U.S. and British bombers hit Germany hard, though the effect of the 'Dambusters', for example, was exaggerated, while the next year was to bring to Britain's skies Germany's V-1 and V-2 'revenge' weapons.

Meanwhile the build up in the U.K. of British and Dominion troops and their American, Free French and Polish allies continued, ahead of the invasion of Europe which would have to happen, it seemed, if the war was eventually to be won.

The movement was not all one way, though: as men, money and materials poured into Britain from the U.S.A, the RAF's Bleddyn Williams, for instance, had to leave his polished rugby boots and those usually snowy-white laces aside as he and others went west to Arizona for pilot training: a powered plane at first, then at home later, a glider – a pointer, it turns out, to plans further ahead ....

7

1944

While the tide of war may have been beginning to run in the direction the Allies would have wanted, there was no overwhelming reason for immediate optimism, so the year's turn was the cause of no great celebration – at Hogmanay in Scotland or elsewhere – and the Sassenachs were once again to see off their northern rivals in both their Services international clashes that spring.

By the time the English made it a hat trick by at last beating Wales in April, the siege of Leningrad had been lifted; the Red Army had taken Sebastopol and reached Romania; Orde Wingate, head of the Burma-based 'behind-the-lines' Chindits, had died in an air crash and the Allied attempts to take or by-pass Monte Cassino in southern Italy were meeting implacable resistance from both geography and the Germans.

One rugby man who was never to forget his experiences in that last theatre of operations was Hawick's man of voice, humour, humanity, rugby balls and mint balls, the BBC's much-loved and long-serving commentator, Bill McLaren. Fewer know him as a 1947 Scottish triallist flanker, a TB victim and a soldier who served in Italy with the Royal Artillery, where as a second lieutenant he fought at Cassino. As a forward spotter in 20/21 Battery, 5 Medium Regiment, he identified enemy targets and relayed the information back by radio.

Bill McLaren

Another wartime experience haunted him all his life: a huge pile of some 1,500 mutilated and unburied corpses in an Italian churchyard, the victims of a massacre. At 21 the sight changed his life and forged his attitude to sport. Rugby was in his blood, he explained, "but in the great scheme of things it really doesn't matter".

STALAG 357

Certificate of Merit

Awarded to

BARRACK 88

RUNNERS - UP
IN THE INTER-BARRACK
SEVEN - A - SIDE

RUGBY TOURNAMENT

GILLIS D.	LOTTER F.
MICHAEL J.	BERRY C.
SMYTHE C.	McLEAN W.
WILSON J. (CAPT)	

CHAIRMAN

CAMP RUGBY COMMITTEE

Camp Sevens Certificate

On his return to Hawick from post-war PE instructor training in Aberdeen he went down with tuberculosis. He spent 19 months in a sanatorium where he was treated with the new 'miracle drug' streptomycin, which saved his life. Always a useful player, McLaren had turned out for Scotland against the Army and played in that Scotland trial, but the onset of TB put paid to any hopes of an international career. Most listeners will have felt grateful that Bill, who died in 2010 aged 86, did the next best thing.

Meanwhile, just like Cardiff's Spence and Wooller and their fellow-prisoners in the Far East, many rugby men were incarcerated in the PoW camps, the 'Stalags', throughout German-held Europe. Mercifully there has been no rugby-based screen equivalent of Sylvester Stallone, Pele and Bobby Moore's *Escape to Victory*, but in the real, often brutally-harsh and at best certainly tedious PoW world, planning and participating in or even observing rugby matches was a life saver of a sort.

An RAF rugby man who escaped death and, on several occasions, his captors, was the stalwart flanker and Welsh trialist Ken Rees, who also captained London Welsh, played for Birkenhead Park, the RAF and Combined Services and starred for Cheshire in their County Championship win of 1950. In fact, many insist Rees was the original 'cooler king', who somehow morphed into the mythical Steve McQueen character in *The Great Escape* (no rugby!)

The diminutive Rees was piloting a Wellington bomber when shot down and crash landing in a lake in Norway and made himself a thorough nuisance at various POW camps before being sent to Stalag Luft III in Silesia. Being short and Welsh it was assumed that he would have some sort of mining skills, and, although in fact a draper by training, he was put in charge of one of the tunnels planned for the mass breakout – the 330 foot long 'Harry' – which in the event was the only one used.

Rees worked at the face of the tunnel most of the time, helping to shift 250 tons of soil before the breakout on the night of March 24-25 1944. Over 200 PoWs were ready to flee but only 76 had exited the tunnel when the Germans realised what was occurring. Rees had to scuttle back along the tunnel to Hut

Ken Rees

104 where after being threatened with summary execution he found himself in the cooler. Again.

Rees always played down his omission from the film and made light of any comparisons with himself and McQueen: "He is taller than I am, I'm heavier than he is, he's American and I'm a Welshman, he rode a motorbike, I don't – the only things we've got in common is that we both seemed to annoy the Germans and ended up doing stretches in the cooler."

Still with the RAF, he later commanded a Valiant V-bomber squadron tasked with delivering an atomic bomb on Moscow should the need arise. After all that excitement he retired to become a postmaster in North Wales, and died in 2014 at the age of 93.

Where allowed, then, rugby and other sports clearly aided the building and maintaining of fitness, interest and morale amongst those many thousands of Allied prisoners of war, as well as active forces. Many stories of and images of rugby behind the high electric fences and watchtowers have emerged since those days, some with the censor's marker still visible, blanking out parts of the picture.

Our pictures are from, amongst others, Stalag 357; Laband for Stalag VIIIB; and Stalags XVIIID and XVIIIA (where Maori PoWs are pictured in Austria). The care taken and the ingenuity shown in preparing for some of the games is

Rugby in the Stalags

Match Programme & SA Team Picture

also well illustrated by the 'internationals' played in at least one German PoW Camp, Stalag IVB, at Muhlberg-on-Elbe. Amongst them were:

May 20 – 'Wales' 3 'South Africa' 17.

Wales – Pen: H. Grant.

South Africa – Tries: A.J. Fabricus 2, Schaefer 2. Con/Pen: Uys.

Referee: RSM Andy Samuels (England). Touch-Judge: C.J.G. Alford (Wales).

The kit and hand-coloured programme were lovingly organised against the odds, a guard bribed to take the team picture and a programme of entertainment for the day laid on.

May 31 – 'South Africa' 9 'The Rest' 0.

South Africa – Tries: C.J. van der Westhuizen, M.L. Moore. Pen: Gus Ackerman.

Referee: Alf Dampier (South Africa).

The South African captain in these matches was Barend Stephanus ('Fiks') van der Merwe, who with typical strength scored the only try in the 3-0 rematch against Wales and went on to play in one 1949 test v New Zealand as a flanker. A police officer, he was born at Craddock 2/1/1917. He played for Northern Transvaal, and died 11/7/2005, aged 88.

As a footnote, when Stalag IVB was liberated, RSM Andy Samuels, the Camp Leader, was the last person on the last lorry to leave. He stayed to make sure everyone was out. He had been a Sgt. in the 5th Battalion of the East Yorkshire Regt. Born in Scotland, he was 14 when he moved to Hull and he joined the Army in 1919, being a regular soldier who was taken prisoner in the Western Desert. He was taken to Italy, then to the Stalag, 40 miles from Leipzig.

As the lorry left the camp following liberation by the Red Army, he saved a young German from the Russians by making him a Private in the regiment and years later the boy, who became a schoolteacher back in his homeland, said he owed his life to Andy, who was one of 'Five Brave Men' to whom the book *'Copper Wire'* was dedicated.

Meanwhile, as secret planning for the invasion of mainland Europe went ahead through the spring of 1944, three 'international' matches were played in the first half of the year, the first at Murrayfield.

England at Scotland, February 1944

February 26 – SCOTLAND 13 ENGLAND 23 (at Murrayfield, Edinburgh). (20,000).

Scotland selected Cpl. George Kinnon Brunton of the Royal Scots as hooker, but he died in an accident eight days before his 'international' debut, having twice played for a Scotland Services XV earlier in the year. He was aged 32, from Walkerburn and was buried at Innerleithen Cemetery. John Hastie replaced him in this game, though coming in to prop with Bob Cowe switching to hooker.

Gloucester wing forward Gordon Hudson had an extraordinary game, scoring four of his side's five tries in a match he would surely never forget.

Fly half Tom Gray kicked Scotland ahead with a penalty, but England then took over with scrum half Jim Parsons and Hudson crossing, plus a conversion of the latter try by Johnny Lawrenson. Then, centre Jim Stott dropped a goal and Hudson scored two more tries, the latter again converted by Lawrenson for a 20-3 lead at half-time.

In the second half, Hudson scored his fourth try after a run by Stott, though Scotland, who moved Russell Bruce to fly half, came back in the last ten minutes and scored ten points with 'Copey' Murdoch converting tries by Gray and scrum half James Blair.

Sadly, Blair, who was probably the best performer for his side, was to be killed in Normandy just five months after this game, which was the first Services International to be played at Murrayfield after derequisition from its supply depot use by the Royal Army Service Corps.

An England change after selection saw Peter Hastings replace Tommy Kemp (shoulder injury) while Scotland lost Ewan Douglas (dislocated shoulder) and Jim Lees to be replaced by Murdoch and Howard Campbell. One report stated that at least 30,000 were present at the game. There were 14 Army representatives in the Scotland side.

Scotland - *+Capt. Murdoch; *+Capt. Innes, +Capt. Munro, +Major Bruce, Cadet Rating Alex E.W. Murray (Oxford University/ Navy); +Lieut. Gray, Lieut. Blair; +Lieut. Howard H. Campbell (Cambridge University/

Autographs from the game

Army), *Lance-Cpl. John D.H. Hastie (Melrose/Army), Cpl. Cowe, *Major Melville, +Capt. Frank H. Coutts (Melrose/Army), *Capt. (GD) Shaw, *Capt. Waters (capt.), CSM J.R. ('Stiffy') McClure (Ayr/Wasps/Army).

Touch-Judge: Major A. ('Jock') Wemyss.

Tries: Blair, Gray. Cons: Murdoch 2. Pen – Gray.

England – Lance-Cpl. (E) Ward; Lieut. Hollis, LAC Lawrenson, Cfn. Stott, Sgt-Inst. Francis; Lieut. Hastings, Sqdn Ldr. Parsons; +Capt. Prescott (capt), *Cpl. Longland, Flt-Sgt. Dustin, +Cpl. Mycock, Lieut. (Schoolmaster) Doherty, Cpl. Hudson, Sgt. Dancer, +Flt-Lieut. Weighill.

Touch-Judge: Capt. H.A. Haigh-Smith.

Tries: Hudson 4, Parsons. Cons: Lawrenson 2. DG: Stott.

Referee: Allan McM. Buchanan (Ireland).

SCOTLAND

ALEXander Elliot W. MURRAY – Wing. Sedbergh School/Christ Church College, Oxford University (Blue 1943)/London Scottish/United Services/ Rosslyn Park. He was a Cadet Rating, then a Sub-Lieut. in the Navy serving on the HMS Victory in February 1946. Born 8/10/1923 West Derby, Liverpool. Died 3rd quarter, 1994 Surrey.

HOWARD Hindmarsh CAMPBELL, MC – Prop. Born Machalos, near Nairobi (Kenya) 10/11/1921. Died Stretlen, near Reading 23/2/2012.Oundle School/ Cambridge University/London Scottish/Army/Barbarians. He was Lieut. in the Royal Engineers, then a Civil Engineer and was capped later in the 2nd and back rows. 4 Caps (1947-48). He played golf at Henley GC.

JOHN Dickson Hart HASTIE – Hooker. Born Peebles 16/3/1902. Died Short, Balding 19/1/1965. Gala Academy/Melrose/Army. 3 caps (1938). Lance-Cpl. in the Army, then a Bank manager.

FRANK Henderson ('The Bing') COUTTS, CBE, DL – 2nd Row. Born Glasgow 8/7/1918. Died Edinburgh 20/10/2008. Glasgow Academy/Melrose/ Barbarians/Army/Kent/London Scottish/Metropolitan Police. 3 caps (1947). He was a Major, then a Brigadier in King's Own Scottish Borderers and became SRU President in 1977-78 and Vice-Patron of the Army RU in 2007. He wrote 'One Blue Bonnet'.

James R. ('Jock', 'Stiffy') McCLURE – Back Row/Hooker. Ayr/Cumnock/ Wasps/London Scottish/Scotland Trials. Army Company Sgt-Major and later a Major. A schoolteacher at Ayr Academy and Cumnock Academy, he played for Ayr RFC until his late 50s.

March 18 – ENGLAND 27 SCOTLAND 15 (at Welford Road, Leicester). (18,000).

Scotland included the England-born Henry Uren, a captain in the Highland Regiment, who had taught at Glasgow Academy and played much of his senior rugby in Glasgow. Uren had not originally been selected, but Alex Murray had withdrawn. 'Jock' McClure came in for John Hastie, who was forced to withdraw.

Only hours before kick-off, England prop Gerry Dancer withdrew with illness and Fred Goddard, the Taunton and Somerset County player, took his place. Tommy Kemp again withdrew with injury so that Peter Hastings played at fly half. Johnny Lawrenson was ill and was replaced by teenager Leo Oakley.

However, despite the late change, the English pack again dominated even though Robin Prescott had an eye closed early in the game. Oakley made a good debut at centre and the reliable Welshman Roy Francis was the fastest man on view.

An Ernest Ward penalty and another Gordon Hudson try – his fifth in two games - was followed by 'Donny' Innes going over for Scotland, but Gerry Hollis quickly replied and Jimmy Stott converted so England led 11-3 at the interval.

In the second half, prop forward R. Cowe kicked a penalty for Scotland, but Oakley raced in for a debut try and Stott converted, yet Scotland, who tackled splendidly, again hit back as 'Copey' Murdoch dropped a goal at 16-10.

England now cut loose with tries by Hastings, Francis and Francis again, plus a Stott conversion with Scotland getting a late consolation try from Frank Coutts, converted by Cowe.

England – Lance-Cpl. Ward; Lieut. Hollis, +Cadet Officer L.F.L. (Leo) Oakley (Bedford/Army), Cfn. Stott, Sgt Inst. Francis; Lieut. Hastings, Sqdn Ldr. Parsons; Lieut Fred C. Goddard (Taunton/Army), *Cpl. Longland, *Capt. Prescott (capt), +Cpl. Mycock, Lieut. (Schoolmaster) Doherty, Cpl. Hudson, +Flt-Lieut. Weighill, Capt. Gilbert.

Touch-Judge – Capt. H.A. Haigh-Smith.

Tries: Francis 2, Hollis, Oakley, Hudson, Hastings. Cons: Stott 3. DG: Ward.

Scotland – *+Capt. Murdoch; *+Capt. Innes, +Capt. Munro, Lieut. Grant, Capt. Henry G. Uren (Glasgow Acads); +Major Bruce, +F/Officer Ernest Anderson (Stewart's College FP/Cambridge University/RAF);

Lieut. Campbell, CSM McClure, Cpl. Cowe, *Major Melville, +Capt. Coutts, +Pte. Jim B. Lees (Gala/Navy), *Capt. Waters (capt), *Capt. (GD) Shaw.
Touch-Judge: Major A. ('Jock') Wemyss.
Tries: Innes, Coutts. Con/Pen: Cowe. DG: Murdoch.
Referee: Wing Cmdr. (CH) Gadney (Leicester).

ENGLAND

Lionel Frederick Lightborn (LEO) OAKLEY – Centre. Born Ramna, Dacca, India 24/1/1926 (some reports say 1925). Died Bedford November 1981. Bedford School/Bedford/Rosslyn Park/Army/Barbarians/East Midlands. He was a fertiliser company sales manager and served in the Royal Artillery, 2nd Indian Airborne Division and 6th Airborne Division (Cadet Officer). He was aged only 18 at the time of this game. 1 cap (1951).

FREDerick Charles GODDARD – Prop. Taunton/Somerset County (47 pre-war apps)/South-East Command. Born Taunton 27/12/1910. Died Claro, Yorkshire in 1st quarter 1985. The son of a college porter, he married Irene Churchill in 1934 and was a Licensed Victualler at the 'Royal Marine' in 45 Silver Street, Taunton in 1939 and then a Lieut. and Capt. in the 5th Wiltshire Regiment. He was awarded the Dutch Bronze Cross and played for the Rhine Army XV and BAOR Combined Services in Germany 1946. His wife died in 1942.

England v Scotland March 1944

SCOTLAND

HENRY George UREN – Wing. Born Plymouth 2nd quarter 1915. Died New Kilpatrick, Glasgow, 5/2/2006. Plymouth College/Plymouth Albion/Glasgow Academicals/Army. He was a Captain in the Highland Regiment and when he served in the 15th Scottish Division he was mentioned in dispatches, later returning to be a schoolteacher at Glasgow Academy, then a Salesman. He was a Devon County cricketer in 1937.

Ernest (ERNIE) ANDERSON – Scrum Half. Born 20/10/1918. Died 27/1/2001. Stewart's College/Edinburgh University/Stewart's College FP/Cambridge University/RAF. He was a Flying/Officer in the RAF, then a Schoolmaster.

James Blanc (JIM) LEES - Back Row. Born Selkirk 11/8/1919. Died Galashiels August 2004. Selkirk High School/Gala/Navy. Private in the Navy, later a Newsagent. 5 caps (1947-48).

April 8 – ENGLAND 20 WALES 8 (at Kingsholm, Gloucester). (16,000).

None of the England backs ever went on to won a full cap and Wales were favourites once again and did most of the attacking, but failed to stay the course on this occasion. Kingsholm was packed to capacity and the gate receipts were around £2,500, all going to Service Charities.

It was just like pre-war games as Welshmen fastened leeks to the posts before the Gloucester Police Force intervened and then the band of the RAF Technical Training Command led the singing of the anthems in a splendid atmosphere.

England opened with a magnificent penalty kicked by Ernest Ward and added another before Coleman scored a try for Wales only for scrum half Jim Parsons to cross for England but again Wales replied as fly half and captain Willie Davies crossed for a solo try that Bill Tamplin converted, yet England led 9-8 at half-time even if Wales led 2-1 on tries.

It remained that way until ten minutes from time with Wales looking likely to win, but England cut loose to score three tries without reply as their pack suddenly came out on top and two of them scored tries from forward rushes.

The game had been contested at a tremendous pace in the first half with excitement at a high pitch though after the interval it slowed down as England's defence was given a great testing and their line had several narrow escapes.

It was a brilliant try by Welsh-born wing Roy Francis that saw England suddenly become unstoppable with their forwards now rampant.

The crowd, that included a large number of British and American Servicemen, now witnessed a grandstand finish by England as both Jim Doherty and Bob Weighill scored tries with one conversion by centre Johnny Lawrenson.

The debutant England forward Peter Walker, playing on his club's ground in a splendid debut, was killed just four months later. He had played in this match as fellow Gloucester forward Gordon Hudson withdrew because of a broken thumb, while Tommy Kemp was picked for the third successive time and yet again withdrew with Peter Hastings once more coming in.

Wales had to make late changes with pre-war cap Arthur Rees replacing Ike Owens and Jack Knowles coming in for Alan Edwards, who had broken a finger. Ernie O. Coleman was shown as R.G. Coleman in the programme.

England – Lance-Cpl. Ward; Lieut. Hollis, Sgt. Lawrenson, Cfn. Stott, Sgt-Inst. Francis; Lieut. Hastings, Sqdn-Ldr. Parsons; Sgt. Dancer, *Cpl. Longland, *Capt. Prescott (capt), +Cpl. Mycock, Lieut. (Schoolmaster) Doherty, Capt. Gilbert, +Flt-Lieut. Weighill, Lieut. Peter N. Walker (Gloucester/Army).

Touch-Judge: Capt H.A. Haigh-Smith.

Tries: Parsons, Doherty, Francis, Weighill. Con: Lawrenson. Pens: Ward 2.

Wales – Sgt. (AA) Davies (stated as Newport); Lance-Cpl. Jack T. Knowles (Newport/Army), *D. Idwal Davies (Swansea/London Welsh/ Leeds RL), Lance-Cpl. Sullivan, *Cpl. (SA) Williams; *Sgt. (WTH) Davies (capt.), *+Lieut. Tanner; *Sgt. Law, *+Sgt. Travers, Sgt. (WG) Jones (Newport), +Gunner Ernie O. Coleman (Newport/Army), Gunner (Rees) Williams, *Arthur M. Rees (Metropolitan Police/London Welsh/ RAF), +Lieut. Tamplin, Sgt Foster.

Tries: Coleman, (WTH) Davies. Con: Tamplin.

Referee: Stanley H. Budd (Knowle, Bristol).

England v Wales Programme, April 1944

ENGLAND

PETER Norman WALKER – Back Row. Born Upton on Severn, Worcestershire 2nd quarter 1923. Killed in action in Normandy 18/7/1944 (aged 21). Worcester GC/Gloucester/Hertford College, Oxford/Oxford University (Blues 1941-42)/ Barbarians/Army. He was a Lieut. in the 4th Batt. of the Royal Welch Fusiliers and is buried in the Brouay War Cemetery (Normandy).

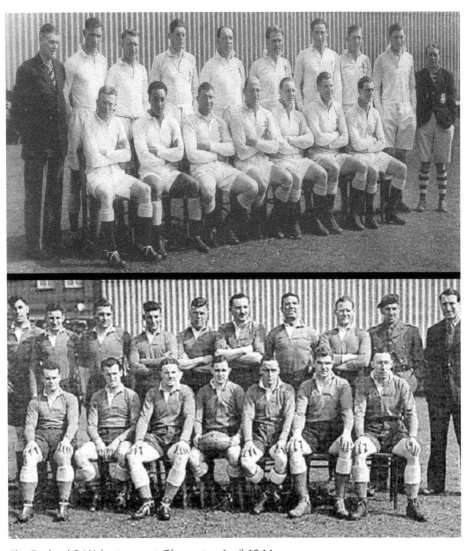

The England & Wales teams at Gloucester, April 1944

WALES

John Thomas (JACK) KNOWLES – Wing. Born 4/8/1915 Newport. Died Hillside Drive, Pontypool 3/5/1996. Newport (126 games, 61 tries, 2 drop goals 1934-35 to 1939-40)/Army/Monmouthshire. He was a Lance-Cpl, then a Capt in the South Wales Borderers and became a Police-Sgt post-war. He played for Newport against New Zealand in 1935.

David IDWAL DAVIES – Centre. Born 10/11/1915. Died Llanelli 7/7/1990. Llanelly County School/Trinity Coll. Carmarthen/Hendy/Pontarddulais/Llangennech/Swansea/London Welsh/RAF/Leeds and Wales RL. A Sgt., then a Flying-Officer in the RAF, he was later a schoolmaster. 1 cap (1939). He was the father of Wales centre D. Brian Davies (3 caps, 1962-63).

Ernest Owain (ERNIE) COLEMAN – Prop/2nd Row. Born Newport 3/11/1917. Died Newport 30/9/1999. Newport/Army. He was a Steelworker who served as a Gunner in the Anti-Aircraft Command. 3 caps (1949).

ARTHUR Morgan REES OBE, CBE, QPM, DL, KstJ – Back Row. Born Llangadog 20/11/1912. Died Oxshott, Surrey 13/5/1998. Llandovery College/Wales Secondary Schools/Cambridge University/RAF/Met. Police/London Welsh/Stoke/Wrexham/Barbarians/Sussex/Middlesex. 13 caps (1934-38). He was a Flt-Lieut., then Sqdn-Ldr., then Wing-Cmdr. in the RAF. He joined the Metropolitan Police, rising to Chief Constable of Denbighshire, then Chief Constable of Stafford and Stoke-on-Trent, Deputy Lieut. of Staffordshire and Freeman of the City of London. He was awarded the OBE (1960), CBE (1963) and the Queen's Police Medal (1970).

Other matches of note that spring included:

Jan 1 – Scotland Services 11 RAF and Dominions 6 (at Myreside, Edinburgh).

Scotland had Wales RL wing Syd Williams and included Coutts, (HH) Campbell and (JB) Lees.

New Zealander Eric Grant skippered the combined RAF/Dominions team, which included Welshmen (IA) Owens and (AS) Edwards.

Jan 8 – South Wales 23 Army 11 (at the Arms Park, Cardiff).

South Wales - *Gwyn Bayliss (Pontypool, but listed as Newport); D. Glyn Jones (Cardiff), S. Howard-Jones, N. Harris, Knowles; +Cleaver, Jim Hawkins (Newport); Ray Bale (Cardiff), Flowers, A.D. Stanley Bowes (Navy/Cardiff), Leslie Smith (Newport), W. Talbot (Abertillery), +Tamplin, J.T. Hickey (Cardiff), Foster.

Tries: Knowles 2, Foster, Howard-Jones, Cleaver. Cons: Cleaver 2. DG: Hawkins.

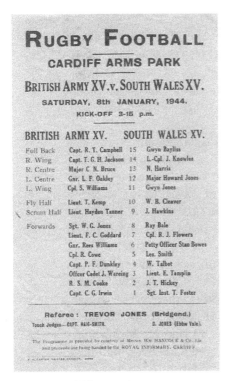

RUGBY FOOTBALL

CARDIFF ARMS PARK

BRITISH ARMY XV. v. SOUTH WALES XV.

SATURDAY, 8th JANUARY, 1944.

KICK-OFF 3-15 p.m.

BRITISH ARMY XV.			SOUTH WALES XV.
Full Back	Capt. R. T. Campbell	15	Gwyn Bayliss
R. Wing	Capt. T. G. H. Jackson	14	L.-Cpl. J. Knowles
R. Centre	Major C. N. Bruce	13	N. Harris
L. Centre	Gnr. L. F. Oakley	12	Major Howard Jones
L. Wing	Cpl. S. Williams	11	Gwyn Jones
Fly Half	Lieut. T. Kemp	10	W. B. Cleaver
Scrum Half	Lieut. Hayden Tanner	9	J. Hawkins
Forwards	Sgt. W. G. Jones	8	Ray Bale
	Lieut. F. C. Goddard	7	Cpl. R. J. Flowers
	Gnr. Rees Williams	6	Petty Officer Stan Bowes
	Cpl. R. Cowe	5	Les. Smith
	Capt. P. F. Dunkley	4	W. Talbot
	Officer Cadet J. Wareing	3	Lieut. E. Tamplin
	R. S. M. Cooke	2	J. T. Hickey
	Capt. C. G. Irwin	1	Sgt. Inst. T. Foster

Referee : TREVOR JONES (Bridgend.)

Touch Judges—CAPT. HAIG-SMITH.   D. JONES (Ebbw Vale).

The Programme is provided by courtesy of Messrs. Wm. HANCOCK & Co. Ltd. and proceeds are being handed to the ROYAL INFIRMARY, CARDIFF.

S Wales v British Army Programme

The Army side, captained by (CR) Bruce, included Welshmen Syd Williams, (HJC) Rees, Tanner, (WG) Jones and (Rees) Williams.

Tries: (Syd) Williams, (CR) Bruce, (CG) Irwin. Con: (FC) Goddard.

Jan 22 – Scotland Services 12 Anti-Aircraft Command 21 (at Inverleith).

The Anti-Aircraft side included Welshmen (VGJ) Jenkins, (Rees) Williams and Coleman.

Jan 29 – Army 8 RAF 11 (at Richmond Athletic Ground).

The crowd of 4,546 was the highest at the ground since the 1920 Hospitals Cup was watched by King George V. RAF hooker, A/C Tommy Armitt (Swinton/Hull/GB/England RL), lost his way and arrived too late to play, Bob Weighill being summoned from the crowd and given boots!

Army – Try: Prescott. Pen: Risman.

RAF – Tries: Lawrenson, (Cliff) Evans, (WTH) Davies. Con: Lawrenson.

Referee: (SH) Budd.

February 12 - An Ireland XV 0 GB Army XV 15 (at Ravenhill, Belfast).

Ireland - *+(CJ) Murphy; *Frederick George Moran (Clontarf/Ireland 9 caps 1936-39), L. O'Brien (University College, Cork), Gerry T. Quinn (Old Belvedere), N.J. Burke (Lansdowne); Greer, J.W. Adrian (NIFC); (F) Cromey, W. Moynihan (Dublin University), +James Crothmans (Jimmy) Corcoran (University College, Cork/Ireland 2 caps 1947-48), +Keeffe, +James Edward (Jimmy) Nelson (Malone/Ireland 16 caps 1947-54 & B Lions 1950 - 2 tests v NZ, 2 tests v Aust), *(DB) O'Loughlin, (K) O'Brien, P.J. (Tom) Halfpenny (University College, Dublin).

GB Army - Ward; Francis, +Munro, Risman (now Lieut.), *(SA) Williams; +Gray, *+Tanner; +Coleman, *+Travers, Sgt. F.E. Morris (Newport), C.G. Irwin (Queens University, Belfast), +Coutts, *(GD) Shaw, Cowe, Foster.

Tries: Travers, Tanner, Foster. Pens: Gray, Tamplin.

Referee: R.W. Jeffares.

Feb 19 – RAF 14 Civil Defence 29 (at Leicester).

Civil Defence had Kenneth C. Fyfe (Sale/Cambridge Univ./Scotland) as centre and captain; (Arthur) Bassett wing; (EC) Davey centre; Lesley Smith (Newport), (AR) Taylor and (Will) Davies (Neath) in the pack.

Feb 26 – Oxford University 6 Cambridge University 5 (at Iffley Road, Oxford).

Oxford broke a run of eight Cambridge victories (they played twice a year in wartime). Oxford was skippered by Garton-Sprenger. Their tries were scored by wings J.K. Pearce and the fine Harlequin player, Dennis A. Barker.

Cambridge were captained by J.M. Langham. Their scorers were Newport High School centre C.D. Phillips (try) and (JF) Bance (conversion). They also included (RH) Lloyd-Davies, Eric Bole, Pat Sykes, D. Brian Vaughan and New Zealander L.R. Wallace (Massey University). Micky Steele-Bodger could not play after selection, while the fly half was Ian Douglas Freeman Coutts, who won another Blue in 1951 and gained two caps for Scotland (1951-52).

Ireland v British Army Programme, Feb 1944

Mar 4 – Northern Command 37 Scotland Services 5 (at Headingley, Leeds).

Northern Command – Tries: Francis 2, Risman, Foster 2, (JB) Lees, (JM) Blair, Walford. Cons: 5/Pen: Risman.

Scotland Services – Try: (E) Anderson. Con: Murdoch.

Mar 11 – RAAF 3 RNZAF 0 (at Richmond Athletic Ground).

A try by 22-year-old wing Flt/Sgt. Kenneth John Taubman from Marrickwille, NSW (Sydney University) won the game: however he died in an aircraft accident in Ireland on 8/8/1944. The Australian team included Flt-Sgt. Kenneth Howard (Ken) Kearney of Parramatta (3/5/1924-18/8/2006), who hooked for NSW, Australia (1947-48, 7 caps) and then played for Leeds and Australia RL.

RAAF full back, Flight-Sgt. George Kilpatrick, a wireless operator in 218 squadron, played splendidly, but died on 22/4/1945 when the Lancaster he was in crashed on take-off from RAF Chedburgh for a raid on Lubeck. He was buried in Cambridge Cemetery.

Mar 25 – South Wales 42 Dominions 19 (at St Helen's, Swansea). (15,000).

Dominions had to make several late changes. Music was provided by the Band of the 12th Btln. Glamorgan Home Guard, Swansea.

South Wales – (RH) Lloyd-Davies; L/Cpl. Knowles, F/O (J. Idwal) Davies, Sgt. (T) Sullivan, (A) Bassett; Cleaver, Sgt. Cliff Evans (Neath/RAF/Leeds RL); (Will) Davies, Sgt. (W) Travers, (DRG) Williams, Bdr. (Rees) Williams, (J) Hopkins, Lance/Bdr. Allan Jones (Llanelli/RHA), Lieut. Tamplin, Sgt. (I) Owens.

Touch-Judge: Ivor Jones (Llanelli/Wales/GB 1930).

Tries: Owens 3, (JI) Davies 2, Knowles, Bassett, (DRG) Williams, (A) Jones, (R) Williams.

Cons: Tamplin 4 (plus 2 more by unknown kicker).

Dominions – 2nd Lieut. (MP) Ackermann; Flt/Sgt. (KJ) Taubman, F/O M.A. Milich, DFC, F/O R.E. Lelong DFC (Auckland), P/O (JH) MacDonald; Sgt. Norman Emery (Australia), Flt/Lieut. B.R. Miles (Newcastle/Manly); F/O L.A.A. Kilgour (Palmerston North/King Country/RNZAF), Flt/Sgt. (K) Kearney, 2nd Lieut. (later Capt.) E.E. Swales VC (Durban HS/Durban HSOB/Natal/Griqualand West), F/O F.W. Crisp (Auckland University/RNZAF), 2nd Lieut. (later Lieut.) G.R. Lacey (Northern Transvaal), F/O (RA) Dalton, Flt-Sgt. I. Osborne (Combined PSRU Australia), Sqdn Ldr. (JB) Nicholls (capt.).

S Wales v Dominions & Programme, March 1944

Touch-Judge – Flight-Lieut. (Eric) Grant.

Tries: Lelong, MacDonald, Osborne.

Con: Emery (plus 1 by unknown kicker). Pens: Ackermann, MacDonald.

Referee: Fred G. Phillips (Pontarddulais).

Leonard Albert Arthur Kilgour was killed in action on 23/7/1944 (see note in 1943 Chapter).

Mate Alexander Milich, DFC, from Kataia was born at Waiharara 10/4/1921 and was killed in action on 8/12/1944. He was in the RNZAF, though had served earlier in the NZ Home Guard. He was in 198 squadron and was shot down over Holland and buried at Woudenberg Cemetery in Utrecht, Netherlands.

Roy Emile Lelong gained the DFC and bar. He appeared for the RAF XV in 1947. Born Auckland 12/12/1917. Died Hampshire (GB) 1977. He was in 644 and 605 squadrons and was a brilliant pilot, later fighting on loan to the United States Air Force in Korea. He joined the RNZAF in January 1942, transferring after the war to the RAF. In 1955 he returned to GB to command 257 squadron.

Gordon R. Lacey was a South African pilot in 630 squadron that attacked an oil refinery at Rositz near Leipzig. He was shot down on 15/2/1945 but his remains were not identified until 1948 and then reinterred at Heveren War Cemetery, Leuven. Only one other of his six crew was identified in 1948.

Edwin (Ted) Essery Swales (born 3/7/1915 Indana, Durban, Natal) joined the SA Infantry as a Sgt-Major and fought in Africa with the 8th Army. He then switched to the SAAF, being awarded the DFC with 582 Squadron and on 23/2/1945 led an attack on Pforzein. His plane went down near Limburg in Belgium, but he had ordered all his crew to bale out, though he crashed and died at the controls. He was awarded the Victoria Cross posthumously.

Mar 26 – Championship final – Perpignan 20 Aviron Bayonnais 5 (at Parc des Princes, Paris).

Apr 15 – In the first-ever match of its kind to be held in Britain, the NZ 'Pakehas' (White men) beat the NZ Maoris 13-11 (at Richmond Athletic Ground).

Apr 22 – Middlesex Sevens Final: St Mary's Hospital 15 RAF (Jurby) 5 (at Richmond). The Trophy was presented by W.J. Jordan, the NZ High Commissioner. In Round 4, RNZAF lost 3-13 to Notts and RAAF lost 3-8 to Guy's Hospital.

Apr 29 – Rugby League XV 15 Rugby Union XV 10 (Odsal, Bradford). (14,000).

League v Union Programme, April 1944

Doug V Phillips & Bob Weighill

In the second such big cross-code 'Union' clash, the League stars again deservedly prevailed.

RL – Ward; Francis, Lawrenson, Stott, Edwards; Brogden, Royal; (DR) Prosser, Driver (LL) White, LAC Chris Brererton (Halifax/RAF), Sgt. D. Murphy (Bramley/Army), (EV) Watkins, Owens, Sgt. (WG) Chapman, Foster (capt).

Tries: Lawrenson, Owens, Brogden. Cons: Ward 3.

RU – CSM R. Frank Trott (Penarth/Cardiff/Army); Hollis, Sullivan, Tanner, Lieut. Eddie F. Simpson (Headingley/Bradford RU/Yorkshire/Navy/HMS Fabius, Yorkshire president 1955); Gray, Parsons; Dancer, Longland, Prescott, Cpl. Douglas Versailles Phillips (Skewen, Swansea, Army RU/Oldham, Belle Vue Rangers, Wales & GB RL), (PN) Walker, (GD) Shaw (capt), Waters, Weighill.

Tries: Gray, Phillips. Cons: Gray 2.

Touch-Judges: Capt H.A. Haigh-Smith and Maj. E.L. Thompson (Harlequins/Army N.Command).

Referee: Wing-Cmdr (CH) Gadney.

Other official NZ Services games played that spring were:

Jan 22 – Beat South African Air Force 8-3 (at Richmond). This was the first UK appearance by a South African XV post-WW1. They were loaned a set of green jerseys by the Welsh Guards.

RNZAF – Tries: G.N. Hewitt, A.G. Cooper. Con: (unknown). SAAF – Pen: R. Ackermann.

Feb 12 – Beat Guy's Hospital 13-11 (at Honor Oak Park).
Feb 26 – Beat Guy's Hospital 9-8 (at Honor Oak Park).
Mar 4 – Beat Sutton 12-0 (at Cheam).
Mar 18 – Lost to St Mary's Hospital 0-19 (at Richmond).
Apr 1 – Beat Rosslyn Park 9-5 (at Richmond).

Miscellaneous:

Civil Defence sides included (Ted) Ward centre, and Cyril Challinor (Neath and Wales 1939), back-row forward.

Coventry reached February 1943 having been unbeaten since November 1941, when they had lost to Northampton and the run was to go on.

Rosslyn Park sides included Private Theodore Obolensky of the Royal Fusiliers, the younger brother of the late Prince Alexander Obolensky. Theodore, born in Paddington, London in 1919, also played in an Army trial match.

Ex-England centre Len Corbett had played against Wales centre Claude Davey: now Davey directly opposed Len's son Michael in a match between Rosslyn Park and a Public Schools XV.

London District included second row forward Bruce Alan Neale, an Army major in the Royal Artillery, who went on to gain three caps for England in 1951.

RL players to appear included Clifford J. Carter (Newport RU/Batley, Leeds, Cardiff RL, hooker), Lockwood (York, full back), A. McDonald (Leeds, forward) and Trevor H. Smith (Bradford Northern forward, from the Westminster Dragoons).

A useful wing for Bedford, Moseley and Rosslyn Park was Peter Henry Waterkeyn, who joined the RAF and as a navigator he escaped a crash with minor injuries, being made Sqdn-Ldr., then Wing-Cmdr. at RAF Cardington in 1961. He was born 29/10/1919 in Kingston, Surrey; married 1944 in Worcester and died in Marlborough, Wiltshire on 21/5/2004. His father was from Antwerp but had married in Wimbledon.

RUGBY LEAGUE:

Feb 28 – England 9 Wales 9 at Central Park, Wigan.

Apr 15 – RL Challenge Cup final – (1st leg) Wigan 3 Bradford 0 at Central Park, Wigan. Apr 22 – RL Challenge Cup final – (2nd leg) Bradford 8 Wigan 0 at Odsal, Bradford. Bradford won 8-3 on aggregate.

Deaths of international representatives during the early months of 1944 included:

Jan 16 – George Holmes Gallie, MC (Scotland, 1 cap, 1939). He was the son of Robert Gallie, MC (8 caps, 1920-21). He was a Major in the 78th Field Regiment, Royal Artillery and was killed in action at Minturno, aged 26. His brother had been killed in 1940.

Jan 26 – Alastair Simpson Bell McNeil (Scotland, 1 cap, 1935). He was a Surg-Lieut. in the Navy and was killed in action at Anzio, aged 28.

May 19 – Jack Hardy Harris (All Blacks, no tests, but played in eight matches in 1925, including the tour of Australia). He was killed in action whilst serving as a Cpl. with the 23rd Battalion in Italy. Aged 40.

Jun 3 - George Fletcher Hart (New Zealand, 11 caps, 1930-36). New Zealand 100 yards champion, 1931. Died at Sora, Italy of wounds received as a Lieut. in the 20th Armoured Regiment. He was hit by a shell during the advance from Cassino to Avezzano. Aged 35.

Jun 15 - William Norman Renwick (Scotland, 2 caps, 1938-39). An Oxford Blue, he was a Capt. in the Royal Horse Artillery, who had fought through North Africa and died in Italy. Aged 29.

Between those last two deaths, of course, what was ultimately to prove the decisive Allied invasion of mainland Europe had begun on D-Day, 6 June; a narrow window of better weather was exploited under Eisenhower and Montgomery to send a gigantic armada to the Normandy beaches, eventually establish bridgeheads, overcome stern initial resistance and start to drive the Germans back eastwards across France.

Meanwhile the US Fifth Army entered Rome, and the next two months saw further Allied progress there and against Japan in the Pacific, and by the Russians into Poland. Late July saw the failure of the Bomb Plot to kill Hitler by senior German Army officers, but August brought the liberation of Paris and the re-establishment of a Polish government.

June had also, though, seen the first of Hitler's 'secret super weapons', the V1 Doodlebug or Buzz Bomb, a jet-powered flying bomb, hit Britain. It would go on to cause more than 20,000 mainly civilian casualties, and from September on the V2 rocket missile joined the bid to wreck London lives, fabric and morale. That one, unlike the V1, couldn't be shot down.

One Welsh international who was, tragically, shot down was a man with claims to be one of the country's finest all-round sportsmen. Major Maurice

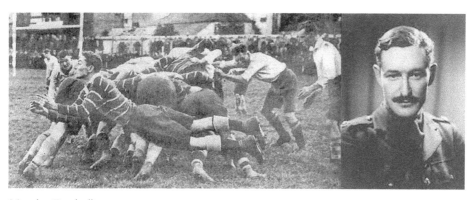

Maurice Turnbull

Tasker Watkins

Turnbull was advancing through Normandy in August when he was killed by machine-gun fire from a German armoured vehicle: see end-of-chapter obituaries.

Another Welsh sportsman in that same August advance survived, through bravery and good fortune, to win the Victoria Cross and eventually become Deputy Chief Justice and for eleven years a much-respected President of the

WRU. The then Lieut., later Major, from Nelson, S. Wales, won his VC for leading a bayonet charge against 50 armed enemy infantry and then single-handedly taking out a machine-gun post to ensure his unit's safety. He was to became The Right Honourable Sir Tasker Watkins, VC GBE QC DL, and died in 2007 aged 88.

November 25 – WALES 28 ENGLAND 11 (at St Helen's, Swansea). (20,000).

The Welsh backs were simply outstanding as they ran England ragged with six tries, of which only one was by a forward. Centre Bleddyn Williams (three tries) and star fly half Gus Risman

In the war-hectic latter half of 1944, only one services international was able to take place:

(13 points) were brilliant in one of the best games seen in South Wales for a long time despite the fact that it had rained solidly for hours before the kick-off.

The English team included Ordinary Seaman John Robins at lock. By 1950 he was playing at prop in the Wales Triple Crown-winning team and then toured with the Lions to NZ and Australia, while England were forced into making a last-minute change on the wing that saw 1938 Empire Games sprint champion Cyril Holmes replace the Frenchman Jacques Remlinger.

Earlier, Gerry Hollis had dropped out causing Ernest ward to move to centre and South African Mike Ackermann to play at full back. Six of the Wales team and eight of the English were new to Service International matches.

Willie Davies was not available, but fellow RL star Risman switched to his place, bringing Idwal Davies in at centre, while Jack Knowles had to come in on the wing for Alan Edwards. Another top League player, wing forward Trevor Foster, was the game's outstanding forward.

Though Ackermann showed a huge boot, he failed with two penalty kicks at goal and it was Risman's kick that opened the scoring. He then sent Bleddyn Williams away for a splendid score and then, when Risman's drop shot failed, wing Syd Williams followed up to touch down. Edgar Bibby opened England's score with a penalty, but Risman replied with a similar score.

Just on the interval scrum half Haydn Tanner sent the supporting Foster over for a 15-3 lead. The second session was almost half over before Wales struck again as a brilliant Risman's reverse pass saw Williams again go clear, with Risman converting. England finally grabbed a try when the two young Australians threequarters combined and Brian Young sent John Simmonds over, but the brilliant Risman ran clear at the other end at 23-6.

Holmes gained a second England try that Bibby converted, but Wales rightly had the last say with Risman breaking and Williams tearing away for his third try that Risman converted.

Wales - +CSM R. Frank Trott (Penarth/Army); Lance/Cpl. (JT) Knowles, *F/O (DI) Davies, +F/O (BL) Williams, *Cpl. (SA) Williams; Sgt. Risman (capt.), *+Lieut. Tanner; Petty Officer A.D. Stan Bowes (Cardiff/Navy), *+Sgt. Travers, *Bdr. Emrys A. Evans (Llanelly/Salford RL/Army), Cpl. Doug V. Phillips (Swansea/Belle Vue Rangers RL/Army), *BSM Harold W. Thomas (Neath/Salford RL/Army), *Flt/Sgt. Eddie V. Watkins (Cardiff/Wigan RL/RAF), Sgt. Owens, Sgt. Foster.

Tries: (BL) Williams 3, Foster, (SA) Wiliams, Risman. 2 Cons/2 Pens: Risman.

England – Lieut. Marthinus (Mike) T.A. Ackermann (SAAF); +CSM Cyril B. Holmes (Army/Manchester), Lance/Cpl. (E) Ward, Sgt. Brian J. Young (RAAF), Flt/Lieut. John A. Simmonds (RAAF); Lieut-Cdr. R.Edgar Bibby (Navy/Birkenhead Park), Sqdn/Ldr. Parsons; *Cpl. Longland, *Sqdn/Ldr. H. Bert Toft (RAF/Manchester University), Capt. F. Phil Dunkley (Army/Harlequins), +Ord/Seaman John D. Robins (Navy/Coventry), +Cpl. Mycock, +Flt/Lieut. Weighill, Lieut. Doherty, Cpl. Hudson.

Tries: Holmes, Simmonds. Con/Pen: Bibby.

Referee: R.A. Beattie (Watsonians).

WALES

Richard FRANK TROTT – Full Back. Born Cardiff 14/3/1915. Died Cardiff 28/3/1987. Llandaff/Penarth/Cardiff/Waterloo/Barbarians/Army. Guardsman, then Company Sgt-Major in the Army. 8 caps (1948-49). He was in Electricity Board admin. and later became Cardiff Athletic Club secretary.

A.D. STANley BOWES – Prop. Born Cardiff 1918. Died Cardiff 1987. Llandaff/Cardiff/Navy. Petty Officer in the Navy, he never married and gave much of his life to Cardiff Rugby Club, playing in the win over New Zealand in 1953, making 184 appearances (1938-39 to 1955-56 – 7 tries)

Wales v England & Programme, Nov 1944

Eddie V Watkins

and serving for many years as a committeeman. He worked as a porter in Whitchurch Mental Hospital and never married.

EMRYS A. EVANS – Prop. Born Gwaun-cae-Gurwen 24/4/1911, Died Bristol 23/6/1983. Cwmgors/Amman Utd/Army/Llanelli/Salford, Wigan and Wales RL. 3 caps (1937-39). He was in the haulage business and was a Bombardier in the Army.

DOUGlas Versailles PHILLIPS – 2nd Row. Born Neath 28/6/1919. Died Neath 28/4/2000. Neath Schools/Skewen/Swansea/Oldham, Broughton Rgs, Belle Vue Rangers, Wales and GB RL. He was a Cpl. and a Trooper in RECCE Corps and later was a Builder. Middle name after the Treaty.

HAROLD Watkin THOMAS – 2nd Row. Born Neath 19/2/1914. Died Neath 10/12/1989. Neath Schools/Briton Ferry/Cimla/Neath/Glamorgan/ Salford and Wales RL. Wales, 6 caps (1936-37). He was a Metal Worker who served as a RSM in the Maritime branch of the Royal Artillery. He was the brother of Wales forward David Leyshon Thomas.

Edward Verdun (EDDIE) WATKINS – Back Row. Born Caerphilly 2/3/1916. Died Cardiff 28/6/1995. Caerphilly Secondary School/Wales Secondary Schools (v Yorkshire 1934)/Bedwas/Cardiff/RAF/Glamorgan & British Police/ Wigan, Belle Vue Rangers and Wales RL. He was a Schoolmaster at Surbiton Grammar School and served in the Special Investigations Branch of the RAF and also a Flight-Sgt. Wales, 8 caps (1935-39). Middle name after the battle.

ENGLAND

Marthinus (MIKE) Theron A. ACKERMANN, DFC – Full Back. Born Cape Town 10/9/1915. Western Province/SAAF/Cape Town University. Also known as 'Ronnie', he was a Lieut. in the South African Air Force, saw duty with 630 Squadron in 1945 and was awarded the DFC in the same year.

CYRIL Butler HOLMES – Wing. Born Bolton 11/1/1916. Died Bolton 21/6/1996. Wrekin College/Manchester University/Army/Manchester/RMC Sandhurst/Lancashire/North-West Counties/UAU/Barbarians. In the Army PT Corps and a CSM Instructor, (Sandhurst), having won the 100 and 220 yards at Sydney's 1938 Empire Games. Later a Director in his family's oil company. He also ran in the 100 metres for GB in the 1936 Olympics in Berlin. England, 3 caps (1947-48).

BRIAN J. YOUNG – Centre. Newcastle (New South Wales)/Randwick RFC/ RAAF. He was a Sgt. in the Royal Australian Air Force.

JOHN A. SIMMONDS – Centre. Parkes (New South Wales)/RAAF. He was a Flying Officer and a Flt-Lieut. in the Royal Australian Air Force.

Robert EDGAR BIBBY, DSO – Fly Half. Died in 1997 (aged 77). Rydal School/ Navy/Birkenhead Park/Cheshire. He was a Lieut-Cmdr. in the Navy on HMS Formidable, was awarded the DSO in 1942 and was also a Navy Fleet Air Arm Pilot in 830 Naval Air Squadron. He later owned Wirral Airways (1946-50).

Henry BERT ('Bloody') TOFT – Hooker. Born Manchester 2/10/1909. Died Chichester 7/7/1987. Manchester Grammar School/RAF/Manchester University/Combined Services/Lancashire/Rosslyn Park/Barbarians. He was a Flt-Lieut. and then a Sqdn-Ldr. in the RAF. He became a Schoolmaster in Manchester Grammar School/Royal Latin School, Buckinghamshire and Bath Technical College and Principal at South-East Berkshire College of Education and later was a Journalist for the Observer. England, 10 caps (1936-39).

F. Philip DUNKLEY – Prop. Harlequins/Army. Captain in the Army and was a brother of Philip Edward ('Pop') Dunkley (England, 6 caps, 1931-36).

And, though Welsh: JOHN Denning ROBINS – 2nd Row (later prop). Born Cardiff 17/5/1926. Died Cardiff 21/2/2007. Navy/Coventry/Loughborough University/Birkenhead Park/Sale/London Welsh/Leicester/Yorkshire/ Barbarians/Cheshire/B & I Lions/Scotland Services. Wales 11 caps (1950-53). GB tour to NZ (3 tests)/Australia (2 tests) 1950. He was an Ordinary-Seaman in the Navy and became a Sportsmaster. Assistant manager of the 1966 B & I Lions to New Zealand/Australia and was a coach at Loughborough College/ Sheffield University/Cardiff University.

Other matches of note in later 1944 included:

> ### In New Zealand:
>
> Aug 26 – North Island 18 South Island 8 (the NZ Inter-Island Services match, at Athletic Park, Wellington).
> North – Tries: O/S D.A. Barchard, A/B B.M. Waldegrave, WO2 R.A. Everest, Chaplain/Major F.J. Green
> Cons: Capt. Tom.C. Morrison 3.
> South – Tries: A/C2 T.R. O'Callaghan, WO2 A.R. Cochrane. Con: O'Callaghan.
> (O'Callaghan was injured and A/C2 H.E. (Bert) Cook (later Kiwis and Leeds RL) replaced him.
> Referee: H.B. Simmons (Wellington).

Sept 16 – North Island 28 South Island 3 (The NZ Inter-Island match at Lancaster Park Oval, Christchurch).

North – Tries: R.J. Fox 2. Sgt. Ken G. Elliott, John M. Dunn, F/O G.W. ('Red') Delamore.

5 Cons/Pen: Morrison.

South – Try: L.W. Hewitt.

Referee: C.C. Crawford (Canterbury).

Sept 30 – A NZ XV 19 NZ Combined Services 22 (at Athletic Park, Wellington).

NZ XV – Tries: Percy L. Tetzlaff, R.B. McIntosh, L.D.A. Abbott, J.A. Gunning.

Cons: D.H. Murdoch, R.S. Sewell. Pen: Sewell.

NZ Comb Services – Tries: Cpl. A.V. Wiles 2, Barchard, Delamore, Pte. W.P. McHugh.

Cons: Morrison, O'Callaghan. Pen: O'Callaghan.

A host of players on view were All Blacks of the past or future, with the NZ XV including Des Christian, E. ('Has') Catley, Leo Connolly, Dunn, Morrie McHugh

North Island v South Island Programme

and Tetzlaff (captain), while the NZ Combined Services included Delamore, Elliott, AC/2 Harry Frazer, AC/2 Jack McLean, Morrison and O'Callaghan.

Referee: D.S.B. Heather (Waikato).

Sept 30 – Back in the UK, a NZ Inter-Island match was played at Richmond Athletic Ground, with North Island defeating South Island 22-14. The teams are not known, but Eric Grant scored a try for North Island.

Oct 7 – South Wales 3 RAF 22 (at St Helen's, Swansea).

South Wales – Lloyd-Davies; Bassett (now Derby RFC), Sullivan, John Morgan (Cwmavon/Cardiff), Knowles; Cleaver, Tanner (capt); (Will) Davies (Neath), W.T. Pritchard (Ebbw Vale), D.R.G. Williams (Llanelli/Pontarddulais), (Rees) Williams, Bowes, (AR) Taylor, Tamplin, Sedley Davies (now Bridgend).

Pen: Tamplin.

RAF – Sqdn-Ldr. Keith Irvine Geddes, DFC (Cambridge University/ Scotland); Edwards, (BL) Williams, Lawrenson, A/C T.L. (Peter) Blandy (Oxford University); (WTH) Davies, Parsons; Dancer, Toft (capt.), Longland, (EV) Watkins, Mycock, Owens, Weighill, (WT) Reynolds.

Scores were 5 tries, 2 cons, 1 pen.

Tries: Foster 2, Risman plus 2 others. 3 Cons/Pen: Risman.

Referee: Ivor David (Neath).

Oct 21 – RAAF 8 NZ Forces 6 (at Richmond).

RAAF – included Ken Kearney, Young and Simmonds, the latter two having played for England Services. At centre was E.M. Butler (New South Wales), while skipper, Sqdn-Ldr. and later Wing-Cmdr. John B. Nicholls (New South Wales), a back-rower, later played for Scotland Services.

Tries – Nicholls, Butler. Con – Butler.

S Wales v the Army Programme, Swansea 1944

RAAF v NZ Forces, with Mr. Jordan, NZ High Commissioner, for whose trophy this inter-dominion series was played from October to January

The winning RAF side aiding charities v S Wales

Oct 21 – South Wales 8 Army 24 (at St Helen's, Swansea).

Bleddyn Williams, Mycock and Owens had switched sides within a fortnight, but Tanner went to the Army team. Ernie Coleman and Rees Williams were late additions to the Army side when Capt. Vivian G. Weston (Kelvinside Acads/London Scottish/Scotland 1 cap 1936) and Capt. P.B. Stewart (London Scottish) could not appear.

South Wales – Lloyd-Davies; Knowles, Sullivan, (John) Morgan, Ordinary-Seaman Norman Sparrow (Swansea/Navy); (BL) Williams, F/Officer Cliff Evans (Resolven/Neath/RAF/Salford, Leeds, & Wales RL); (DRG) Williams, (WT) Pritchard, Bowes, Mycock, (HW) Thomas, Owens, (AR) Taylor, (DV) Phillips.

Scores: 2 tries, 1 con.

Touch-Judge: W Rowe Harding (Swansea/Cambridge University/Wales 17 caps 1923-28; GB to South Africa 1924 – 3 tests).

Army – Trott; Sgt. A.W. Guest (Castleford RL), (CR) Bruce, Staff Sgt Inst. John Thomas (Aberavon), Cpl. Albert E. Johnson (Warrington and England RL); Risman, Tanner, Coleman, Capt. (JDH) Hastie, (Emrys A) Evans, Lees, (Rees) Williams, Sgt. W..Elvet Jones (Cardiff), Lieut. G.B. Franks (RMC Sandhurst), Foster.

Army v RAF Programme, Nov 1944

NZ Forces were skippered by (Eric) Grant and included full back J.H. MacDonald who had played for England Services.

Try: Lieut. G. Harris (wing). Pen: MacDonald.

Oct 28 – RAAF 14 SAAF 11 (at Murrayfield). (8,000). Referee: (RA) Beattie.

Nov 4 – Army 18 RAF 15 (at Richmond).

The Army included John Arthur (Jack) Gregory the 1948 Olympic sprinter and 1949 England wing (one cap), then with Sale.

The RAF included forward P/O R.U. (Ronny) Reynolds (Sale) and wing Flt-Lieut. J.J. Remlinger, DFC (Wasps), a Frenchman who claimed to have destroyed Erwin Rommel's car and wounded him. Jacques J. Remlinger was born 3/1/1923 and died in London in 2002. He was educated at Harrow School, flew with the Free French Air Force and then continued living in London.

Army – Tries: Hastings, Tanner, (SA) Williams, Foster. Con: Ward. DG: Risman.
RAF – Tries: (JA) Simmonds 2, Young, (WTH) Davies. Pen: Geddes.

Nov 4 – South Wales 34 NZ RAF/Services 14 (at St Helen's, Swansea, 5,000).

South Wales – Lloyd-Davies; Bassett, (J) Matthews, (D. Idwal) Davies, Sparrow; Cpl. (WE) Jones, Sgt. Ivor Davies (Bridgend); (DRG) Williams, Pritchard, Bowes, Tom Rees (Tumble), (J) Hopkins, (AR) Taylor, Tamplin, Sub-Lieut. J. Williams (Llanelli).

Tries: Bassett 3, (DI) Davies 2, Taylor, Rees, Matthews. Cons: Tamplin 5.

NZ Services – F/O (JH) MacDonald (Marlborough); Lieut. (G).Harris (Poverty Bay), Flt-Lieut. (E) Grant (Auckland), +Sgt. (MP) Goddard (South Canterbury), P/O G. Childs (Waikotua); P/O J.L. Grayburn (South Canterbury), Lieut. R.W. Brinsden (Auckland); F/O A. Haydon (East Coast), Lieut. B. Hay (Canterbury), Sgt. A.W. Wordley (North Auckland/ Maoris), F/O F.W. Crist (Auckland Univ.), W/O A.T. Kofoed (Taranaki/ Wellington), Flt-Sgt. G.L. Breed (Wanganui/NZ RL), Pte. R.M. McKenzie (Manawatu), Sub-Lieut. C.J. Phelps (Wellington).

Touch-Judge: P/O Geary (Otago University).

Tries: Grayburn, Harris, Kofoed. Con/Pen: MacDonald.

Referee: (FG) Phillips (Pontarddulais).

ST. HELEN'S GROUND, SWANSEA, SATURDAY, NOV. 4th, 1944, kick-off 3-30

SOUTH WALES — SEMI-INTERNATIONAL RUGBY MATCH (In aid of War Charities) OFFICIAL PROGRAMME 3d. — NEW ZEALAND R. A. F.

Match programme & NZ/Scot/RAF Grant

With Paris liberated, de Gaulle feted, and despite Arnhem's 'Bridge Too Far' the Allies driving towards the Rhine, the city celebrated WW1's Armistice Day with some rugby as well as the parades and the flowers.

Paris v the RAF, November 1944: wing J Remlinger's own artwork, Delmas on the charge, programme and Eddie Watkins' invite and menu

Nov 11 – Paris XV 6 RAF 26 (at Parc des Princes, Paris).

Paris - Tries: J. Delmas 2.

Jacques Michel Pierre Chaban-Delmas was a general and played as left wing and captain. Born Delmas 7/3/1915 in Paris, he died there on 10/11/2000. He became French Prime Minister 1969-72 and had eight terms as Mayor of Bordeaux. He added Chaban to his name as it was his code name as a Resistance Leader.

RAF – Geddes; Remlinger, (DI) Davies, (BJ) Young, (JA) Simmonds; (WTH) Davies, Parsons; (RU) Reynolds, Toft (capt), Longland, Mycock, (EV) Watkins, (WT) Reynolds, Hudson, Owens.

Tries: Hudson 2, Young 2, (RU) Reynolds 2. Cons: Geddes 4.

Referee: (CH) Gadney.

In the programme, Bleddyn Williams and Bob Weighill were included, but Williams had been posted to a glider pilot's course and Weighill had a broken wrist. They were replaced by (DI) Davies and (WT) Reynolds.

Nov 11 – South African Services 11 NZ Services 8 (at Richmond Athletic Ground).

SA Services – Tries: Lieut. (GR) Lacey, Wing-Cmdr. P. Hopkins. Con/Pen: Lieut. (MT) Ackermann.

NZ Services – Tries: Goddard, Macdonald. Con: Macdonald. Referee: Cadet W.V. Wright (NZ).

Nov 25 – South African Services 16 NZ Services 8 (at Richmond).

SA Services – Tries: E F Westman, J F Rudd, P D Jones. 2 Cons/Pen: Westman.

NZ Services – Tries: Goddard, Grayburn. Con: Macdonald.

Dec 2 – Oxford University 3 Cambridge University 3 (at Oxford).

Oxford – Try: J.K. Pearce. Captain: A.H. Campbell.

Cambridge – Try: Steele-Bodger. Captain: (DB) Vaughan. (The pack included Bole, Bance and L.R. Wallace from Massey University, NZ).

Dec 9 – RAF 24 Dominions 13 (at Richmond Athletic Ground).

RAF included Sgt. D. Griffiths (Ebbw Vale) at centre; Cpl. J.G. Shaddock (Wellington, RNZAF) at fly half and Cpl. Peter O'K. Plumpton (Downside School/ RAF Halton) at prop. Bleddyn Williams scored one of the six RAF tries.

A close encounter at the Richmond Athletic Ground

Dec 26 – J.E. Thorneloe's XV 11 Barbarians 23 (at Leicester).

Barbarians – Trott; Derek L. Marriott (Christ's Hospital/Old Blues/Harlequins), Heaton, Scott, R.F. Harris (a late replacement); (BL) Williams, Tanner (capt.); (FP) Dunkley, Longland, C. Browse (St Mary's Hospital), A.B. Lees (Guy's Hospital), D.J.B. Johnston (St Mary's Hospital), (JB) Nicholls, Weighill, Hudson.

The club of Harris was never recorded, but it seems he was a Leicestershire County player.

Tries: Scott 2, Tanner, Weighill, Hudson, Nicholls, Trott. Con: Heaton.

The Barbarians report stated that (BL) Williams scored one of the tries credited to Scott.

Thorneloe's v Baabaas, Dec 1944

> J.E. Thorneloe's XV included (JA) Gregory and (H) Greasley as wings, Nim Hall at fly half, (J) Parsons at scrum half and skipper Gilthorpe as hooker with (AM) Rees in the back row.
> Tries: Greasley, C.S. Harris (Coventry); Con/Pen: Hall.
> Referee: R.F. Barradel (Leicester Society).

Dec 30 – Scottish Combined Services 14 RAF 26 (at Murrayfield).

Scottish Combined Services – Tries: Risman, (SA) Williams, scrum half K.P.P. Goldschmidt. Con/Pen: Risman.

Keith Geddes was captain, while Major (later Lieut-Col.) Kenneth Philip Parlane Goldschmidt was the scrum half. The latter was born 6/5/1916 and died 18/4/1994 in Bath, for whom he had also played. A pupil of Stowe School, who appeared for Hampshire County, he was in the Royal Leicestershire Regiment.

The RAF included P/O John Henry Orr (later Sir Harry Orr), OBE, of Heriot's FP/Scotland (2 caps, 1947) and wing A/C R.J. Forbes (RAF Heaton Park).

Tries: (D. Idwal) Davies 3, Hudson 2, Remlinger. Cons: Gilthorpe 4.

TEAMS

SCOTTISH SERVICES
(DARK BLUE JERSEYS)

Full Back
15 Squadron Leader K. I. Geddes (Wasps, Cambridge University, and R.A.F.) (captain)

Three-Quarters
14 Lieut. D. S. Ritchie (Edin. Acads. and Cambridge University)
13 Cpl. S. A. Williams (Salford, Wales, and Army)
12 Lieut. A. J. Risman (Salford, Wales R.L., and Army)
11 Sub.-Lieut. A. E. Murray (Oxford University)*

Half Backs
10 2nd Lieut. J. D. Cowie (Fettesians)
9 Major K. P. P. Goldschmidt (Hampshire and Barbarians)

Forwards
8 C.S.M.I. J. R. M'Clure (Ayr and Wasps)*
7 Flight Sgt. K. H. Kearney (Royal Australian Air Force)
6 Officer Cadet C. G. Bannatyne (Lorettonians)
5 Sub.-Lieut. C. Wilhelm (South African Services)
4 Pte. R. M. M'Kenzie (New Zealand)
3 Pte. J. B. Lees (Gala and Army)*
2 Capt. D. M'Gill (Kilmarnock and Aldershot Services)
1 Sub.-Lieut. G. W. Thomson (Watsonians)

Touch Judge—A. B. Kinnear (Stewart's College F.P.)

ROYAL AIR FORCE
(PALE BLUE JERSEYS)

Full Back
15 Lieut. M. T. Ackermann (Western Province S.A.)*

Three-Quarters
14 A/C R. J. Forbes (Heaton Park)
13 Flying Officer B. L. Williams (Cardiff)*
12 Pilot Officer I. Davies (Swansea and Wales)
11 Flight Lieut. J. J. Remlinger (Wasps)

Half Backs
10 Sgt. W. H. T. Davies (Swansea, Bradford Northern, and Wales) (captain)
9 Squadron Leader J. Parsons (Wasps)*

Forwards
8 Cpl. R. J. Longland (Northampton and England)*
7 Squadron Leader C. G. Gilthorpe (Wasps)*
6 Cpl. P. Plumpton (Downside School)
5 Cpl. J. Mycock (Harlequins)*
4 Flight Sgt. E. Watkins (Cardiff)*
3 Sgt. E. Bedford (Hull Kingston Rovers)
2 Flight Lieut. R. G. J. Weighill (Waterloo)*
1 Cpl. G. Hudson (Gloucester)*

Touch Judge—Flight Lieut. A. D. G. Matthews (Northampton)

Referee—Mr R. A. Beattie (Watsonians)

* Denotes Services International Players.

A SELECTION OF MUSIC WILL BE PLAYED BY THE BAND OF THE 1st ROYAL DRAGOONS BY KIND PERMISSION OF THE OFFICER COMMANDING

Scottish Services v RAF programme, Dec 1944

> **Other official NZ Services games played in the UK in later 1944 were:**
>
> Oct 28 – Lost to Wasps 9-20 (at Sudbury).
> Dec 2 – Beat Anti-Aircraft Command 16-0 (at Richmond).
> Dec 16 – Beat OCTU Sandhurst 16-5 (at Sandhurst).

While V2s created fear and damage in London, the Germans' mighty *Tirpitz* had been sunk, and further afield, despite the heat of the conflict in Italy, in the desert and in the jungle, Australian, New Zealand and South African troops still managed to get in some rugby, while closer to home the provinces of Ireland continued to play each other and to combine against the British Army XV and their own Defence Forces.

In the South Pacific the NZ 3rd Division was based in Nouméa, New Caledonia, from 1942 to 1944. Their commander emulated Freyberg by providing his Harold Barrowclough Cup for rugby competition between divisional units, and other sports were also encouraged. New Zealand troops stationed in Fiji from 1940 to 1942 had played rugby and cricket, while the Aussies feature here in two rugby pictures: from the Middle East, patently staged, and the Far East, clearly not.

Collection of Irish wartime programmes

The 6th South African Armoured Division, when not in the vanguard of efforts in the North African Desert and Italy, were quick to organize their rugby activities, which were recently recorded in detail just before his untimely passing by Gideon Nieman in his *Khaki-Clad Springboks*. This followed the earlier *Khaki All Blacks* by Mike Whatman, Paul Donoghue's *Rugby against Rommel* and A C Swan & A H Carman's *Five Seasons of NZ Services Rugby* as splendidly-researched resources.

Australian Rugby in the Middle and Far East

Rugby against Rommel

South African and New Zealand forces were always keen to lock horns and had done so, after trials, in three games in Cairo in 1943-4, the 'Boks Division winning 2-1. Then they were off to Italy and the real battles, but after the fall of Rome and further advances, matches were again organized and in late December the S African United Defence Force, with many Air Force personnel to the fore, beat the NZ Advanced Base XV 8-5 in Rome. The rivalry between the two nations, their banter about 'The Book' of Rugby, mythical or otherwise (Nieman proffered three alternatives), and who were better read at the game, grew ever stronger, though generally good natured off the field.

The New Zealanders, generally pushing up the peninsula further east, also played amongst themselves or rivals, as the programme from Ancona shows; while the 22nd Battalion team drink from the Freyberg Cup, won at Forli on 8 December 1944.

Meanwhile, in Northern Europe a race for Antwerp had been won by the Allies and a team of airmen from 34 Wing 2 ATAF was pictured with their Belgian National Team opponents at Anderlecht Stadium before the flyers' 5-0 win.

Freyberg Cup winners 1944 & and veteran squad member Ray Potier

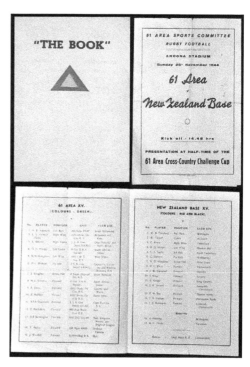

Rosslyn Park programme

1 Area v NZ Base XV Programme & 'The Book' (?)

Camborne programmes 1944

The No 34 Wing 2 ATAF (Belgium) and the Belgium National teams prior to their match in the Stade Anderlecht, Brussels in 1944. The Airmen won 5-0.

Airmen v Belgium, 1944

Christmas in a prosperous peacetime can often be characterised as 'the Battle of the Bulge': less danger of that in rationed, luxury-starved Britain as 1944 ended, and as a very real and bloody struggle, known by that name, saw the Germans' last throw of the offensive dice in the snowy Ardennes forest.

It failed – just – and at home, meanwhile, as the year closed, Bleddyn Williams found himself playing alongside anther great Welsh centre, this one from pre-war days. The crash-tackling legend Claud Davey turned out with the young fly-half-cum-centre in a number of games for the enterprising Rosslyn Park Club. The RAAF, an Oxbridge XV and the Public Schools (programme pictured) were amongst their games.

A long way indeed from south west London, the far south west of England still kept some of its rugby (and also its charitable intent) too, as the pictured selection of three programmes from Camborne shows. The Home Guard were twice on parade, we see, with Boxing Day seeing a bigger clash, against Devonport Services.

Deaths of international Caps in later 1944 included:

Jul 1 – John Howard (Australia, 2 caps, 1938). One of the first two Aborigines to be capped. He died in a Japanese Prisoner of War Camp. Aged 29.

Jul 19 – James Michael Blair (Scotland Services) died of his wounds at Normandy. Lieut. in the Army Reconaissance Corps he had been at Oxford University when he enlisted. He had played in the Services Internationals. Aged 21.

Aug 5 – Maurice Joseph Lawson Turnbull (Wales, 2 caps, 1933) was killed in action by machine gun fire in the French village of Montchamp in Normandy. A major in the 1st Battalion of the Welsh Guards, he had also won three Wales hockey and amateur soccer caps, played rugby (no Blue, injuries), hockey and cricket for Cambridge University, whom he captained in 1929; rugby for Cardiff, London Welsh, Glamorganshire and Wales; cricket for Glamorgan (also Captain and Hon. Sec.), and England (9 tests) and was a Wales Squash Champion. His brother, Bernard Ruel Turnbull won 6 caps (1925-30). Aged 38.

Sept 12 – Winston Philip James ('Blow') Ide (Australia, 2 caps, 1938). He served in the 8th Division of the Australian Imperial Forces, being torpedoed by a United States submarine whilst on board a Japanese Prison ship. He had been a Prisoner of War in Singapore. He toured GB with the 1939 Australians, who returned home without playing a game. Aged 29.

Oct 8 – William Nicol Carson, MC (All Blacks, 3 matches in 1938, but no tests). He earned a Military Cross during the Battle of Mareth, but was wounded in Italy and then contracted jaundice while recovering. He died on board a hospital ship while at sea and was buried in Egypt. Aged 28.

Dec 29 – Allan H. ('Le Sioux') Muhr (France, 3 caps, 1906-07). Born in Philadelphia (or Chicago), USA. He was at Pearl Harbour, but died when an internee of the Germans in Neuengamme, near Hamburg. He had worked for the US Red Cross as in Interpreter and was aged 62. He played for France against England and NZ in 1906 and England in 1907 and refereed French finals in 1906 and 1907, also playing for France in Davis Cup tennis. He was a founder and President of the French Rugby Federation; a US Army commander; was awarded a War Cross while with the US Field Ambulance in France, and, posthumously, a Commander of the Légion d'Honneur.

8

1945

Three Services International matches were played in the first half of the year:

February 24 – ENGLAND 11 SCOTLAND 18 (at Welford Road, Leicester). (20,000).

Numerous changes were forced on the sides with Welshman John Robins now in the back row for England, who introduced Morrie Goddard, who was to be capped post-war by New Zealand. That's the war for you: nowadays there are rules (made to be regularly limit-tested!).

Twelve of the Scotland side were newcomers and their Australian forward, John Nicholls, was forced to play as a wing, while four of the Englishmen were debutants. The result was a surprise, with the English halves playing poorly and the new Scotland backs far superior.

The New Zealand-born forward Rod McKenzie scored the opening try with skipper Keith Geddes converting and after an Ernest Ward penalty, another New Zealander, Eric Grant, side-stepped and touched down with Geddes again adding the extras.

Rod McKenzie

In the second half a try by wing Bill MacLennan made it 13-3, but England fought back with first Ward and then the splendid Goddard crossing, hooker George Gilthorpe converting the latter: but John Orr's try, between the English touchdowns, again goaled by Geddes, settled it.

The England touch-judge was a South African, Maxwell Davies, while the Gloucestershire Regiment provided the music.

England – Lance-Cpl. Ward; LAC R.J. Forbes (Wasps/RAF), +Sgt. Morrie P.Goddard (RNZAF), A/B Ernest Ruston (Hunslet RL/Navy), Lieut. Hollis (capt.); Lieut-Cmdr. Bibby, Sqdn-Ldr. Parsons; *Cpl Longland, Sqdn-Ldr. Gilthorpe, Capt. Dunkley, +Cpl. Mycock, Schoolmaster Doherty, Sgt. E. (Ted) Bedford (Hull KR, Keighley RL/RAF), +Ordinary-Seaman (JD) Robins, +Flight-Lieut. Weighill.

Touch-Judge: Capt L. Maxwell Davies.

Scotland – +Sqdn Ldr. Keith I.Geddes (capt.) (Wasps/Cambridge University/RAF); Sqdn-Ldr. John B. Nicholls (New South Wales/RAAF), Capt. Jim R. Henderson, MC (Glasgow Acads/Army), +Surg-Lieut. W.D. (Bill) MacLennan (Watsonians/Navy)), Flt-Lieut. Grant; +P/O David D. McKenzie (Merchistonians/RAF), +Officer Cadet Angus W. Black (Edinburgh University/RAF); CSM McClure, *Cpl. Hastie, +Marine Cadet Tom P.L. McGlashan (Royal HSFP/Navy), Sub-Lieut. C. Wilhelm (South African Services), *Pte. Rod M. McKenzie (NZ Services/NZ), +P/O John H. Orr

(Heriot's FP/RAF), F/O Andrew M.L. Barcroft (Heriot's FP/RAF), *Capt. J. David A. Thom (Hawick).

Touch-Judge: Major A. ('Jock') Wemyss.

Tries: (RM) McKenzie, Grant, MacLennan, Orr. Cons: Geddes 3.

Referee: Trevor Jones (Llangynwyd, Maesteg).

ENGLAND

R.J. FORBES – Wing. Wasps/RAF. He was a Leading Aircraftsman in the RAF at Heaton Park and appears to have been from the Manchester area.

Maurice Patrick (MORRIE) GODDARD – Centre. Born Timaru, NZ 28/9/1921. Died Christchurch, NZ 19/6/1974. Marist Brothers School/Timaru Boys HS/Ashburton County/South Canterbury/South Island/RNZAF/RAF. 5 caps for NZ (1946-49). He was a Sgt. in the RNZAF, then a Furrier and menswear store owner.

Ernest ('SONNY') RUSTON – Centre/Fly Half, born 1923 in Hunslet. Hunslet RL/Navy/Northern Command. He was an A/B in the Navy and may still be alive in 2018.

Edward (TED) BEDFORD – Back Row. Hull KR (47 apps, 10 tries), Hull and Keighley RL/RAF. He was a Sgt. in the RAF.

SCOTLAND

KEITH Irvine GEDDES, DFC – Full Back. Born Woking 25/10/1918. Died while skiing in France, but buried in Dorset, 30/3/1991. Loretto School/Cambridge University (Blue 1938)/London Scottish/Wasps/RAF/Middlesex. He was a Sqdn-Ldr. (and a fighter ace) in the RAF's 604 Squadron, then a Farmer and a Shipping Executive. 4 caps (1947). He was the son of I.C. Geddes (6 caps, 1906-08).

JOHN Bernard NICHOLLS, DFC – Wing, but later a Forward. He is believed to have died flying at Warragamba (NSW) 21/9/1969, aged 57. RAAF/Drummoyne/Northern Suburbs (NSW). Flt-Lieut. then Sqdn-Ldr., then Wing-Cmdr. in 35th Squadron, RAAF. He was awarded the Coronation Medal in Australia 1953 and flew a Lancaster from Sydney to Biggin Hill in 1965.

James Rae (JIM) HENDERSON, MC – Centre. Born 28/10/1917. Died 19/9/2005 at Lochranza on Arran, aged 87. Glasgow Academy/Glasgow Academicals. He was a Gunner and later a Capt. in the 51st Highland Regiment, enlisting in 1939. He fought at El Alamein, being wounded in Egypt 1942; was awarded the Military Cross at Tripoli in 1943 and then saw action in Sicily, the Normandy landings, Holland and Germany. He ran for Scotland (winning the 220 and 100 yards at Ibrox and Teamsport) and also played cricket for his country, including a game against Australia in 1948, when he bowled against Don Bradman. He was a stockbroker pre-war and later worked for J.K. Mills; Thomas Boag and Co; Scott and Robertson; Cameron MacLatchie and British Polythene Industries. He died at 87, soon after a birdie 2 at Shiskine GC, in Arran.

Scotland v England, Leicester, Feb 1944

William Donald (BILL) MacLENNAN – Centre. Born Edinburgh 4/4/1921. Died Haddington 29/9/2002. George Watson's College/Watsonians/Edinburgh University/United Services, Portsmouth/Navy. He was a Surgeon-Lieut. in the Navy on HMS Collingwood.

DAVID Douglas McKENZIE – Fly Half (later Wing). Born Wallsend-on-Tyne 28/12/1921. Died Vancouver (Canada) 4/8/2005. Merchiston Castle School/ Merchistonians/RAF/Barbarians/Edinburgh University. He was a Pilot-Officer, then a Flying-Officer in the RAF and later a Headmaster. 6 caps (1947-48). He also was listed in a programme as from the Navy! Having emigrated to Canada, he refereed the British Lions against British Columbia All-Stars in 1959.

ANGUS William BLACK – Scrum Half. Born Dunfermline 6/5/1925. Died 14/2/2018 Fife aged 92. Dollar Academy/Edinburgh University/RAF/ Barbarians/British Lions. He was an Officer-Cadet in the RAF. 6 caps (1947-50). Lions to NZ (2 tests)/Australia 1950. He became a Doctor and in 2016 was the oldest-living Lion, aged 90.

Thomas Perry Lang (TOM) McGLASHAN – Prop. Born Edinburgh 29/12/1925. Royal HS/Navy/Royal HSFP/Edinburgh University. He was a Marine Cadet in the Navy and later a Dentist. 8 caps (1947-54).

C.WILHELM – 2nd Row. Western Province/SAAF. He played for the SA Air Force but was also a Sub-Lieut, in the Navy, mentioned as SANF (Naval Forces). Born Burgersdorp (SA), July 1922.

RODerick McCulloch McKENZIE – 2nd Row. Born Rakaia, NZ 16/9/1909. Died Auckland, NZ 24/3/2000. Kakariki School/Fielding Convent School/

Scotland v England, March 1945

Manawatu/North Island/NZ Services/NZ. He was a Private in the NZ Services, had won 9 caps for NZ (1934-38) and had toured GB with the 1935 All Blacks. He became a Post Office Mail Room Supervisor.

(SIR) JOHN Henry ORR, OBE, QPM – Back Row. Born Edinburgh 13/6/1918. Died Edinburgh 26/9/1995. Heriot's College/Heriot's FP/RAF/Edinburgh City Police/British Police. He was a Pilot Officer in the RAF, being awarded the OBE in 1972 and was Knighted in 1979, having become Chief Constable of several Police Forces and SRU President in 1975-76. 2 caps (1947).

ANDREW Michael Leigh BARCROFT – Back Row. Born 22/1/1922. Heriot's College/Heriot's FP/RAF. He was a Flt-Lieut. and Flying-Officer in the RAF and became an agricultural officer, making trips to Malaysia and Singapore. He married in Maidstone, 1974 and was last known to be living there.

J. DAVID Alexander THOM – Back Row. Born Hawick 16/2/1910. Died in 1982. Hawick HS/Hawick/London Scottish/Barbarians/Middlesex. He was a Captain in the Army and was SRU President in 1965-66. 5 caps (1934-35).

March 17 – SCOTLAND 5 ENGLAND 16 (at Murrayfield, Edinburgh). (20,000).

Murrayfield's biggest war-time crowd saw Ernest Ward, now playing at centre, have a huge part in England's win. Late changes included the moving of the Australian John Nicholls from backs to forwards for Scotland, while scrum half Jim Parsons pulled out of the England team at the last moment and Pat Sykes came in.

The England touch-judge was the twice-capped 1934 England wing Antony Lawley ('Tim') Warr of Oxford University, who was a captain in the Royal Gloucestershire Hussars. Music was provided by the Royal Scots and the Queen Victoria School in Dunblane.

The young South African full back, Mike Ackermann, was faultless for England, though his opposite number Keith Geddes also had a fine game, but it was Ward who stood out in front of all others.

First Ward engineered a try for skipper Gerry Hollis and soon the pair repeated it, with Ward converting the second. Then, Scotland centre Bill MacLennan score a spectacular try, beating half the English side for Geddes to convert.

England was on top after the interval, as Ward cross-kicked for Hollis to complete his hat-trick and wing forward Gordon Hudson added a fourth try, converted by hooker George Gilthorpe.

Scotland – +Sqdn/Ldr. Geddes (capt); Flt-Lieut. Grant, Capt. (JR) Henderson, MC, +Surgeon-Lieut. MacLennan, +Cadet Doug W.C.

Smith(Aberdeen University/RAMC); +F/O (DD) McKenzie, +Officer-Cadet Black; CSM McClure, *Cpl. Hastie, +Marine Cadet McGlashan, Lieut. Erik A. Melling (Old Sedberghians/Norwegian Army), *Pte. (RM) McKenzie, +P/O Orr, Sqdn-Ldr. Nicholls, F/O (AML) Barcroft.

Touch-Judge: Major A. ('Jock') Wemyss.

Try: MacLennan. Con: Geddes.

England – Lieut Ackermann; LAC Forbes, +Sgt Goddard, Lance-Cpl Ward, Lieut Hollis (capt); A/B Ruston, +A/C W.Pat Sykes (Wasps/Cambridge University/RAF); *Cpl Longland, Wing Cmdr Gilthorpe, Cpl Peter O'K. Plumpton (RAF/Downside), +Cpl Mycock, Schoolmaster Doherty, Cpl Hudson, +Flt-Lieut. Weighill, Sgt. Bedford.

Touch-Judge: Capt Antony Lawley (Tim) Warr.

Tries: Hollis 3, Hudson. Con: Ward, Gilthorpe.

Referee: Allan McM. Buchanan (Ireland).

SCOTLAND

DOUGlas William Cumming SMITH – Wing. Born Aberdeen 27/10/1924. Died Midhurst, London 22/9/1998. Aberdeen GS/Aberdeen University/RAMC/Army/London Scottish/Barbarians. He was a Cadet, then a Lieut. in the Army. 8 caps (1949-50). British Lions 1950 (0 tests vs NZ, 1 test vs Australia). Lions Manager to NZ/Australia in 1971. He was a Doctor and became SRU President in 1986-87.

ERIK Arne MELLING – 2nd Row. Born Newcastle 25/9/1918. Died Newcastle 1st quarter 2004. Aged 85. Sedbergh School/Old Sedberghians. He

England v Scotland at Murrayfield, March 1945

was a Lieut. in the Norwegian Army and his father, a Norwegian, came to England in 1910 and founded E.J. Melling Ltd, Paper and Polythene Packaging, which Erik took over in the 1960s.

ENGLAND

William PATrick SYKES – Scrum Half. Born Vancouver (Canada) 3/3/1925. He is believed to have died on 14/1/2014 in England's West Country, probably Devon. St John's School, Leatherhead/Cambridge University/Wasps/RAF/ Combined Services/London Counties/Eastern Counties/Middlesex/Barbarians. He was an Air Craftsman in the RAF and later was an Artificial Flower Company employee, then Branch manager of Burroughs Machines. 7 caps (1948-53).

PETER O'Keeffe PLUMPTON – Prop. Born London 25/2/1920. Died 1/4/1995. Downside School/RAF. He was a Cpl., then a Flying-Officer, then a Flt-Lieut. in the RAF, being stationed at RAF Halton/Cosford/Cranwell and retired from active service in 1975.

April 7 – ENGLAND 9 WALES 24 (at Kingsholm, Gloucester). (18,000).

This was the last of the Services Internationals, and the Welsh backs proved too fast for the English with Willie Davies and his cousin, Haydn Tanner, in charge at half-back and Gus Risman, moved back to centre, also excelling with young Bleddyn Williams alongside him.

It was all over by half-time as Wales led by 16-3 by with wing Alan Edwards scoring an opening try and Tanner dropping a rare goal. Risman placed a penalty and then came tries by Ike Owens and Tanner before Ernest Ward opened England's account with a penalty.

After the break, Morrie Goddard's interception sent Gerry Hollis over but Edwards pounced again and Risman converted at 21-6. Wales forward Emrys Evans scored his side's fifth try before Ward replied with another penalty.

Several players from either side withdrew after selection, including Idwal Davies, the Welsh centre, and Joe Mycock, the England second row, with the latter having an abcess in his ear.

England – Lieut. Ackermann; Lieut. Hollis (capt), +Sgt. Goddard, Lance-Cpl. Ward, Cpl. Albert E. Johnson (Warrington & GB RL/Army); A/B Ruston, Sqdn-Ldr. Parsons; *Cpl. Longland, Wing-Cmdr. Gilthorpe, Cpl. Plumpton, Capt. Dunkley, LAC H. Ron Peel (Bedford/Headingley/ RAF), Cpl. Hudson, +Flt-Lieut. Weighill, Sgt. Bedford.

Try: Hollis. Pens: Ward 2.

Wales – +CSM Trott; A/C Edwards, Sgt. Risman, +F/O (BL) Williams, F/O Clifford Evans (Salford & Leeds RL/RAF); *Sgt. (WTH) Davies (capt), *+Lieut. Tanner; Petty Officer Bowes, *+Sgt. Travers, *Bdr. (EA) Evans, *Cpl. (DV) Phillips, *BSM (HW) Thomas, *Flt-Sgt. (EV) Watkins, +Lieut. Tamplin, Sgt. Owens.

Tries: Edwards 2, Owens, Tanner, (EA) Evans. Con/Pen: Risman. DG: Tanner.

Referee: R.A. Beattie (Watsonians).

ENGLAND

ALBERT E.JOHNSON – Wing. Warrington (112 tries in 198 apps, 1939-1951), Wigan (guest) and GB RL/Army. He was a Corporal in the West Yorkshire Regiment and may have emigrated to Australia in 1955.

Harry RONald PEEL – 2nd Row. Born Morningside district of Edinburgh 9/8/1914. Died Exeter 12/1/2000. Leeds GS/Bramley Old Boys (1934-37)/ Headingley(1937-39 and 1945-47)/Bedford (1943-45)/RAF/Cumberland (1947)/Carlisle (1946-47)/Yorkshire. Leading Air Craftsman in the RAF. Retired from the game, December 1947.

WALES

CLIFFord EVANS – Wing. Born Resolven 14/7/1913. Died July 1982 Wiltshire. Wales Schools/Resolven/Neath/RAF/Salford, Leeds and Wales RL. He was a Flying Officer in the RAF and became a coach of Swinton, St Helen's and Salford RL.

The Welsh Rugby Football XV.

Here is the Welsh team, winners of the eighth wartime Services Rugby International. On ground: H. Tanner, W. H. T. Davies. Sitting: Cliff Evans, F. Trott, B. L. Williams, A. J. Risman (captain), D. Phillipps, Alan Edwards, E. V. Watkins. Standing: A. D. S. Bowes, I. Owen, E. Evans, H. Thomas, W. E. Tamplin, W. H. Travers, F/Lt. A. Mathews (touch judge)

The English Rugby Football XV.

The English team, which lost to Wales, defeated Scotland at Edinburgh a month ago. Sitting: M. P. Goddard, F. P. Dunkley, R. Longland, G. Hollis (captain), C. G. Gilthorpe, A. E. Johnson, E. Raston. Standing: M. T. Ackermann, P. Plumpton, G. Hudson, R. Peel, E. Ward, E. Bedford, R. G. H. Weighill, J. Parsons, S/Ldr. Kain (touch judge)

The Welsh and English sides at Gloucester, April 1945

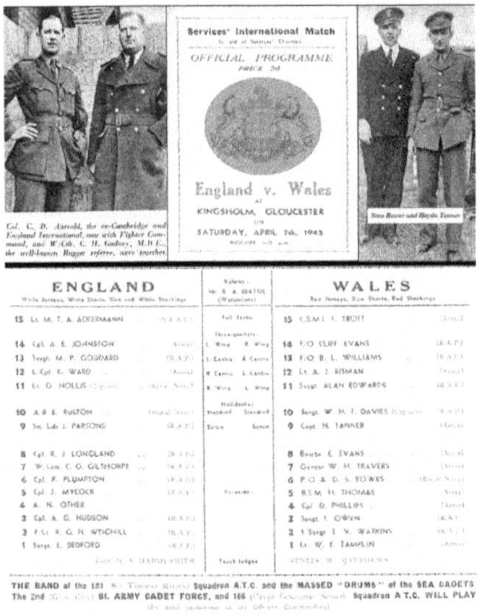
Services' International Match

OFFICIAL PROGRAMME

England v. Wales

AT

KINGSHOLM, GLOUCESTER

ON

SATURDAY, APRIL 7th, 1945

Col. C. D. Aarvold, the ex-Cambridge and England International, now with Fighter Command, and W/Cdr. C. H. Gadney, M.B.E., the well-known Rugger referee, were together.

Stan Bowes and Haydn Tanner

ENGLAND			WALES	
15 Lt. M. T. A. ACKERMANN		Full Backs	15 C.S.M.I. F. TROTT	
14 Cpl. A. E. JOHNSTON	(Army)		14 F/O CLIFF EVANS	(R.A.F.)
13 Sergt. M. P. GODDARD	(R.A.F.)		13 F/O B. L. WILLIAMS	(R.A.F.)
12 L/Cpl. E. WARD	(Army)		12 Lt. A. J. RISMAN	(Army)
11 Lt. D. HOLLIS			11 Sergt. ALAN EDWARDS	(R.A.F.)
10 A.B. E. RUSTON			10 Sergt. W. H. T. DAVIES	(R.A.F.)
9 Sq. Ldr. J. PARSONS	(R.A.F.)		9 Capt. H. TANNER	(Army)
8 Cpl. R. J. LONGLAND			8 Bombr. E. EVANS	(Army)
7 W/Com. C. O. GILTHORPE	(R.A.F.)		7 Gunner W. H. TRAVERS	(Army)
6 Cpl. F. PLUMPTON	(R.A.F.)	Forwards	6 P/O A. D. S. BOWES	
5 Cpl. J. MYCOCK	(R.A.F.)		5 B.S.M. H. THOMAS	(Army)
4 A. N. OTHER			4 Cpl. D. PHILLIPS	(Army)
3 Cpl. A. G. HUDSON	(R.A.F.)		3 Sergt. J. OWEN	(R.A.F.)
2 F/Lt. R. G. H. WEIGHILL	(R.A.F.)		2 F/Sergt. I. V. WATKINS	(R.A.F.)
1 Sergt. E. BEDFORD	(R.A.F.)		1 Lt. W. E. TAMPLIN	(Army)
		Touch Judges		

THE BAND of the 181 Squadron A.T.C. and the MASSED "DRUMS" of the SEA CADETS The 2nd Bt. ARMY CADET FORCE, and 186 Squadron A.T.C. WILL PLAY

Programme, courtesy of Bleddyn's family, players & others at the match

February 10 – Ireland XV 5 Army 9 (at Ravenhill, Belfast). (20,000).

Pre-war cap Fred Moran ran in from halfway, converted by Kevin Quinn, to give Ireland a 5-0 half-time lead before Gus Risman placed two penalties and Jack Knowles added a try to give the Army the victory.

Ireland - *+(CJ) Murphy (capt.); *Moran, (GT) Quinn, +Kevin Joseph Quinn (Old Belvedere – 5 caps, 1947-53), +William Henry Jordan 'Harry' Millar (UC Cork – 5 caps, 1951-52); Carry, Eddie O'Mullane (UC Cork); +Corcoran, John (Jack) Belton (Old Belvedere), H.G.G. Dudgeon (Collegians), +Colm Patrick Callan (Lansdowne – 10 caps, 1947-49),

OFFICIAL PROGRAMME

Price - Threepence (at least)

IRISH RUGBY FOOTBALL UNION

BRITISH ARMY XV

v.

AN IRISH XV

AT RAVENHILL - - BELFAST

SATURDAY, 10th FEBRUARY, 1945

KICK-OFF 3 P.M.

The total proceeds from the sale of these Programmes will be devoted to the funds of LOCAL HOSPITALS.

R. W. JEFFARES, Secretary, I.R.F.U.

W. A. B. DOUGLAS, Hon. Secretary, Ulster Branch, I.R.F.U.

Here comes Kyle! The Army v an Irish XV, 1945

+Nelson, *O'Loughlin, Guiney (now Bective Rangers), +Donal Joseph Hingerty (Lansdowne – 4 caps, 1947).

Try: Moran. Con: (KJ) Quinn.

Army - +Trott; Knowles, Sullivan, Ward, (AE) Johnson; Risman, *+Tanner; *(EA) Evans, Dunkley, A.C. Reid (Yorkshire), McClure, *(DV) Phillips, +Lees, G.B. Frank (Rosslyn Park), Foster.

Try: Knowles. Pens: Risman 2.

Other matches of note in the spring of 1945 included:

Jan 1 – French Services 21 Army 9 (at Parc des Princes, Paris).

Centre Jean Dauger (Bayonne, 3 caps in 1945) was the French star, while Jean Prat (Lourdes, 51 caps 1945-55) and Robert Soro (Lourdes, 21 caps 1945-49) were in a French pack for the first time.

Tries: Dauger 2, wing Georges Baladie (Agen, 6 caps in 1945-46), prop Jean Prin-Clary (Brive, 10 caps 1947-57), back-row forward Andre Sahuc (Metro, 2 caps in 1945).

Cons: Centre Joseph Desclaux (Perpignan, 3 caps in 1949) 2, Soro.

Remembering & raising funds for the Boys in Burma

The Army fielded a star-studded side with Risman and Tanner at half back and only two 'new' faces in Cardiff centre Captain T. Lyn Williams and second row Vivian George Weston (Scotland, 2 caps, 1936) from Kelvinside Acads., who was a 2nd-Lieut., then Capt. in the Royal Artillery. The skipper was Robin Prescott.

Tries: Risman, (TL) Williams, (CB) Holmes.

Referee: H.A. Fry (England).

Jan 13 – South Wales 5 Sir Robert Webber's XV 8 (at Arms Park, Cardiff) (10,000).

Cricketer Willie Jones scored the South Wales try, converted by the great pre-war RL full back Jim ('Buller') Sullivan.

Sir Robert Webber (well-known Cardiff businessman)'s XV – Surg-Lieut. G.B. Davies (Moseley/Navy); Hollis, Ldg. Seaman S. Wilson (Navy/Hull RL), (BL) Williams, Petty-Officer R.F. Weedall (Old Caledonians/Brighton/Navy); Bibby, N. Steel (Birkenhead Park); Bowes, Travers, Chief Petty-Officer R.G. Stovell (Navy/HMS Black Swan), (DV) Phillips, Doherty, Willshire, Tamplin, L. Jeffreys (Bristol).

Touch-Judge: Brice H. Jenkins (Cardiff RFC Official).

Tries: Hollis 2. Con: Tamplin.

South Wales – J. Sullivan (Cardiff, Barbarians RU/Wigan, Wales, GB RL); Ordinary Seaman N. Sparrow (Swansea), Sgt. (Randall) Lewis, Sgt. D. Griffiths (Ebbw Vale/RAF), Knowles; Cpl. (WE) Jones (Neath/RAF), Tanner (capt.); (Will) Davies, W.T. Pritchard (Ebbw Vale), Wilf J. Evans (Pontypool/Wales), Les Smith (Newport), Kenyon William James Jones (Oxford University/Wales 1 cap, 1934), (AR) Taylor, F/O Hubert Johnson (Cardiff/Bath), (AM) Rees.

Touch-Judge: C. Grey Williams (Swansea). Referee: (Trevor) Jones (Llangynwyd, Maesteg).

James (Jim) Sullivan, from Splott in Cardiff, turned to RL at the age of 17, while still having played for the Barbarians at Union and being capped at Baseball for Wales. He was possibly the greatest-ever full back at either Union or League. Born 2/12/1903 Cardiff. Died 1/11/1977 in Wigan. He was aged 41 at the time of the game above.

Reginald Gordon Stovell, a prop, appears to be named later in the famous Yangtse Incident of 1949 as a Telegraphist (mentioned in despatches) on an assisting ship (Black Swan), while he previously served on HMS Drake and played for the Navy.

Jan 20 – St. Mary's Hospital 8 Coventry 3 (at Teddington).

This was Coventry's first defeat since 1941. Aided by the retention of men of service age in the munitions and engineering industries of the city, the club had achieved 72 successive wins, scoring 1,712 points against 254. The Hospital fly half (Nim) Hall, later to be capped by England, dropped two four-point goals.

Jan 20 – SAAF 13 RAF 8 (at Richmond Athletic Ground).

Jan 27 – An Army XV met an RAF XV at the Vomero Stadium in Naples, but the result is not known.

Army XV – F. Miller (Hull RL); J.W. Winston (Old Whitgiftians), A.J. Pimblett (St Helen's RL), H. Germaine (Dewsbury RL), C. Ritchie (Edinburgh Acads); *(RB) Bruce Lockhart (Cambridge University/Scotland), Maurice W. Daddy (Hull KR RL – 134 apps, 22 tries); R.C. Duthie (Stewart's College FP), J.A. Ransom (Civil Service), Major J.A. Dingwall-Fordyce (Liverpool/Cameroons), A.J. Morrison (Dumfries Academy), H.D. Philip (Aldershot Services), D. Barnes (Blackheath), C.M. Burge (Heriot's FP), *Ivor Bennett (Aberavon, Glamorgan Police, Wales RU/Warrington and Bridgend RL).

Freddie Miller (born 1915, died 1960, aged 45 at Patrington, North Yorkshire) was a Hull RL player at 18 and stayed for 17 years (1,185 points in 385 games) before spending three seasons at Featherstone and scoring 496 points in 92 games (1950-53) before retiring. The club built a Memorial Gate to him.

RAF XV – Wayman; Oberholzer (both 205 Group); Puter (214 Group), Du Toit (MACAF), Skinner (MAAF); Evans, Arnot (both MACAF); Mackenzie (BAF), Tucker (MACAF), Van der Walt (BAF), Pohl, Price (both 214 Group), Staines (MAAF), Mackley (BAF), Rees (MAAF).

Referee: *A.L. Gracie (Harlequins/Scotland). Music was played by the No 2 RAC Band.

Feb 10 – Scottish Services 14 RAAF 10 (at Murrayfield)

The airmen faced a pretty full Scots side, but ran them close.

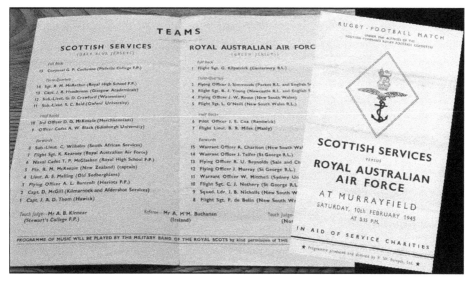

Match programme

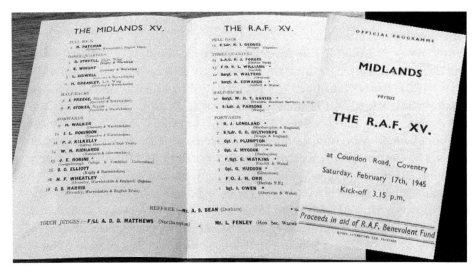

Match programme

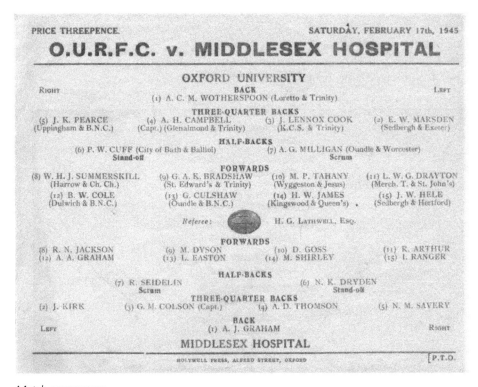

Match programme

Feb 10 – Civil Defence Services 10 RAF 6 (at Gloucester)

The winners fielded eight past or future internationals from three different countries.

Feb 17 – Midlands 10 RAF 10 (at Coventry).

Coventry's renowned Harrys – Wheatley and Walker – were in the 'home' side.

Feb 17 – Oxford University 14 v Middlesex Hospital 0

Feb 24 – Cardiff 16 NZ XV 9 (at Arms Park, Cardiff).

Cardiff – Tries: (GG) Hale, T. Lyn Williams, V. Roberts, (WB) Cleaver. Cons: Hale 2.

NZ XV – Tries: Hunter, Bryant. Pen: P. Eggleston.

Feb 24 – RAAF XV v French Air Force XV, arranged at Batley by Mayor Auty for Forces Charities.

Referee: Ivor David (Neath).

RUGBY FOOTBALL MATCH

ARRANGED BY

HIS WORSHIP THE MAYOR OF BATLEY,
(Councillor F. Wilfrid H. Auty).

ROYAL AUSTRALIAN AIR FORCE XV

v.

FRENCH AIR FORCE XV

AT

MOUNT PLEASANT, BATLEY

(by kind permission of the Directors).

Saturday, 24th February, 1945.

Kick-off 3·15 p.m.

Proceeds for Forces Charities.

The Batley Old Prize Band will play selections before the match.

A 'One-off' at Batley

Mar 3 – RAF 8 Army 6 (at St Helen's, Swansea) (20,000).

Army - +Trott; Knowles, (T) Sullivan, Pte J. Lowrey (Border Regt.), Johnson; Risman (capt.), *+Tanner; *(EA) Evans, *+Travers, Dunkley, (DV) Phillips, *(HW) Thomas, +Tamplin, +Lees, (W. Elvet) Jones.

The RAF down the Army at Swansea, March 1945, Pic Courtesy of Bleddyn Williams' family

Tries: (EA) Evans, Knowles.

RAF - +Geddes (capt.); Forbes, +(BL) Williams, (H) Walters, *(D. Idwal) Davies; *(WTH) Davies, Parsons; *Longland, Gilthorpe, Plumpton, *(EV) Watkins, +Mycock, Hudson, +Orr, Owens.

Tries: (DI) Davies, Owens. Con: Geddes.

Referee: (Ivor) David (Neath).

The Swansea and West Wales Rugby Charity Committee had by the time of this game, the sixth between the sides at the St. Helen's Ground, raised £16,600 for Services and War charities rom those, the four S Wales v the Army clashes and various others. So, as the war in Europe looked to be drawing to a close, the Inter-Services Rugby Committee decided the entire proceeds from this clash should go to aid the revival, post-war, of the Swansea RFC.

Mar 3 – Cambridge University 16 Oxford University 4 (at Cambridge).

Cambridge included Steele-Bodger, Bole and Bance in the pack.

Tries: J. Hall, J.W. MacLeod, C.M.A. Vallance and captain (DB) Vaughan. Cons: Bance 2.

For Oxford, captained by A.H. Campbell, DG: Tom W. Cuff (Bath).

Referee: Lieut-Col. (later Col.) L.H.F. Sanderson.

The RU War Emergency Committee refused to allow London to meet Paris at Stade Colombes on 17/3/45 on the grounds that hostilities were still in progress.

Mar 24 – RNZAF 20 RAAF 13 (at Old Deer Park).

GB v Dominions Programme, March 1945

RNZAF – Tries: (E) Grant, (MP) Goddard, Cpl. M.V.H. Hill, G.S.R. MacDonald.

Cons: Ordinary-Seaman J.D. Ridland 2. DG: Goddard.

RAAF – Tries: (JB) Nicholls, Flt-Sgt. J. Todman, F/Officer Alan S. Roper. Cons: Flt-Sgt. W. Cameron 2.

Referee: (Trevor) Jones.

RNZAF included Flt-Lieut. Raymond Alfred Dalton (2 caps NZ 1947). His son, Andy, later captained NZ.

Mar 31 – Great Britain 36 Dominions 13 (at Welford Road, Leicester).

The four centres were outstanding, with Morrie Goddard and Australian, F/Officer Percival Albert Clifton Dermond (462 Squadron, RAAF), who played RL for New South Wales/Eastern Suburbs opposing Ernest Ward and Bleddyn Williams, whose famous story tells how, having crash-landed his glider behind enemy lines with supplies for the Rhine crossing, he spent a week sleeping in German ditches and slit trenches, using an American parachute to keep warm.

He recalls bumping into his commanding officer, Hugh Bartlett, DFC (the dashing Sussex batsman) one Friday morning: "Williams, aren't you meant to be at Welford Road [Leicester] tomorrow playing for Great Britain against the Dominions? They need you. Pack your bags!"

The GB XV and Willie Davies on the move!

"He drove me to the Rhine, which I crossed on a barge, and then on to the base in Eindoven. From Holland I got the last supply plane to Brize Norton, where my CO picked me up and flew me back to base camp at Rivenhall, where I arrived around midnight and surprised my newly-wed wife Violet.

She thought I had been killed, as she was told only two of the glider pilots on that mission had survived – but we made it by train to Leicester by lunchtime, I scored a try and Great Britain won the match." Boys' Own stuff indeed.

GB – Trott; MacLennan, (BL) Williams, Ward, Hollis; (WTH) Davies, Tanner; Longland, Gilthorpe, (Emrys) Evans, Mycock, (DV) Phillips, Hudson, (HW) Thomas, Owens.

Referee: H.G. Lathwell (London).

Tries: (E) Evans 2, Hollis 2, (WTH) Davies, Hudson, MacLennan, Ward, (BL) Williams.

The Dominions XV and Willie Davies still on the move!

3 Cons/Pen: Ward.

Dominions had selected Ordinary Seaman Roy Alfred Roper (5 caps, NZ 1949-50) at fly half, but he had to withdraw.

Team – Ackermann; (E) Grant (capt.), Goddard, Dermond, Nicholls, F/O C. Geary (RNZAF); Sgt. H.O.A. Stewart (NZ Army); O/Cadet R.W. Squire (RNZAF), O/S L. Wallace (RNZ Navy), (RU) Reynolds, P/O G.F. Brice (RNZAF), Wilhelm, (RM) Mackenzie, F/O F.L.de Belin (RAAF), Sub-Lieut. G.S.R. MacDonald (RNZ Navy).

Tries: de Belin, Nicholls. 2 Cons/Pen: Ackermann.

Referee: (HG) Lathwell.

Frederick Leslie de Belin, who won 8 RL caps for Australia (1948-50), died 11/2/2006, aged 85.

Apr 7 – French Championship final – Agen 7 Lourdes 3 (at Parc des Princes, Paris). Guy Basquet and Jean Matheu played in the Agen pack while Jean Prat and Robert Soro played for Lourdes.

Apr 14 – Army 13 RAF 8 (at Richmond).

Army included centre Cadet Michael D. Corbett (Downside School), the son of Bristol/England centre Len Corbett. The referee was (HG) Lathwell.

In these dying days of the war in Europe, North Africa saw a typically competitive local 'international services' tournament at the Alamein Club, Cairo. Both the SAAF and Wales Services had won 2 and drawn 1 in games with each other, England and the NZ Services. Les Manfield had captained Wales to a St David's Day win over England. In the play-off for the title (some dubbed it the 'World Cup!) South Africa edged Wales 9-6. It was reportedly watched by some 15,000 and NZ Services defeated England for third place. Also at Cairo, NZ and SA combined as the 'Kiboks' and lost 13-11 to a combined GB Army-RAF XV.

Apr 15 – In the Middlesex Sevens preliminary rounds at Thames Ditton and Colindale, NZ Services 'A' beat Handley Page 13-0, Middlesex Hospital 2nds 22-8 and Old Blues 16-5 to qualify for the finals with NZ Services 'B' losing 8-13 to Wasps 2nds.

Apr 21 – Middlesex Sevens final – Nottingham 6 St Mary's Hospital 3 (at Richmond Athletic Ground) A crowd of 6,000 saw Jack Heaton skipper Notts to victory. In Round 4, NZ Services 'A' lost 0-3 to Rosslyn Park; the RAAF lost

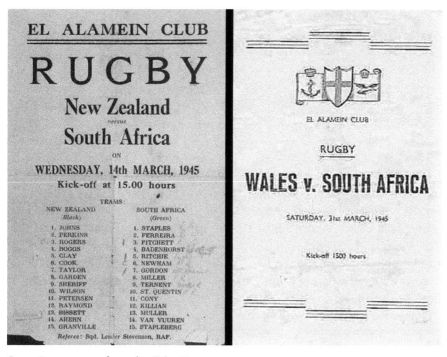

Some Programmes from the Cairo Tournament

0-5 to Rugby and the South African Services lost 3-13 to a Twickenham seven. (Bleddyn) Williams appeared for Rosslyn Park, who reached the semi-finals while (RH) Lloyd-Davies played for RAF (Jurby).

Apr 28 – British Empire Services XV 27 French Services 6 (at Richmond Athletic Ground).

Programme from the match

Empire - +Geddes; Hollis, +(BL) Williams, Risman, Brogden; *(WTH) Davies, *+Tanner (capt.); *(EA) Evans, *+Travers, McClure, (DV) Phillips, *(HW) Thomas, de Belin, +Mycock, Owens.

Tries: Owens 2, Hollis 2, Risman 2, Brogden. Cons: Risman 3.

The first French side in England since 1930 were awarded caps by their country for this game.

Team – Lucien M. Rouffia (Narbonne/RL); Georges Baladie (St Agen/RL), Jean Dauger (Aviron Bayonnais/RL), Louis Junquas (St Vincent de Tyrosse), Brig-Gen. J.M. Chaban-Delmas (CASG Paris); Andre J. Alvarez (Aviron Bayonnais), Gaston Combes (Fumel/RL); Jean M.G. Massare (Paris University), Jean Villagra (Vienne), Jean M. Prin-Clary (SU Cavillon), Robert P.V. Soro (Lourdes), Alban Moga (Begles), Pierre M.B. Thiers (Montferrand, capt.), Andre Sahuc (US Metro, Paris), Jean Prat (Lourdes).

Try: Massare. Pen: Prat.

In charge of the team were Rene Crabos and Adolphe Jaurreguy. Ike Owens was the outstanding Empire player in this last major wartime clash, 10 days before VE Day.

Referee: R.A. Beattie (Watsonians).

Miscellaneous:

Bristol fielded Dr. Jack Matthews v the RAAF, and he led Welsh Academicals v a NZ Army XV at Abercynon.

Waterloo at times included 1948 Olympic sprinter (JA) Gregory.

A Civil Defence XV could include (EC) Davey, Fyfe (captain), Bassett, Harry Walker (Coventry, later England), Harold F. Wheatley (Coventry/England), Will Davies (Neath), Leslie Smith (Newport), Heaton, (Nim) Hall and (AR) Taylor.

Rosslyn Park again included those two great Welsh centres from different eras - Claud Davey and Bleddyn Williams, plus the 18-years-old wing Christopher Elliott Winn from KCS Wimbledon, who was to go on to Oxford University and play eight times for England (1952-54).

Harlequins included scrum half Hugh de Lacy from Raneclagh College in Athlone and Trinity College in Dublin, who became a Barbarian and won two caps for Ireland in 1948.

The RAF included centre Sgt. Haydn Walters (Swansea), back from duty abroad.

Several RL players appeared in Union games, including full back H. Lockwood (Halifax/England RL), G.S. Brown (Batley/Army), Cpl. Edward

The Welsh 'Accies' v a NZ Army XV

John D Robins, later Lion

(Ted) Tattersfield (Leeds/England RL) and A.W. Guest (Castleford/Army).

John Walker Sinclair Irwin, who gained five caps for Ireland (1938-39) was released by the Germans after being a Prisoner of War. He went on to live until 13/8/2004 when he died in Belfast, aged 91. He had been captured at Lapane near Dunkirk in 1940, being a Captain in the RAMC, and later worked as a doctor in Ireland, becoming IRFU President in 1969-70. His father, Sir Samuel Thompson Irwin, was also an international with nine caps (1900-03) and also an IRFU President (1935-36), living until 1961, aged 83.

On 3/3/45 John D. Robins, as noted, completed the second part of what was to be a seemingly unique triple, when he played for the Scottish Services against Northern Command at Murrayfield. Having already played for England Services, he was to be fully capped by Wales in 1950, when he also toured with the British Lions.

Official NZ Services games played in the spring of 1945 were:

Jan 6 – Beat Sutton 49-0 (at Cheam).

Jan 13 – Lost to Newport 15-18 (at Rodney Parade, Newport).

Newport – Tries: W.C. Walbyoff 2, (DH) Steer, M. Reese. Con: Walbyoff. DG: Jim Hawkins.

NZ – Tries: (E) Grant 2, (Roy) Roper. Cons: F/O W.F. Crist 2, Sgt. N.A. Elmes.

Feb 3 – Beat Rosslyn Park 19-6 (at Richmond).

Feb 10 – Lost to Warwickshire 6-11 (at Coventry). At prop for this game and the next three was Ordinary Seaman L.R. Wallace (RNZ Navy), who gained Blues at Cambridge University.

Feb 14 – Beat Cambridge University 22-19 (at Cambridge).

Feb 17 – Beat Guy's Hospital 17-9 (at Honor Oak Park).

Feb 24 – Beat Oxford University 14-11 (at Oxford).

Mar 3 – Lost to Paris University 11-12 (at Parc des Princes, Paris).

Mar 10 – Lost to Cardiff 11-22 (at Arms Park, Cardiff) (6,000).

Cardiff – Tries: Cleaver 3, Hale 2. 2 Cons/Pen: Tamplin.

NZ – Tries: (E) Grant, M.V. Hill. Con/Pen: (RM) McKenzie.

Mar 24 – Beat Royal Australian Air Force 20-13 (at Richmond).

Apr 2 – Lost to Newbridge 0-11 (at Newbridge).

Newbridge – Tries: S. Harris, K. Gumer. Con: Clem Davies. Pen: J. Bearshall.

Apr 7 – Beat a Somerset XV 22-10 (at Bridgwater).

May 5 – Drew with Abertillery 3-3 (at Abertillery Park).

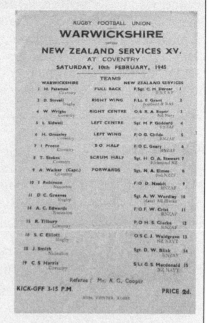

Warwickshire v NZ Services Programme

NZ – Try: P/O Ian J. Botting. A wing from the RNZAF and Otago, hetoured with the All Blacks to South Africa in 1949, then played for Oxford University and was later capped by England.

Deaths of international representatives in the first part of 1945:

Feb 21 - Eric Henry Liddell (Scotland, 7 caps, 1922-23). Born in Tientsin, China 16/1/1902. He won the 1924 Olympic 400 metres gold, was the 200 metres bronze medallist and became a Medical Missionary, but died in of a brain tumor in the Weishsien (Japanese) internment camp at Weifang, in China, aged 43. He was the inspiration for the Oscar winning 'Chariots of Fire' British film.

Mar 13 – Etienne Piquiral (France, 19 caps, 1924-28). He was a Capt. of the Regiment of Artillery and died behind enemy lines at Lubeck, aged 43. He played in the 1924 Olympics.

Apr 11 – Ian Henry Dustin (England Services, 1943-44). He was a New Zealander who was a P/Officer in the RNZAF – 502 Squadron of RAF Coastal Command out of Stornoway. He was shot down with no trace of all eight airmen on board during an anti-shipping raid in Norway, aged 26.

May 12 - Robert Mackenzie (Mike) Marshall, DSC (England, 5 caps, 1938-39). He was a Lieut-Cmdr. in the RNVR, whose P11 gunboat in MGB Flotilla was mined at sea, near Skagerrak. He was awarded the DSC in 1944 and Bar in 1945. Aged 27.

RUGBY LEAGUE:

Mar 10 – England 18 Wales 8 at Central Park, Wigan.

Apr 28 – RL Challenge Cup final – (1st leg) Huddersfield 7 Bradford 4 at Fartown, Huddersfield.

May 5 – RL Challenge Cup final – (2nd leg) Bradford 5 Huddersfield 6 at Odsal, Bradford. Huddersfield won 13-9 on aggregate.

The Allies' spring advance across Europe from both west and east succeeded, though not without cost, obstacles and the horrifying discovery of the Nazi Death Camps. In a bizarre juxtaposition we have the news of the Red Army closing in on the Nazi leader's Berlin Bunker while, as the programme pictures show, there was almost normality about the rugby in Cornwall and Somerset: though it was the 'older and younger' in those Home Guard ranks.

With Hitler dead by his own hand at the end of April, the European war over by May 8th – VE Day – and the Japanese conflict ended by September after the horrors of Hiroshima and Nagasaki (letting Japan's charismatic Mr. Rugby, 'Shiggy' Konno, off the kamikaze hook), peace was restored, and war hero Churchill found himself elected out of his PM's office with Attlee and Labour's summer victory.

'No panicking' in the West Country

In rugby, 'Services' Internationals were to be replaced by 'Victory' Internationals, with France returning to the fold, though only two of these matches were played before the year was out, with the rest in 1946. The series, with rather ad hoc arrangements and no championship involved, also included the 'Kiwis' (the 2nd NZ Expeditionary Force rugby squad) touring Great Britain, France and Germany in 1945 and 1946.

They played 'internationals' with four of the 'five nations' and became one of the best and most-loved sides ever to make a long tour of the UK. Rather as happened at the end of World War One, with NZ's 'First XV' (the winning King's Cup squad) and those next best below in their ranks both touring, the NZ Services of 1945-6 thus became effectively a reserve side to the Kiwis, and the Services' record is included below.

For the Kiwis, only scrum half and captain Major Charlie Saxton (3 NZ caps 1938) was a pre-war international player, but many of the party went on to gain full NZ honours. Their matches and their players are outlined in another chapter, but the England match is shown below.

November 24 – ENGLAND 3 KIWIS 18 (at Twickenham).

It was thought that England would be the team to halt the unbeaten run of the New Zealanders, but instead it was the tourists who gained a decisive victory in front of a crowd of over 30,000 at rugby's headquarters in the first representative match there for seven years. England made one change from the selected side as 2nd row Joe Mycock withdrew and Ron Peel replaced him.

Though no caps were awarded it still had the feel of a full international and England had to defend grimly to half the tide of the Kiwi runners, particularly through their strong pack. Behind the scrum, full back Bert Cook was outstanding and Fred Allen was a superb controller, but England, meanwhile, had few chances to attack their opponents.

The Kiwis scored first when Allen gave wing Jim Sherratt a clear run in and Cook converted and the latter added a penalty before the break was taken at 8-0. Skipper Jack Heaton opened the second half with a penalty, but it was the superior fitness of the visitors that told late on.

First, Keith Arnold went over with three defenders hanging on to him with Cook converting. Then, a huge kick by Cook took the Kiwis to the corner and scrum half Charlie Saxton sent Sherratt over again with Cook landing his fourth successful goal attempt.

England – G.H. (Harry) Pateman (Coventry); Derek L. Marriott (Old Blues), *+Heaton (capt), +E. Keith Scott (St Mary's Hospital), Hollis; +'Nim' M. Hall (St Mary's Hospital), + Sykes; +Geoff A. Kelly (Bedford), W. Owen Chadwick (Blackheath), +Tom W. Price (Gloucester), +D. Brian Vaughan (Harlequins/Navy), Peel, Hudson, *Harry F. Wheatley (Coventry), Eric Bole (Waterloo/Cambridge University).

England v the Kiwis ephemera

Pen: Heaton.
The Kiwis' line-up is detailed in the final chapter.
Tries: Sherratt 2, Arnold. 3 Cons/Pen: Cook.
Referee: R.A. Beattie (Watsonians).

ENGLAND

George Henry (HARRY) PATEMAN – Full Back. Coventry/Warwickshire. Born Coventry 1915. Died Coventry 1994.

DEREK L. MARRIOTT – Wing. Born Islington 30/5/1924. St Mary's Hospital/Old Blues/Rosslyn Park/Harlequins/England Universities/London XV/London University/Barbarians/Middlesex/R.V. Stanley's XV/Civil Defence. He was Vice-President of the Old Blues in 2009-10 and lived in Southgate. No death date found, would be 94 if still alive in 2018.

Edward KEITH SCOTT, MRCS – Centre. Born Truro 14/6/1918. Died Truro 3/6/1995. Clifton College/Oxford Univ./St. Mary's Hospital/Redruth/Harlequins/Barbarians/London Counties/Cornwall. He was a 12th man for England in a 'Victory' Cricket test. 5 caps (1947-48). A doctor, he was the son of Frank S. Scott (1 cap, 1907).

Norman Macleod (NIM) HALL – Fly Half. Born Huddersfield 2/8/1925. Died London 26/6/1972. Worksop College/St. Mary's Hospital/Army/Huddersfield/Combined Services/Barbarians/Richmond/Yorkshire/Middlesex. 17 caps (1947-55). He was a Medical Student/Insurance Broker/Licensee and served in the Army with the Royal Signals, Catterick.

GEOFFrey Arnold KELLY – Prop. Born Royston 9/2/1914. Died Cambridge 9/3/1997. Perse School, Letchworth/Bedford/Barbarians/East Midlands/Eastern Counties. 4 caps (1947-48). He was a Fertiliser sales representative and President of Royston RFC.

William OWEN CHADWICK – Hooker. Born Bromley 20/5/1916. Died Canterbury 17/7/2015, aged 99 years 2 months. Tonbridge School/St John's College, Cambridge Univ./Blackheath/Barbarians/Richmond/GB tour of Argentina 1936. He won Blues for Rugby in 1936, 1937 and 1938 (captain) and attended Cuddesdon College (1940-41), then becoming Curate at St John's Church, Huddersfield and Chaplain at Wellington College until the end of the war. He became an Honorary Fellow at St John's College, Cambridge, in 1964, and was Master of Selwyn College, Cambridge (1956-83); Dixie Professor of Ecclesiastical History (1958-68) and Regius Professor of History (1968-83). He was also Hensley Henson Lecturer in Theology at Oxford University (1975-76) and Ford Lecturer in English History at Oxford (1980-81). He was also President of the British Academy (1981-85) and Chancellor of East Anglia University (1984-94).

Thomas William (TOM) PRICE – Prop. Born 26/7/1914. Died Gloucester 11/7/1991. St Mark's School, Gloucester/Gloucester/Cheltenham/Gloucestershire/Barbarians. 6 caps (1948-49). He was a Laundry employee and also worked in an Aircraft factory.

Douglas BRIAN VAUGHAN – 2nd Row, later Back Row. Born Wrexham 15/7/1925. Died Peel, Isle of Man 19/4/1977. Luton School/Cambridge Univ./Navy/Harlequins/Devonport Services/United Services, Portsmouth/ Barbarians/Yorkshire/Hampshire/Devon/Kendal. RNE College, Keyham then Navy, but invalided out 1964, then a Company Director and Schoolteacher at Sedbergh School, being also British Lions manager to South Africa in 1962. 8 caps (1948-50).

Harold Frederick (HARRY) WHEATLEY – Back Row. Born Coventry 26/12/1912. Died Coventry 10/4/2003. King Henry VIII School, Coventry/ Coventry/Warwickshire/Midland Counties/Barbarians/Kenilworth. He was a Haulier and Lorry Driver. 7 caps as a prop (1936-39). His brother, Arthur A. Wheatley, won 5 caps at lock (1937-38).

ERIC BOLE – Back Row. Born Liverpool 2nd quarter 1925. Died Lincolville, Maine (USA) 2/9/1988, aged 63. Wycliffe College/Magdalen College, Cambridge University (Blues in 1945-46-47{captain})/Waterloo/Barbarians. He was a schoolteacher living in New Brighton, who emigrated to the USA in 1954, marrying there and becoming the headmaster of the Principia School, St Louis, Missouri.

December 22 – WALES 8 FRANCE 0 (at St Helen's, Swansea). (10,000).

Driving rain cut down the size of the crowd and made the pitch a sea of mud with passing difficult. Wales centre Bleddyn Williams overcame it all however in a masterly display and made both the tries, though the match was mostly confined to the forwards.

France full back Lucien Rouffia was in fine form and Britain first saw the huge locks Robert Soro and Alban Moga, plus a wonderful back row of Jean Prat, Guy Basquet and Jean Matheu.

A superb run by the 22-year-old Williams eluded his marker, French skipper Louis Junquas, and sent Cardiff club-mate and fellow centre Jack Matthews over and then Williams ran well and cross-kicked for forward Sedley Davies to score with hooker Maldwyn James converting.

France, who had twice awarded caps against the British Army, now did so again. Scrum half Billy Darch was a late replacement for the selected Haydn Tanner. It was the first French international team to play in Britain since 1931.

Wales – R. Hugh Lloyd-Davies (Cambridge University/RAF); D. Glyn Jones (Cardiff/RAF), +(J) Matthews (capt.), +F/O (BL) Williams, Graham G. Hale (Cardiff/Welsh Guards); +W.B. (Billy) Cleaver (Cardiff), W.J. (Billy) Darch (Cardiff); Elwyn Gwyther (Belle Vue Rangers and Leeds RL),

+D. Maldwyn James (Cardiff), +Griff W. Bevan (Llanelli/Navy), +(WJ) Evans, Sedley J.G. Davies (Maesteg), W. Elvet Jones (Swansea/Llanelli), *+Manfield, +R.T. (Bob) Evans (Newport).

Tries: Matthews, (SJG) Davies. Con: James.

Programmes: Wales v France 'Victory' international and Wales' earlier trial

France – +Lucien M. Rouffia (Narbonne/Romans); +Elie Pebeyre (Fumel/Brive), +Georges Baladie (Bergerac), +Louis Junquas (Tyrosse/ Bayonne/Lyon, capt.), +Henri Dutrain (Toulouse); +Maurice Terreau (Bourg/Toulouse), +Yves R. Bergougnan (Toulouse); +Jean M. Prin-Clary (Covillon/Toulon/Brive), +Marcel Volot (Stade Francais), +Jean M.G. Massare (Paris University), +Robert P.V. Soro (Lourdes/Romans), +Alban Moga (Begles), +Jean Matheu (Agen/Castres), +Guy Basquet (Agen), +Jean Prat (Lourdes).

Referee: Alan S. Bean (Sunderland).

WALES

Rheinalt HUGH LLOYD-DAVIES – Full Back. Born Ammanford Hospital (parents lived in Tycroes) March 1925. Died Islington or Lambeth July-September 1983. Amman Valley Grammar School/London Welsh/Cambridge

University (he read law at Trinity Hall and gained a Rugby Blue in 1947)/Harlequins/RAF/Barrow RL. He was a Leading Air Craftsman and a F/Officer in the RAF and his real name was Rheinallt Lloyd Hughes Davies. He also worked as a Gardener for Islington Council and was the first Varsity Blue to join Rugby League. He was jailed in France and died penniless, sleeping rough and calling himself 'Colonel'. Hugh's father was a bus conductor and he had a brother and a sister, but was brought up by his grandparents. A heavy drinker, he was sent down by Cambridge, temporarily joined Gray's Inn and was jailed for nine months for pawning stolen jewellery.

David GLYN JONES – Wing. Born Aberdare 28/12/1920. Died Glasgow 14/7/2008. Monmouth School/Church Village School/Cardiff Univ./Cardiff Medicals/RAF Halton/Cardiff (30 games, 28 tries, 1945-46 and 1946-47). He was a Doctor and served in the RAF. He left Cardiff for Sheffield in 1949 and then worked in an ENT hospital in Glasgow from 1955. He also played outside half for Harlequins and was in the Cardiff side that won the 1939 Middlesex Sevens.

GRAHAM George HALE – Wing. Born Cardiff 29/2/1920. Cardiff High School/Cardiff HSOB/Cardiff (59 games from 1938-39 until 1946-47). He served in the Welsh Guards and was a Prisoner of War in Benghazi, North Africa, taken then to Italy, but was ill and was allowed to be invalided home by ship. Died 8/1/2018 Cardiff, a month short of his 98th birthday. He played in the Cardiff side that won the 1939 Middlesex Sevens.

William Benjamin (BILLY) CLEAVER – Fly Half. Born Treorchy 15/9/1921. Died Rhiwbina, Cardiff 29/9/2003. Pentre School/University College Cardiff/Treorchy/Pentre/Bridgend/Cardiff/Newbridge/Llanelli/Barbarians/British Lions. 14 caps at fly half/full back/centre (1947-50). Lions (3 tests v NZ; 0 tests v Australia 1950). He was a Mining Engineer and became Deputy Director of Mining for South Wales.

William James (BILLY) DARCH – Scrum Half. Born Trealaw, Rhondda 2nd quarter 1923. Died in the Sunrise Senior Living Home, Astolat Way, Guildford on 20/1/2014. Trealaw Elementary School/Porth Secondary School/Cardiff University/Cardiff (68 games, 1945-46 to 1948-49)/Aberavon. He worked for many years as BP's Director in charge of laying pipelines in Anchorage, Alaska, then became President of the consortium that built the Trans-Alaska pipeline. He worked in Canada and finally in Melbourne (Australia) for Bechtel (USA). He retired to Meadow Rise, Sketty in Swansea until late 2012, but spent his last days in Guildford, his wife, Kathleen, having predeceased him. He was injured during Cardiff's 1939 Middlesex Sevens victory and did not play in the semi-final or final.

ELWYN GWYTHER – Prop. Born Penclawdd, Gower 8/3/1921. Died Llanelli 21/3/1996, aged 75. Penclawdd/Llanelli/Belle Vue Rangers, Leeds, Wales and

GB RL (1946 Australia/NZ tour). Ex-colliery worker. His wife died in 2003 in Pontyberem: they had a son and three daughters.

David MALDWYN JAMES – Hooker. Born Cilfynydd 28/6/1913. Died Aberdare 19/7/2003. Pontypridd Grammar School/ Cilfynydd/Pontypridd/Cardiff/Mountain Ash. 5 caps (1947-48). He was a National Coal Board employee.

GRIFFith Wilfred BEVAN – Prop. Born Burry Port 15/8/1914. Died Burry Port 25/10/2004. Burry Port/Birmingham Welsh/Llanelli/Devonport Services/ Furnace Utd/Navy. 1 cap (1947). He served in the Navy and was a Steelworker.

SEDLEY James G DAVIES – 2nd Row. Born Aberkenfig 14/9/1919. Died (while living in Maesteg) at the Princess of Wales Hospital, Bridgend, June 1996, aged 76. St Robert's School, Aberkenfig/ Tondu Schools/Wales Schools Under 16s

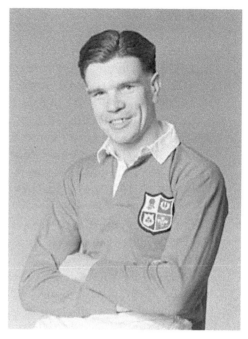

R T 'Bob' Evans, later Lion

(1933)/Aberavon/Maesteg (played in their Invincible season of 1949-50). He worked for the Tondu Brick Company and was a Miner at Duffryn Rhondda Colliery. His grandson, Ian Greenslade, hooked for Cardiff/Bridgend. His wife Connie died in 1992, leaving four children - Alan (S Wales Police prop), Gareth, Carol and Jeff. His father, W.J. Davies, was in the Maesteg side of 1912-13, while Sedley captained Maesteg in 1945-46 and 1948-49, making 189 appearances.

Watkin ELVET JONES – Blind-side wing forward. Born Pontarddulais 4/10/1920. Died Swansea 4/3/2012. Wales Secondary Schools (1939 vs Yorkshire)/Swansea/Llanelli/Cardiff/Neath. He also played for the Army against the RAF whilst being a Cpl. in the Royal Artillery and later worked in Penarth Boys Club and was Deputy Head of Glamorgan Farm School for juvenile delinquents in Neath. He predeceased his wife.

Robert Thomas (BOB) EVANS – Open-side wing forward. Born Rhymney 16/2/1921. Died Abergavenny 14/4/2003. Rhymney School/Rhymney/ Abergavenny/Newport/Monmouthshire/Welsh & British Police/British Lions. 10 caps (1947-51). Lions 1950 to NZ (4 tests)/Australia (2 tests). He had served in the RAF and became a Det. Chief Superintendent in the Gwent Police.

FRANCE

LUCIEN M. ROUFFIA – Full Back. Born Narbonne 6/1/1924. Died Romans 8/3/1980. Narbonne/Romans. 4 caps (1945-48).

ELIE PEBEYRE – Wing. Born Seilhac 27/1/1923. Died Brive-la-Gaillarde 12/12/2008. Fumel/Brive. 8 caps (1945-47).

GEORGES BALADIE – Centre. Born Ville d'Avray 20/5/1917. Died November 1988. Agen/Bergerac. 6 caps (1945-46).

LOUIS JUNQUAS – Centre. Born St Vincent-de-Tyrosse, Landes 11/11/1920. Died 23/5/2002. Tyrosse/Bayonne/Lyon. 13 caps (1945-48).

HENRI DUTRAIN – Wing, later centre. Born Toulouse 3/7/1922. Toulouse. 8 caps (1945-49).

MAURICE TERREAU – Fly Half, later centre. Born Bourg-en-Bresse 30/1/1923. Died Bourg-en-Bresse 22/12/2000. Bourg/Toulouse. 17 caps (1945-51).

YVES R. BERGOUGNAN – Scrum Half. Born Toulouse 8/5/1924. Died Toulouse 15/4/2006. Toulouse. He scored the last four-point drop goal in an international against England in 1948. 17 caps (1945-49).

JEAN M. PRIN-CLARY – Prop, later 2nd Row. Born Marseilles 15/7/1912. Cavillon/Toulon/Brive. 10 caps (1945-47). Death date unknown.

MARCEL VOLOT – Hooker. Born Gonfreville l'Orcher 27/6/1917. Died 28/8/2014, aged 97. Stade Francais.

JEAN M.G. MASSARE – Prop. Born Fontenay-sous-Bois 29/8/1922. Paris University. 6 caps (1945-46).

ROBERT P.V. SORO – 2nd Row. Born Odos 28/11/1922. Died Arreau 28/4/2013. Lourdes/Romans. 21 caps (1945-49).

ALBAN ('Bamby') MOGA – 2nd Row. Born Bordeaux 1/5/1923. Died Bordeaux 5/4/1983. Begles. 22 caps (1945-49).

JEAN MATHEU – Back Row. Born Gelos 23/6/1920. Died Castres 26/5/1989. Agen/Castres. 24 caps (1945-51). His real name was Jean Matheu-Cambas.

GUY BASQUET – No 8. Born Layrac 13/7/1921. Died Agen January 2006. Agen. 33 caps (1945-52).

JEAN PRAT – Back Row. Born Lourdes 1/8/1923. Died Lourdes 25/2/2005. Lourdes. 51 caps (1945-55). He was an Hotelier while his brother (Maurice) won 31 caps as a centre (1951-58).

December 15 - An Ireland XV 19 British Army 3 (at Ravenhill, Belfast).

The Army made three late changes as F.D. Jeffries, Reg Brown and (WT) Reynolds came in the pack in place of *E A Evans, *H W Thomas and Elvet Jones. There was an interesting selection at fly half for the Irish: one Jack Kyle.

Ireland - *+(CJ) Murphy (capt); *Moran, Greer, +(KJ) Quinn, +Brendan Thomas Quinn (Old Belvedere); +John Wilson (Jack) Kyle, Desmond Thorpe (Old Belvedere); Belton, +Karl Daniel Mullen (Old Belvedere), +Corcoran, +Robert Dunlop (Bob) Agar ((Malone), +Callan, Dudgeon, Guiney, +Desmond McCourt (Queens University, Belfast).

Tries: (KJ) Quinn 2, Moran, Kyle. 2 Cons/Pen: Thorpe.

British Army - +Trott;

OFFICIAL PROGRAMME

Price - Threepence (at least)

IRISH RUGBY FOOTBALL UNION

ULSTER BRANCH

BRITISH ARMY XV.
(GREAT BRITAIN)

v.

AN IRISH XV.

At RAVENHILL, BELFAST

SATURDAY, 15th DECEMBER, 1945

KICK-OFF 2-30 P.M.

TOTAL PROCEEDS FROM THE SALE OF THESE PROGRAMMES WILL BE DEVOTED TO THE FUNDS OF LOCAL HOSPITALS

R. W. JEFFARES, Secretary, I.R.F.U.

W. A. B. DOUGLAS, Hon. Secretary, Ulster Branch, I.R.F.U.

Ireland XV v British Army 1945

(AE) Johnson, +Charles William Drummond (Melrose), +Lawrence Gjers Gloag (Seaforth Highlanders), Jack ('Darcy') Anderson (London Scottish/Hawick); Risman, Keith H.S. Wilson (London Scottish); 2nd Lieut. F.D. Jeffries (Warwickshire Rgt), +Hastie, (WG) Jones (Newport/Royal Artillery), Reg A. Brown (Mitcham/Rosslyn Park), (DV) Phillips, (WT) Reynolds, R.M.P. Fenning (Royal Artillery/Bristol), Thomas Priest (Bristol).

Pen: Risman.

With the war finally at an end, other matches of note in later 1945 included:

Sept 15 – Cardiff 28 RAAF 3 (at the Arms Park, Cardiff).

Sept 20 – Newport 18 RAAF 3 (at Rodney Parade, Newport).

9th Match

v. Royal Australian Air Force

At Richmond, November 7, 1945.

Match Drawn—8 to 8.

NEW ZEALAND SERVICES:

Tpr. H. E. Johns
(Army)

F/O. I. J. Botting   F/Sgt. M. P. Goddard   Pte. J. R. O'Hearn
(R.N.Z.A.F.)   (R.N.Z.A.F.)   (Army)

Pte. A. F. Bullick
(Army)

F/O. T. F. C. Geary (C)
(R.N.Z.A.F.)

F/Sgt. J. Holmes
(R.N.Z.A.F.)

F/Lt. R. A. Dalton
(R.N.Z.A.F.)

F/Sgt. D. W. Blick   S/Lt. A. M. Henderson
(R.N.Z.A.F.)   (R.N.Z. Navy)

Lieut. K. D. Rankin   Sgt. L. A. Grant
(Army)   (Army)

Dvr. W. C. Porter   Pte. M. S. Ingpen   Pte. C. L. Hardie
(Army)   (Army)   (Army)

W/O. J. West   W/O. K. H. Kearney   F/O. A. Roper (C)
F/O. C. Nethery   F/O. J. McBride   F/O. G. Horton   F/Lt. A. Dennett
F/O. F. de Belin

W/O. N. Crozier
W/O. T. Ryan
F/O. J. McGilvray   F/O. A. Lewis   W/O. A. Fitzsimons   W/O. A. Browne
W/O. W. Cameron

ROYAL AUSTRALIAN AIR FORCE:

For New Zealand Services: M. P. Goddard and I. J. Botting, tries; H. E. Johns, conversion.

For Royal Australian Air Force: A. Browne and A. Dennett, tries; J. McGilvray, conversion.

Referee: WO/1. J. Hore (New Zealand).

The teams in Swan & Carman's book

Sept 22 – Penzance and Newlyn RFC played its first post-war match, against Guy's Hospital on the Mennaye Field.

Former England wing and GB tourist Barrie Bennetts kicked off.

Oct 20 – Stade Francais 3 Rosslyn Park 6 (at Parc des Princes, Paris).

Nov 3 – Cardiff 14 NZ Services 3 (at the Arms Park, Cardiff).

NZ Services turned out two teams that day (see below).

Cardiff – Tries: (D. Glyn) Jones 2, (Bleddyn) Williams, Darch. Con: Tamplin.

NZ Services – Pen: Trooper Herbert E. (Bert) Johns (full back).

Nov 7 – NZ Services 8 RAAF 8 (at Richmond) (2,000).

NZ Services – Tries: Flight-Sgt. (MP) Goddard, F/O (IJ) Botting. Con: Johns.

RAAF – Tries: A. Browne, A. Dennett. Con: G. McGilvray.

Nov 10 – Newbridge, another club whose wartime 'reserved occupation' miners greatly assisted their rise and post-war strength, were the first Welsh outfit to play in France since 1939 when they travelled to beat Clermont-Ferrand 17-9.

Dec 1 – Wales trial – Reds 20 Whites 11 (at Cardiff Arms Park).

Dec 12 – Oxford University 8 Cambridge University 11 (at Twickenham).

Their Majesties the King and Queen, as well as Princess Elizabeth, were present for the first Varsity match since 1938 to be played at Twickenham.

Oxford were skippered by wing J.K. Pearce and included South Africans (JO) Newton-Thompson (later an England cap), A.B. Harcourt and D.H. Sampson with P.B.C. Moore (later England) and wing forward C. Derek Williams of Cardiff Technical College/London Welsh, who much later played for Cardiff/Neath/Wales.

Try: Newton-Thompson. Con/Pen: J. McGlashan.

Cambridge, led by Eric Bole, included Logie Bruce Lockhart in the centre with New Zealander H.M. Kimberley, while J. Thomas (Lampeter School) was prop and three forwards later played for England – Steele-Bodger, Bance and hooker Alan P. Henderson (9 caps, 1947-49).

Tries: Bole, G.B.R. Oswald, J. Fairgrieve. Con: T.K.M. Kirby.

Referee: (CH) Gadney.

Dec 26 – Leicester 0 Barbarians 3 (at Leicester).

Barbarians - +Trott; Marriott, P.H. Till (Wasps), +Scott, Peter R. Graham (St Mary's Hospital); +Hall, +(JO) Newton-Thompson; *Longland, Gilthorpe, +Kelly, Fenning, D.J.B. Johnston (St Mary's Hospital, capt), Hudson, Bole, A.A. Venniker (St Mary's Hospital/Middlesex).

Try: Graham.

Dec 29 – English Schools 18 Scottish Schools 10 (at Richmond).

English Schools included Brian Boobbyer (Uppingham) at centre, while Scottish Schools had Ian Douglas Freeman Coutts (Dulwich) at full back, Ian S. Gloag (Oundle) wing and Norman G.R. Mair (Merchiston Castle) hooker. Two of them went on to win senior Scotland caps – Coutts (2 caps, 1951-52) and future rugby journalist Mair (4 caps, 1951). Gloag was a Scotland trialist and his brother, Lawrence Gjers Gloag, was capped four times in 1948.

Referee: (CH) Gadney.

Dec 31 – Stade Nantais UC 8 Cardiff 29 (at Nantes).

Miscellaneous:

Richmond and Blackheath combined to play their matches, while pre-war Wales captain Claud Davey was appointed London Welsh skipper and London Scottish, on 29/9/1945, made their first appearance since the end of the 1938-39 season, when they defeated London Irish by 27-0. London Scottish included Geddes as captain, plus (AE) Murray, the Services wing and (KHS) Wilson, who became a Services international.

Northampton included Don White and Lewis Cannell, who both later won England caps.

Harlequins teams included pre-war cap Arthur Godfrey Butler (England, 2 caps, 1937), plus Steele-Bodger, Weighill, de Lacy, Vaughan and Dunkley.

London Welsh included (AM) Rees, Tanner, Lloyd-Davies, (EC) Davey (captain) and forward, Alun Meredith (Wales, three caps 1949). Davey even played at scrum half for the 'Exiles'.

Sale included the pre-war England wing Hal F. Sever (10 caps, 1936-38).

Edinburgh University's half backs, Ranald MacDonald and (AW) Black were 1950 British Lions.

The RAF included Flt-Lieut (Bill) Fallowfield, who became Rugby Football League secretary.

On December 1, Wilfred Wooller returned from being a Prisoner of War at the hands of the Japanese to play what was to be his last game for Cardiff. It was at Richmond against the combined Richmond-Blackheath team and

Cardiff won 16-9 with Wooller beginning at full back and playing centre after half-time.

In the Scotland trial of December 15 at Murrayfield, that young Hawick back-row forward, William B. (Bill) McLaren, who as we recalled, later became one of the greatest-ever TV commentators, played for The Rest, who lost 25-3 to Scotland.

The pre-war England wing H.L.V. Day (Leicester) refereed Guy's Hospital against Paris University at Honor Oak Park on December 19. Paris won 3-0.

The Northern Services fielded several RL players against the 'Kiwis', including Gareth Price (Llanelli/Leeds RL/Army), Cliff Evans (Leeds RL/RAF) and J.H. Fox (Castleford RL/Army). On December 8 Northampton beat Bath 12-6 and it was reported that play was held up while a pig, which had strayed on to the field, was chased off.

After their contribution to Allied success in Italy, the South African 6th Armoured Division had a short tour in Britain and their side included Gunner Stephen Fry (later a Springbok captain and a 1951-52 tourist to GB/France), wing Corporal Cecil Moss (a 1949 Springbok cap), full back Lieutenant George Alfred Cary Smith (1 cap South Africa 1938) and Trooper Alwyn ('Nelles') Vintcent, who later played for Oxford University. The manager was J.H.Burger and the trainer was the great pre-war Springbok forward M.M. ('Boy') Louw.

Vintcent was from Diocesan College, Rondebosch and was a Rhodes Scholar to Trinity College, Oxford. He won a Blue in 1948 and skippered the 'Dark Blues' in 1949, became Managing Director and Chairman of Prince, Vintcent and Company (1968-95), living in Mossel Bay. Born 24/12/1925. Died 13/4/2011, aged 85.

Dec 8 – Beat Combined Guards Brigade 16-0 at Caterham.

Tries: Vintcent, Corporal F.F. Kingswall, Lieut I. Frylinck. Cons: Smith 2. Pen: Swanson.

Dec 11 – Beat St Mary's Hospital 17-5 at Richmond Athletic Ground.

Dec 15 – Drew with Royal Australian Air Force 10-10 at the White City, London.

SA – Try: Frylinck. DG: Smith. Pen: Swanson.

RAAF – Tries: F/O Fred L. de Belin, J.W.T. McBride.

Cons: (AS) Roper 2.

John William Terrence (Terry) McBride, then a forward, played as a wing for the 1947-48 Australian tourists to GB/France. Norm Emery and Ken Kearney also went on to play on the Wallabies tour.

The team at Oxford's iconic Elmer Cotton sports shop near Jesus College (rear) in the Turl

Dec 19 – Lost to NZ Services 6-9 at Richmond Athletic Ground.

SA - Try: Pte J.C. Morkel. Pen: Swanson.

NZ Services – Tries: Goddard, Botting. Pen: Johns.

Dec 22 – Lost to Guy's Hospital 0-3. Referee: (Trevor) Jones.

Guy's – Pen: D. le Clus. Guy's included five South Africans.

This was not the strongest of SA sides, and some back home were concerned that they should not be judged in strict comparison with the very successful contemporaneous Kiwis in the UK. They went on to visit and play in France and Germany before returning to Egypt and, eventually, home.

The RAAF played 22 games in the UK: Won 16, Drew 3, Lost 3 (Pts 320-105). The losses were to Newbridge (0-3), Sale (12-13) and London Irish (8-10). They selected from 4,000 Australian airmen based in Britain. Their final game was on December 15 (see above).

The official NZ Services games played were:

Sept 22 – Beat Wasps 14-3 at Sudbury.

Oct 6 – Beat St Mary's Hospital 14-0 at Teddington.

Oct 13 – Beat Glynneath 11-0 at Abernant Park, Glynneath.

Oct 20 – Beat Abertillery 8-3 at Abertillery Park.

Pre-war Wales international Albert G. Fear (4 caps, 1934-35) and a young fly half Ernie Lewis (later of Ebbw Vale, a leading referee and father of Steve Lewis, Ebbw Vale, Oxford University, Bath, and later WRU Chief Executive) were in the home side.

Oct 25 – Beat A Commandos XV 39-0 at Welford Road, Leicester.

Oct 27 – Beat Tonbridge 36-0 at Tonbridge.

Nov 3 – NZ Services fielded two sides, losing to Cardiff 3-14 (see above), but beating Northampton 11-6 (at Northampton). Cannell, Fallowfield, White and Longland (captain) played for Northampton, with White kicking two penalties.

Nov 7 – Drew with RAAF 8 at Richmond (see above).

Nov 10 – Beat Oxford University 8-3 at Iffley Road, Oxford.

(CD) Williams, (PBC) Moore and (JO) Newton-Thompson played for Oxford, as did wing P.W. Day, who later appeared for the NZ Services.

Nov 15 – Beat A.S. Montferrandaise 19-16 at Clermont Ferrand.

Nov 18 – Beat Lyons Olympic University Sports Club 17-8 at Lyons.

Lyons full back Robien was later found to be G.H. Robinson of the New Zealand Navy!!

Nov 19 – Beat Selection Romans-Dauphine 11-6 at Romans.

Nov 28 – Beat Cambridge University 42-5 at Grange Road, Cambridge.

Bance, Steele-Bodger, Bole (capt) and (Logie) Bruce Lockhart all played for Cambridge, as did centre (HM) Kimberley, who later appeared for the NZ Services.

Dec 1 – Beat Barnstaple 22-5 at Barnstaple.

Barnstaple captain, Herbert Arthur Jones, was capped twice by England in 1950.

On Thursday, December 6 the NZ Services returned to Abernant Park to play a second match against Glynneath, but this was never recorded in the official tour record.

Glynneath won by 14-5 scoring two converted tries and a drop goal against a converted try. The game was recorded by the Aberdare Leader on December 15, 1945 and showed that Glynneath had made many changes from the first meeting. It was refereed by Mr. Fred Phillips of the Swansea Valley RU, who was a WRU vice-president.

For Glynneath, captained by scrum half David Galsworthy, centre Levi Davies dropped a goal while the tries were scored by wing Will Winter (Cwmgwrach) and wing forward David B. Evans (Resolven) and both converted by centre Jack Hamer, though Cpl. B.M. McKenzie (NZ Army) scored his side's try and Bob Scott (Kiwis) converted.

Team manager Major Jack Henley admitted that it was hard to find 15 players for the game, but Mr. and Mrs. Stan Davies provided after-match food at the Rock Hotel and a social evening followed, including tenor Emrys Thomas (Aberdare), comedian Jeff Pritchard, the Cwmgwrach 'brothers' James and Williams at the piano and A. Sailor (!) as a singer.

The Services team sang 'The Kiwis Farewell' and 'The Kiwis Battle-Cry' and were loudly applauded. Most of them stayed in Glynneath homes and reappeared the following night at the Crosffordd Hotel for a dance, with war cries given by both sides!!

Dec 8 – Beat Maesteg 6-4 at Llynfi Road, Maesteg.

Sedley Davies skippered the home side with Billy Banks, later a GB RL player, at scrum half.

Referee: Ivor David (Neath)

Maesteg v the Kiwis Programme, Dec 1945

Dec 13 – Beat Oxford and District XV 12-7 at Oxford.

The District included full back Nigel Gibbs (England, 2 caps, 1954) and scrum half Martin Paterson ('Squib') Donnelly, a New Zealander, who played 59 times for his country from 1937-49 and won an England rugby cap in 1947 as well as appearing for NZ as a cricketer. He was a Major in the 49th Armoured Brigade.

Dec 19 – Beat South African 6th Armoured Division 9-6 at Richmond Athletic Ground (see above).

Beat SA Services, lost at Old Belvedere

Dec 22 – Lost to Old Belvedere Selection 6-12 at Lansdowne Road, Dublin.

Karl Mullen, Moran and three Quinns - BT, KJ and GJ – all played for Old Belvedere.

Dec 27 – Beat Leicester 19-3 at Welford Road, Leicester.

Leicester included William Kenneth Thomas ('Bill') Moore (England, 7 caps, 1947-50); John Thomas Wade ('Tom') Berry (England, 3 caps, 1939) and Francis G. Edwards, the 1940 Red Cross 'cap'.

No-one would call the season which began in September 1945 normal, while war had barely ended and when there were many, many thousands of young rugby men still in uniform and scattered worldwide. However there were beginnings; and, of course, there continued to be keen competition in those distant camps, as seen in the pictured example from Germany.

While many clubs large and small would struggle to get funds, regular sides, satisfactory facilities and the old range of fixtures, there was plenty about which to be hopeful. The appetite for attractive, skilful rugby had been whetted by the quality of the big games played by the Union and often particularly League men during the war years, as the large crowds testified, and the Victory matches were also to prove 'box-office'.

Swansea, for example, scene of some of the best charity games, seem to have used well the profits from that last forces match, getting back into action in September as the pictured season ticket shows. There was some county rugby, too, and Yorkshire had a second row with a good name when they met Roses rivals Lancashire at Manchester in October!

Perhaps the most optimistic sign was the cluster of schoolboy matches and trials looking to the future. Spot your own programme favourite who went on to even greater things: the Welsh halfbacks, the Davieses? – more later; Sid Judd, magnificent schoolboy and later senior Welsh cap who was to die sadly young?; Christopher Winn, English wing and Sussex cricketer?; Alun Thomas, Welsh utility back, later WRU President and Lions manager 1974? or......?

Things could happen very quickly, too, for those who had been robbed of years of

Combined Services (Germany) v the Army in the UK

their potential rugby careers by the war. Rhymney's R T 'Bob' Evans, 18 and eager for sport in 1939, returned from the RAF in 1945 to be elected skipper of his hometown club ready for the new season in September.

'I was the first captain to be elected post-war. The meeting was held in the Institute Library on Surgery Hill. I was on demob. leave, having left the RAF

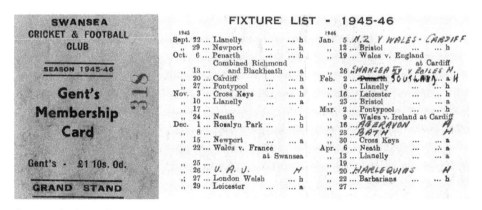

Swansea's planned postwar season

LANCASHIRE COUNTY RUGBY FOOTBALL UNION.

Lancashire v. Yorkshire

at the Manchester R.U.F.C., Moor Lane, Kersal.
Saturday, October 20, 1945. Kick-off 2.45 p.m.

Lancashire (BLUE)   Yorkshire (WHITE)

Full Backs
16. Lt. M. T. Ackerman   15. S. A. F. Comer
    (England and South Africa)   (Halifax)

Three Quarter Backs
15. J. Walkley   14. R. Pollard
    (Waterloo)   (Huddersfield Old Boys)
14. J. Heaton (L'pool)   13. Alex. Gray
    (Waterloo and England)   (Trafford)
13. Cpl. W. Gornall   12. J. B. Womersley
    (Preston & England Reserve)   (Headingley)
11. C.S.M.I. C. B. Holmes   11. Lt. Gerry Hollis (Capt.)
    (Manchester and England)   (Hull & E.R. & England)

Half Backs
10. A. Openshaw   10. P.O. A. C. Towell
    (Leigh)   (Middlesbrough)
9. P. R. B. Jones   9. Lt. W. J. Ellis
    (Waterloo)   (Headingley)

Forwards
8. Maj. J. P. Dunkerley   8. Drv. A. Cave
   (Harlequins and England)   (R.A.S.C.)
7. E. Evans   7. L.Cpl. J. D. H. Hastie
   (Sale)   (Scotn. Command & Scotl'd)
6. Dr. Logan   6. G. H. Bottomley
   (Waterloo)   (Huddersfield Old Boys)
5. P. M. Rhodes   5. Pte. J. B. Lees
   (Manchester)   (Army Command & Scotl'd)
4. D. P. Sheedy   4. P. Atkinson
   (Sale)   (Hull and E.R.)
3. H. F. Luya   3. Ron. Peel
   (Waterloo)   (Headingley)
2. Sgt. J. Mycock   2. Lt. Gordon Frank
   (Sale and England)   (Harrogate Old Boys)
1. E. P. Coislett   1. L.Cpl. D. J. Reynolds
   (Broughton Park)   (Northern Command)

Referee : P. D. COATMAN

November 3rd: LANCASHIRE v. CHESHIRE, at Waterloo.
Nov 30th: MANCHESTER v. BROUGHTON PARK, at Moor Lane.

Programme 2d.

Roses Rugby, October 1945

on V.J. Day. It was a vote between Tommy Bowen, ex-Lawn School, who came from New Tredegar and later Caerleon Training College, and myself'. Evans' talents, nurtured with some Police and Forces wartime rugby, would have been welcome indeed, but he was obviously destined for higher things.

Recruited by Newport before September was out, (Tommy Bowen taking the skipper's role after all), within four months Rhymney's "skipper-that-was" was playing in the Welsh jersey. He gained the first of five "Victory" international selections he was to enjoy in 1946, and at Twickenham his inter-passing with Haydn Tanner brought the thrilling single-try victory. The future Newport skipper and chairman and Police Superintendent was also to be a noted 1950 British Lion.

Death: Nov 20 – Herbert Michael Moran, the captain of the 1908 Australian team to Britain, died of melanoma in Cambridge, England, aged 60. A surgeon, he was born at Darlington in Sydney on April 26, 1885. He was the son of an Irish baker and Australian mother. The game against Wales was his only cap and his dislocated shoulder caused him to miss the Olympic Games match against Cornwall. His career lay in cancer research, studying in Edinburgh and working in London and Dublin hospitals. He was married in 1914, and was a Lieutenant at No. 23 Stationary Hospital, Indian Expeditionary Forces in Mesopotamia and Captain in the Australian RAMC. His notable career included working at the Paris cancer research centre. He spoke Italian, German and French and met Mussolini during his time in Italy. In 1940-45 he served with the RAMC again, being a Lieut-Col. based in Colchester.

All the major rugby playing Allies had lost rugby men aplenty, and all save South Africa at least one capped player. Australia was the only nation to have lost more internationals in the second war than in the first, which illustrates the scale and type of the fighting in the Far East.

There was surprise, though, in 2002, when Jed Smith and Ross Hamilton, then at the Twickenham World Rugby Museum, revealed which country had most international rugby players killed in action between 1939 and 1945. The answer was Germany, as the pair, preparing for an exhibition commemorating

A Schools 'Selection'

the sport's war dead, uncovered the identities of 16 German caps who lost their lives in service.

Their high number of casualties revealed the country's largely forgotten place in the sport's history. 'We were certainly surprised, but perhaps we shouldn't have been,' they said. 'Germany was quite a powerful rugby nation during the 1930s, defeating Italy on five occasions and recording a number of victories over France, who at that time had been expelled from the Five Nations.'

RUGBY LEAGUE:

Nov 24 – Wales 11 England 3 at St Helen's, Swansea.

By Christmas of 1945, too, the Kiwis tour of these islands was well under its exhilarating way: but first, the rest of the action up to the end of the 1945-6 season......

9
1946

The new year, then, saw plenty of rugby scheduled but, unsurprisingly in a British winter, not all of it went unpostponed. For instance, the Scotland v England match set for Murrayfield on January 5 was delayed until April 13 due to frost.

The Kiwis were luckier on that date, though, and scrum half and captain Major Charlie Saxton's team started 1946 with a trip to Wales. Only the skipper (3 caps in 1938) had been capped pre-war, though more were to become All Blacks later. Their games and players are outlined in a dedicated chapter, but the games against Wales and Scotland are shown below.

January 5 – WALES 3 KIWIS 11 (at Arms Park, Cardiff). (28,000).

The low attendance was due to the North Stand being closed as it had been damaged by that 1941 bomb. In the Welsh side, Billy Darch replaced Haydn Tanner, who was on Army duty in Austria; Jack Matthews withdrew and Les Williams moved to centre allowing Billy Williams to play on the wing, while Glyn Jones was not available on the other wing, so Graham Hale, previously a Prisoner of War, played.

Wales were thus not expected to win, yet led 3-0 from a superb penalty by Hugh Lloyd-Davies with just ten minutes remaining. Then, hero turned villain as the Welsh full-back failed to find touch and the ball went into the arms of the magnificent Kiwi right wing, Jim Sherratt, who ran some 50 yards along the touchline, passing Lloyd-Davies on the way, on the South Stand side and behind the posts at the Westgate Street end of the ground for a try that full back Bob Scott converted.

Scott followed by placing two penalty goals in the final minutes to seal the victory. Wales had defended gallantly with Lloyd-Davies and Hale outstanding and it was scoreless in a rather poor game at half-time. Five

---

minutes later came the Welsh penalty from halfway while Scott had missed twice with penalty shots.

However, Wales had been poor in attack and Charlie Saxton outplayed Darch at the base of the scrum, with Wales handling badly and only going close after a foot rush by front-row forwards 'Bunner' Travers and Bill Jones, before Billy Cleaver missed with a drop shot.

Wales – (RH) Lloyd-Davies; William E. Williams (Newport/Swinton RL), +W. Les T. Williams (Llanelli/Navy), +(BL) Williams (capt.), (GG) Hale; +(WB) Cleaver, (WJ) Darch; (WG) Jones (Newport), *+(W) Travers, (LM) Thomas, Graham B. Hughes (Neath/Swinton RL), +(WJ) Evans, L. Morlais Thomas (Neath), *+(L) Manfield, +J. Rees G. Stephens (Neath).

Pen: Lloyd-Davies.

Kiwis team in next chapter.

Try: Sherratt. Con/2 Pens: Scott.

Referee: J.B.G. Whittaker (Lancashire).

WALES

William Eric ('BILLY') WILLIAMS – Wing. Born Cwmtillery 28/3/1925. Died Broadstairs, Kent 27/12/2007, aged 82. Newport (41 games, 25 tries, 1944-45 to 1946-47)/Swinton RL. Miner/Lecturer at Loughborough College/Grammar School (1950-62). He was a Schoolteacher in Broadstairs (Maths and PE) and

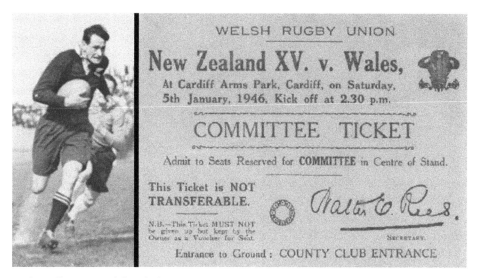

Wales v Sherratt and the Kiwis, 1946

at St Lawrence College, Ramsgate. Played for Dai Gent's XV against the NZ Services 1946. He married in Swansea in 1948 and had a daughter, who was born in Loughborough.

William LESlie Thomas WILLIAMS – Centre (later Wing). Born Mynyddygarreg 15/5/1922. Died Falmouth 27/1/2006. 7 caps (1947-49). Cardiff Training Coll./Trimsaran Boys Club/Devonport Services/Combined Services/Navy/Llanelli/Cardiff/Burry Port/Furnace Utd./Devon/Cornwall/Hunslet and Wales RL. Served in the Navy on HMS Raleigh and later was a PE teacher.

GRAHAM Bagnall HUGHES - 2nd Row. Born 14/2/1917. Died 1st quarter, 1998. Neath. British Steel worker and Fireman in Port Talbot. His brother Raymond (Aberavon) joined him later in the Wales second row.

L. MORLAIS THOMAS (Neath) Back Row. Dates of Birth/Death unknown. Neath Schools captain 1938-39. He played for Neath/Aberavon vs Australia 1947 and Neath vs the 'Kiwis' in 1945.

John REES Glyn STEPHENS – Back Row (later 2nd Row). Born Neath 16/4/1922. Died Neath 4/2/1998. Llandovery College/Wales Schools/Tonmawr/Neath/Barbarians/British Lions. 32 caps (1947-57), Lions to NZ (0 tests)/Australia (2 tests) 1950. Mine owner/Farmer and Café proprietor. Son of Glyn Stephens (10 caps, 1912-19), who became WRU President, as, in turn, did Rees.

January 19 – SCOTLAND 11 KIWIS 6 (at Murrayfield, Edinburgh). (30,000).

This was the first of only two defeats that the tourists suffered in Britain and it was the first time that a Scottish team had beaten a team from New Zealand.

The forwards held and harried with Douglas Elliot outstanding; the backs tackled firmly and skipper Keith Geddes was a rock at full back even though the Kiwis had been favourites to win.

For the tourists, Bert Cook at full back was outstanding; skipper Charlie Saxton threw out passes of great length and the pack won the scrummages, but it was to no avail.

They did however take an expected lead when Stan Woolley, a late replacement for Pat Rhind, scored a try from a forward rush, though Bert Cook failed to convert, and that was the only score of the first half.

Then, Scotland levelled at 3-3 with a try by wing Jack Anderson from a Russell Bruce opening and though Geddes missed the conversion, almost immediately Angus Black and John Orr sent Billy Munro over with Doug Smith converting for an 8-3 lead.

Douglas Elliot & Keith Geddes

The Kiwis came back with a Cook penalty, but Scotland were not finished and Anderson collected a Bruce cross-kick (that may have been a missed drop at goal!) to score his second try in the final minute of the game with Smith's failure to convert being irrelevant.

Within 24 hours of this match, Anderson had not only signed for Rugby League, but also was fully demobilized from the Army.

Scotland had originally included wing forward Gordon B.R. Oswald (Loretto/Trinity Hall College, Cambridge University), but he was unable to play and sadly, died in Poole, Dorset in 1950, aged 24.

Scotland – +Geddes (capt.); Jack ('Darcy') Anderson (London Scottish), +Munro, +Bruce, +(DWC) Smith; +Ian J.M. Lumsden (Watsonians), +Black; *+Ian C. Henderson (Edinburgh Acads./Wdrs.), +George C. Lyall (Gala), +Richie Aitken (London Scottish), +A. Gordon M. Watt (Edinburgh Acads./Wdrs.), J. Kirk (Edinburgh Acads./Wdrs.), +Orr, +David W .Deas (Heriot's FP), +W.I. Douglas Elliot (Edinburgh Acads/Wdrs).

Touch-Judge: F.J.C. Moffat.

Tries: Anderson 2, Munro. Con: Smith.

Kiwis team in next chapter.

Try: Woolley. Pen: Cook.

Referee: Cyril H. Gadney (Leicester).

Scotland v the NZ Kiwis, 1946

SCOTLAND

John ('Jock', 'Darcy', 'Jack') ANDERSON – Wing. Born c. 1920. Died 2003 in Scotland. Hawick/Army/London Scottish/Huddersfield RL (128 games, 84 tries). PoW in Czechoslovakia for three years, he joined Huddersfield one day after this match and demobilised from the Army the next day.

IAN James Michael LUMSDEN – Fly Half (later Full Back). Born Bruntsfield, Edinburgh 6/4/1923. George Watson's College/Watsonians/Bath/Bury/RAF/ Birkenhead Park/Somerset/Cheshire. 7 caps (1947-49). He emigrated to Fremantle, Western Australia with his wife (Dorothy) and two sons (Michael and Stuart) in 1955. RAF/Doctor. Cricket for Scotland.

IAN Cowe HENDERSON – Prop (also hooker). Born 31/10/1918. Died 1991 Haddington. Edinburgh Academy/Edinburgh Acads./Edinburgh Wdrs/ Barbarians. 8 caps (1939-48). Farmer. His brother James McLaren Henderson – died 5/3/2009, aged 101, capped 3 times in 1933.

GEORGE C. ('Dod') LYALL – Hooker. Born Galashiels 23/5/1921. Died Galashiels 23/8/2009. Gala RFC. 5 caps (1947-48). Plumber.

RICHIE AITKEN – Prop. Born Dunbar 29/6/1914. Died North Berwick 2000 (aged 85). London Scottish/Navy/Barbarians.1 cap (1947). Navy (HMS Mercury).

Alexander GORDON Mitchell WATT – 2nd Row (later front and back rows). Born Dorset or Wiltshire 19/12/1916. Died 16/4/1982. Edinburgh Academy/ Edinburgh Acads./Edinburgh Wdrs/Army/Royal Army Medical Corps. Doctor. 6 caps (1947-48).

Wales v England, 'Victory' Series, 1946

J. KIRK – 2nd Row. Edinburgh Academy/Edinburgh Acads./Edinburgh Wanderers/Army(RAMC). Doctor.

DAVID Wallace DEAS – Back Row (later 2nd Row). Born 30/3/1919. Died Edinburgh 7/12/2001, aged 82. Heriot's College/Heriot's FP/Royal Dick Veterinary College. 2 caps (1947). Vet.

William Irving DOUGLAS ELLIOT – Back Row. Born Stow, Midlothian 18/4/1923. Died Melrose 12/3/2005. Edinburgh Academy/Edinburgh Acads./Wdrs./Barbarians. 29 caps (1947-54). Farmer, then joined an Oil Firm. He was an uncle of caps Mike and Alastair Biggar and a brother-in-law of England cap Tom Peart.

> **January 19 – WALES 13 ENGLAND 25 (at Arms Park, Cardiff). (28,000).**
>
> Three four-point dropped goals made up the 12-point difference as both sides scored three tries and converted two.
>
> For Wales, Haydn Tanner, 'Bunner' Travers and Doug Steer withdrew after selection to be replaced by Wynford Davies, Alfie Brickell and Elvet Jones. Travers had announced his retirement from all rugby. Fly half Glyn Davies was still in school and his half-back partner Wynford Davies (no relation) had only just left school to go to Cardiff University.
>
> England lost Ivor Preece (leg injury) and Harold Wheatley after selection and they were replaced by Nim Hall and Geoff Kelly. Hay was heaped onto

the pitch to prevent frost and England confounded the critics by racing into a 22-0 half-time lead with wing 'Dicky' Guest being the outstanding performer and even contributing one of the drop goals.

It was Guest who opened the scoring with a try after gathering skipper Jack Heaton's punt ahead. Heaton converted and then Nim Hall dropped a goal before Eric Bole sent Mickey Steele-Bodger over and Guest grabbed his second by latching on to Keith Scott's kick ahead. Heaton converted and Guest dropped a goal just on the interval.

Wales came back after the break with Bleddyn Williams outstanding and Les Manfield whipping up his pack. Bleddyn and co-centre Jack Matthews combined to send wing Les Williams flying in and Bill Tamplin kicked a fine conversion.

Again the centres combined and Bleddyn went over for a try with Tamplin again converting, but Hall replied with his second drop goal to make it 25-10, though Wales had the final say when Bleddyn sent Les Williams in for his second try. The wing was eventually to join Bleddyn at the Arms Park by transferring from Llanelli to Cardiff, but later turned to RL after signing on a Sunday morning in Bleddyn's Bristol flat. eaton conver

Wales – Lloyd-Davies; Hale, +(J) Matthews, +(BL) Williams, +(WLT) Williams; +Glyn Davies (Pontypridd County School/Pontypridd), Wynford Davies (Pontypridd/Cardiff University); (WG) Jones (Newport), Alfie T. Brickell (Abertillery), +Bevan, (GB) Hughes, +Stephens, +Tamplin, *+Manfield (capt.), (W. Elvet) Jones.

Touch-Judge: Ivor Jones.

Tries: (WLT) Williams 2, (BL) Williams. Cons: Tamplin 2.

England – Pateman; Harold F. Greasley (Coventry), *+Heaton (capt.), +Scott, *+Guest; +Hall, Norman J. Stock (Coventry); +Price, Gilthorpe, +Kelly, +Vaughan, Peel, +Micky R. Steele-Bodger (Cambridge University), John W. Thornton (Gloucester), Bole.

Tries: Guest 2, Steele-Bodger. Cons: Heaton 2. DG: Hall 2, Guest.

Referee: R.A. Beattie (Watsonians).

WALES

GLYN DAVIES – Fly Half. Born Cilfynydd 24/8/1927. Died Bristol 7/11/1976. Pontypridd County School/Welsh Secondary Schools/St Catharine's College, Cambridge University (Blues 1948-49-50{captain})/Cilfynydd/Cardiff/Glam. Wanderers/Pontypridd/Bristol/Army/Clifton/Newport Barbarians/Yorkshire.

Glyn Davies & Wales' 'Pontypridd Schoolboy Halves'

11 caps (1947-49). Lieut in the Royal Signals/Wine Merchant/Director of Harvey's Bristol Cream.

WYNFORD DAVIES – Scrum Half. Born Maesycoed 22/11/1926. Died 5/9/2014 Christchurch (NZ), aged 87. Pontypridd County School/Wales Secondary Schools/Pontypridd/Cardiff University/Newport. Vicar (in England, then in New Zealand).

Alfred ('ALFIE') Thomas BRICKELL – Hooker. Born Abertillery 22/8/1910. Died Abertillery 22/8/1989. Abertillery. Son (Martin, 'Alfie') and grandson (Sean, now a WRU referee) also played for Abertillery.

ENGLAND

HAROLD Frederick GREASLEY – Wing. Born 15/12/1924 Solihull. Died 2nd quarter 1979 Macclesfield. England Schools (as a scrum half)/Coventry/Warwickshire. Worked for Coventry Chain.

NORMAN J. STOCK – Scrum Half. Born Hillfields, Coventry 9/3/1918. Died Coventry August 2001 (aged 83). Coventry/Warwickshire. Draughtsman then Public House landlord in Cheylesmore.

Michael Roland ('MICKY') STEELE-BODGER – Back Row. Born Tamworth 4/9/1925. Rugby School/Cambridge Univ./Edinburgh University/Harlequins/Moseley/Co-optimists/Barbarians/Army/East Midlands. 9 caps (1947-48). Veterinary Surgeon. Barbarians' veteran supremo, 93 at the time of writing.

John William (JOHNNY) THORNTON – Back Row. Born 17/3/1917 Gloucester. Died 3rd quarter, 1992 Cheltenham, aged 75. Gloucester/England Trials. Landlord of the Marquis of Granby in Eastgate Street, Gloucester.

> ### January 26 – IRELAND 3 FRANCE 4 (at Lansdowne Road, Dublin).
>
> France shocked Ireland, particularly at forward, in the first international played in Dublin since 1939 and the first against France for 15 years. The referee's whistle was too frequent with the result that the game was slow and the French back row of Jean Matheu, Jean Prat and Guy Basquet proved the stars.
>
> Scrum half Yves Bergougnan's drop goal just before the interval proved to be the match-winner with his opposite number Des Thorpe landing a penalty for the home side late in the game.
>
> In 1947, Bergougnan was to drop a goal against England which was the last four-point drop-goal ever to be registered in a full international match. Paddy Reid came in for Ireland at short notice as the original choice, Kevin Quinn, was forced to withdraw.
>
> Ireland – *+Con J.Murphy (Lansdowne, capt.); *F.George Moran (Clontarf), +Paddy J.Reid (Garryowen), Hugh Greer (NIFC), +Kevin P.O'Flanagan (London Irish), +Jackie W.Kyle (Queen's University, Belfast), Des Thorpe (Old Belvedere); Jack Belton (Old Belvedere), +Karl D.Mullen (Old Belvedere), +Matthew R.Neely (Queen's University, Belfast), +Colm P.Callan (Lansdowne), Hugh C.Dolan (University College, Dublin), +Des McCourt (Queen's University, Belfast), *Dave B.O'Loughlin (University College, Cork), Jack J.Guiney (Clontarf).
>
> Pen: Thorpe.
>
> France - +A.J. Alvarez; +E. Pebeyre, +G. Baladie, +L. Junquas (capt.), +H. Dutrain; +M. Terreau, +Y.R. Bergougnan; +J.M. Prin-Clary, +M. Volot, +M.A.G. Massare, +R.P.V. Soro, +A. Moga, +J. Matheu, +G. Basquet, +J. Prat.
>
> DG: Bergougnan.
>
> Referee: H.G. Lathwell (London Society).

IRELAND

Cornelius Joseph ('CON') MURPHY – Full Back. Born Dublin 19/9/1914. Died Dublin 9/4/2002. CUS Leeson Street/Lansdowne/Barbarians. Accountant. 5 caps (1939-47).

Frederick GEORGE MORAN – Wing. Born 1/7/1913. Died 17/10/1979. Catholic Union School/Clontarf/Barbarians. 9 caps (1936-39). Hotelier/ Wholesale grocer.

Ireland v France, 'Victory' Series, 1946

Patrick Joseph ('PADDY') REID – Centre. Born Limerick 17/3/1924. Died Limerick 8/1/2016. CBC Limerick/Crescent College/Garryowen/Huddersfield and Halifax RL. 4 caps (1947-48). Brewery Rep. He was part of the Ireland's Grand Slam winning team of 1948.

HUGH GREER – Centre. Bangor Grammar School/North of Ireland FC.

KEVIN Patrick O'FLANAGAN – Wing. Born Dublin 10/6/1919. Died Dublin 26/5/2006. CBS Synge Street/University College Dublin/London Irish/ Leinster. 1 cap (1947). Ireland soccer cap. Brother Michael won one Rugby Cap. Doctor. Olympic Long-Jumper.

John Wilson (JACKIE) KYLE – Fly Half. Born Belfast 10/1/1926. Died: 28/11/2014 Bryansford. RBAI/North of Ireland FC/Queen's University, Belfast/Barbarians/British Lions. 46 caps (1947-58). Lions 1950 to NZ (4 tests)/Australia (2 tests). Doctor (Surgeon in Indonesia, Sumatra, Zambia).

DESmond THORPE – Scrum Half. Old Belvedere.

JACK BELTON – Prop. Old Belvedere.

KARL Daniel MULLEN – Hooker. Born Courtown Harbour, Co Wexford 26/11/1926. Died 27/4/2009. Belvedere College/RCSI/Old Belvedere/Derby/

Barbarians/British Lions. Doctor/Obstetrician. 25 caps (1947-52). Lions captain on the 1950 tour to NZ (2 tests)/Australia (1 test).

MATTHEW Robert NEELY – Prop. Born Craigs, Ballymena 24/12/1919. Died 19/10/1997, aged 77. Foyle College/Methodist College, Belfast/Queen's University, Belfast/Collegians/Navy. Doctor-Surgeon Lieut in RNVR (HMS Pembroke). 4 caps (1947).

COLM Patrick CALLAN – 2nd Row. Born Port, Co Louth 6/1/1923. Died Dublin 30/5/2010. 10 caps (1947-49). St Vincent's College, Castleknock/Lansdowne/Barbarians. Insurance Broker.

Hugh C. DOLAN – 2nd Row. Born 1921. Died 26/2/2011, aged 89, in Marley Nursing Home, Dublin, though lived in Blackrock, Dundalk. Blackrock College/Leinster/University College, Dublin (captain 1944-45). Doctor. Chief Medical Officer in Louth for 20 years. Capt and President of Dundalk Golf Club.

DESmond McCOURT – Back Row. Born Portadown 13/12/1923. RBAI/Queen's University, Belfast/North of Ireland FC/Ulster/Instonians. 1 cap (1947). University Administrator.

David Bonaventure (DAVE) O'LOUGHLIN – Back Row (also Prop/2nd Row). Born Killmallock/Limerick 13/7/1916. Died Glebeigh, County Kerry 17/7/1971. 6 caps (1938-39). Blackrock College/University College Cork/Garryowen/Dolphin. Dairy Creamery.

JACK J. GUINEY – Back Row. Born Brosna, County Kerry in 1915. Clontarf/Bective Rangers. In the 1940s he controversially turned his back on the British flag at the singing of the anthem at Ravenhill, Belfast.

FRANCE

ANDRE J.ALVAREZ – Full back (later Fly Half). Born Bayonne 26/5/1923. Died 27/8/2005. Bayonne/Tyrosse/Racing Club de France/Perpignan/Agen. 21 caps (1945-51).

February 2 – WALES 6 SCOTLAND 25 (at St Helen's, Swansea). (30,000).

Entrance fees were raised, but still some 30,000 were present to see Wales thrashed by a splendid Scottish side that played a fast, open game despite the large amount of rain that had fallen in the morning.

It took Scotland just nine minutes to score the first of their six tries with Charlie Drummond, Angus Black and Douglas Elliot always to the fore.

They had run in four of the tries by the interval for a 16-0 lead, though Wales replied with two second-half tries – the first being an interception by teenage fly half Glyn Davies.

Full back Frank Trott played in place of Hugh Lloyd-Davies, who was ill, while reports varied of the Scottish try-scorers.

Scotland gave Wales a huge beating in the forwards and Russell Bruce was outstanding in the centre with Elliot at open-side wing forward being a massive force for the 'Men in Blue'.

Wing Doug Smith was to be manager of the 1971 Lions in New Zealand and John Orr was knighted in 1979 after being the Chief Constable of several police forces.

Wales – +Trott; (WE) Williams, +(J) Matthews (capt.), +(BL) Williams, +(WLT) Williams; +(GR) Davies, (W) Davies; Frank E. Morris (Pill Harriers/Newport), +(DM) James, +Bevan, (Graham) Hughes, H.Raymond Hughes (Aberavon), +Stephens, *+Manfield, Douglas H. Steer (Abercarn/Taunton).

Touch-Judge: Ivor Jones (Gorseinon).

Tries: (GR) Davies, Bevan.

Scotland – +Geddes (capt.); +Charlie W. Drummond (Melrose), +Munro, +Bruce, +(DWC) Smith; +Lumsden, +Black; +(IC) Henderson, +Lyall, +Aitken, Kirk, +Watt, +Orr, +Deas, +Elliot.

Touch-Judge: F.J.C.Moffat.

Tries: Black 2, Bruce, Drummond, Orr, Elliot. 2 Cons/2 Pens: Geddes. NB: Reports differed and some gave Drummond 2, Elliot 2, Black and Bruce as the try-scorers.

Referee: *Harold Lindsey Vernon Day (England). He won four caps (1920-26) and played for Leicester and Mother Country (1919).

SCOTLAND

Charles William (CHARLIE) DRUMMOND – Wing. Born St Boswell's 26/5/1923. Died Black Isle 9/6/1985. Gala Academy/Melrose/Barbarians/Army. Banker. SRU President 1974-75. 11 caps (1947-50). He served in the King's Own Scottish Borderers.

WALES (who wore letters)

FRANK E.C. MORRIS – Prop. Born 31/12/1914 Newport, died 2nd quarter, 1991 Newport, at 76. Pill Harriers/Newport/Army. Lived at 276 Corporation Road, Newport and was a Sereant in the Army.

Wales v Scotland, 'Victory' Series, 1946

Henry RAYMOND HUGHES – 2nd Row. Born 1920. Died c.1998-99. Aberavon/Pontypridd. He was the brother of fellow 2nd Rower, Graham Hughes. Police officer in Pontypridd. Lived in Hopkinstown.

DOUGLAS Haig (or Hale) STEER – Back Row. Born Newport 19/2/1918. Died Taunton 1st quarter, 1999. Abercarn/Newport/Taunton/Somerset Police/ Somerset County. Played for Dai Gent's XV v NZ Services 1946. A Police Officer, he lived at 48 Greenway Avenue, Taunton in 1939 and in 1941 married Miss Mabel Ling, who died on 23/4/2012 (aged 91) at the Orchard Portman Nursing Home in Taunton.

February 9 – IRELAND 6 ENGLAND 14 (at Lansdowne Rd, Dublin).

The first time England had played in Dublin for seven years saw them win after weathering an early Irish storm.

Late changes saw England's Johnny Thornton (influenza) and the Ireland trio of Des McCourt, Hugh Greer and Kevin O'Flanagan all withdrew – the latter after his plane from England was held up in bad weather. Gerry Quinn and pre-war cap George Moran came into the Ireland backs and Donal Hingerty into the back row.

Joe Mycock was outstanding despite having being a late call-up to replace Thornton and being off the field early on after receiving a kick. For Ireland, Jackie Kyle was limping early in the first half and finished on the wing.

Brendan Quinn hacked on three times for a home try, but England hit back with tries by 'Dickie' Guest and Harold Greasley before the interval, the former converted by Jack Heaton.

Moran pulled back a try, but Heaton kicked a penalty and Mycock added a further try to secure the win.

Ireland – *+(CJ) Murphy (capt.); *Moran, Gerry T. Quinn (Old Belvedere), +Kevin J. Quinn (Old Belvedere), +Brendan T. Quinn (Old Belvedere); +Kyle, Thorpe; Belton, +(KD) Mullen, +Neely, +Callan, +Ernest Keeffe (Sunday's Well), +Donal J. Hingerty (Lansdowne), *O'Loughlin, Guiney.

Tries: (BT) Quinn, Moran.

England – Pateman; Greasley, *+Heaton (capt.), +Scott, *+Guest; +Hall, Stock; +Price, Gilthorpe, +Kelly, +Vaughan, Peel, +Steele-Bodger, +Mycock, Bole.

Tries: Guest, Greasley, Mycock. Con/Pen: Heaton.

Referee: J.R. Beattie (Watsonians).

IRELAND

Gerard (GERRY) Thomas QUINN – Centre. Born Gort, Co Galway 10/9/1917. Died 20/11/1968, Dublin (while playing tennis with Karl Mullen), aged 51. Belvedere College/University College, Dublin/Old Belvedere/Leinster. He was the brother of Kevin and the third of four brothers to play cricket for Ireland.

KEVIN Joseph QUINN – Centre. Born Gort, Co Galway 14/3/1923. Died Dublin 1/5/2002. Belvedere College/Old Belvedere/London Irish/Leinster.

Ireland v England, 'Victory' Series, 1946

7 caps for Ireland at Cricket. 5 caps (1947-53). A Doctor and the brother of Gerry.

BRENDAN Thomas QUINN – Wing. Born Dublin 1/8/1919. Died 11/3/2007. 1 cap (1947). Belvedere College/Old Belvedere/Leinster. Worked in Local Government. Seemingly no relation of Gerry and Kevin.

ERNEST KEEFFE – 2nd Row. Born Cork 16/3/1919. Died Cork 30/11/1991. St Nicholas College, Cork/Sunday's Well/Barbarians. Six caps(1947-48). Farmer/Fabricating engineer. Lived in Blackheath.

DONAL Joseph HINGERTY – Back Row. Born Dublin 11/1/1920. Died 12/12/2007. O'Connell CB School/University College, Dublin/Lansdowne. 4 caps (1947). Professor of clinical biochemistry at University College, Dublin.

February 23 – ENGLAND 0 WALES 3 (at Twickenham). (40,000).

A try by Wales scrum half Haydn Tanner decided an uneventful match.

England lost Harry Pateman (knee) and skipper Jack Heaton (ankle) after selection with Harold Uren and Stephen Peel coming in, while Jack Matthews (ankle) and Les Williams withdrew from the Wales team and 'Jack' Davies and Billy Williams replaced them.

Tanner had this time been released from service in Europe and there were many Welsh followers in the crowd who saw him race away from a scrum in the second half and make and take the only score, after getting a return pass from wing forward Bob Evans.

Harold Greasley had halted Evans, but there was no stopping the wily Tanner, who had made his full international debut eleven years earlier. So well did Evans and his fellow wing forward Hubert Jones spoil England's play, that there were cries for changes in the laws of the sport.

Bleddyn Williams and Les Manfield were the only Wales players to appear in every Victory game.

England – Lieut. Harold J.M. Uren (Waterloo/Navy); Greasley, Stephen Peel (Navy/ United Services), +Scott, *+(RH) Guest; +Hall, Stock; +Price, Dunkley, +Kelly, +Mycock, (HR) Peel, +Steele-Bodger, +Vaughan (capt.), Bole.

England v Wales, 'Victory' Series, 1946

Wales – +Trott; (WE) Williams, +(BL) Williams, Eifion A. ('Jack') Davies (Salford RL), (DG) Jones; +Cleaver, *+Tanner (capt.); +(WJ) Evans, +(DM) James, +Cliff Davies (Cardiff), +Stephens, David J.Davies (Swansea), Hubert E. Jones (Cardiff/Navy), *+Manfield, +(RT) Evans.

Try: Tanner.

Referee: R.A. Beattie (Watsonians).

ENGLAND

HAROLD John Morrison ('Boy') UREN – Full back. Born Wirral 9/3/1912. Died Birkenhead February 1993. Navy/Waterloo/GB tour of Argentine 1936.

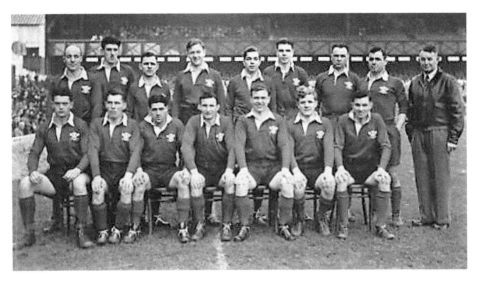

Wales XV v England at Twickenham, 1946

Sub-Lieut 1941, then Temporary Lieut 1942. His brother Richard won 4 England caps (1948-50).

STEPHEN PEEL – Centre (also a full back). Born 25/2/1921 Tynemouth. Died 5/3/2005 South-East Hampshire. Studied medicine at Durham University (M.B., B.S. 1942). Medicals/United Services/Portsmouth/Combined Services/Navy/Hampshire/Northumberland/England Trials. Navy (Surgeon-Lieut. on HMS Tormentor)/Doctor. He lived in Southsea after the war.

WALES

Eifion A. ('JACK') DAVIES – Centre. Penclawdd/London Welsh/Harlequins/Middlesex/Salford (241 apps, 49 tries, 469 goals, 1,085 points), Wales RL (2 caps).

Clifton (CLIFF) DAVIES – Prop. Born Kenfig Hill 12/12/1919. Died Bridgend 28/1/1967. Kenfig Hill Junior & Senior Schools/Kenfig Hill/Steel Company of Wales/Bridgend/Cardiff/Barbarians/British Lions. 16 caps (1947-51) Lions to NZ (1 test)/Australia 1950. Collier/Steelworker.

DAVID John DAVIES – 2nd Row. Swansea (captain 1946-47). Father of Thomas MERVYN Davies (Wales, 36 caps 1969-76; British Lions 1971 to Australia/NZ (4 tests) and to South Africa 1974 (4 tests)).

HUBERT Edward JONES – Back Row. Born Pontypridd 10/3/1924. Died Bangor 15/9/1980, aged 56. Pontypridd Grammar School/University College, Cardiff/Cardiff RFC/Navy. Doctor/Senior Radiologist at Caernarfon and

Jack Davies has fed Wales fly half Billy Cleaver

Anglesey General Hospital in Bangor. He worked at the Welsh National School of Medicine, then at Llandough, Sully and Royal Gwent (Newport) hospitals before joining the Navy, being five years as a Surg-Lieut. and served in the Korean War. He was awarded the Queen's Silver Jubilee Medal in 1977.

> **February 23 – SCOTLAND 9 IRELAND 0 (at Murrayfield, Edinburgh).**
>
> The fast Irish pack tried hard to turn this game, but Scotland, despite facing a fierce gale in the first half, defended splendidly and did not concede a point.
>
> The only try was scored after nine minutes of the first half when the superb wing forward Douglas Elliot kicked ahead and ran 60 yards before linking with scrum half Angus Black, fly half Ian Lumsden and centre 'Billy' Munro, with the latter crossing for captain Keith Geddes to convert.
>
> Ireland, with Austin Carry having played in place of the injured fly half Jackie Kyle, and Terry Coveney replacing Harry Greer at centre, attacked

hard but could not score and they lost scrum half Ernie Strathdee with a bleeding nose for several minutes of the second half.

Both Irish wings were tackled into the corner flags, while Carry kicked too much and home full back Geddes hit the Irish crossbar with a huge penalty from 50 yards. Then, after 62 minutes, a Scottish heel at a scrum enabled Black to feed his partner, Lumsden, who dropped a neat goal.

The closest Ireland came to scoring was just on time when wing George Moran missed with a drop shot. Scotland made one change from the selected side with 'Jock' McClure replacing Gordon Watt in the second row.

Scotland – +Geddes (capt.); +Drummond, +Munro, +Bruce, +(DWC) Smith; +Lumsden, +Black; +(IC) Henderson, +Lyall, +Aitken, Kirk, McClure, +Orr, +Deas, +Elliot.

Touch-Judge: R.M. Meldrum.

Try: Munro. Con: Geddes. DG: Lumsden.

Ireland – *+(CJ) Murphy (capt.); *Moran, Terry A. Coveney (St Mary's College, Dublin), +(KJ) Quinn, +(BT) Quinn; E. Austin Carry (Old Wesley), +Ernie Strathdee (Queen's University, Belfast); +Jimmy C. Corcoran (University College, Cork), +(KD) Mullen, +Neely, +Callan, +Keeffe, +Hingerty, H.G.G. Dudgeon (Collegains), +McCourt.

Touch-Judge: R.W.Jeffares.

Referee: Trevor Jones (Llangynwyd).

IRELAND

Terence (TERRY) A. COVENEY – Centre. St Mary's College, Dublin/Leinster.

Reverend Canon E. AUSTIN CARRY – Fly Half. Born Dublin 24/8/1918. Died Enniskerry, County Wicklow 13/3/2009. Wesley College School/JCT/Trinity College, Dublin/Old Wesley/Old Belvedere. Rector of St Saviour's, Arklow and Holy Trinity, Killiney

Ernest (ERNIE) STRATHDEE – Scrum Half. Born Belfast 26/5/1921. Died Belfast 17/7/1971 (in a hotel fire). Belfast High School/Queen's University, Belfast/Barbarians. 9 caps (1947-49). Presbyterian minister/TV Sports journalist.

James Crothmans (JIMMY) CORCORAN – Prop. Born Cork 14/7/1922. Died Lincoln 5/8/2002, aged 80. President, Brothers College, Cork/University College, Cork/Sunday's Well/London Irish/Munster. 2 caps (1947-48). Doctor in Lincoln, England.

HUGH Gordon G. DUDGEON – Back Row. Collegians/Ulster.

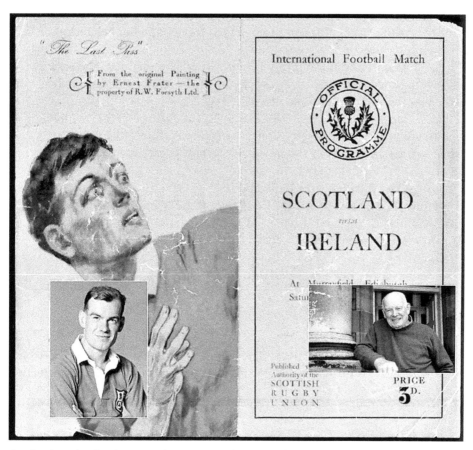

Scotland v Ireland, 'Victory' Series, 1946, with Angus Black (insets)

March 9 – WALES 6 IRELAND 4 (at Arms Park, Cardiff). (32,000).

Ireland certainly shocked Wales to lead by a drop goal from fly half Austin Carry and then, when losing 6-4, he almost put over a similar score to snatch victory, but the attempt sailed just wide.

Winger Billy Williams had raced in at the corner for a grand try by pushing off full back Con Murphy's attempted tackle and then Billy Cleaver sent Bleddyn Williams clear for what proved the winning score, though hooker Maldwyn James failed to convert them.

Three players named Quinn were in the Ireland three-quarters and they were opposed by three named Williams, with the latter trio being unrelated, while Wales also had three named Davies and hooker Jack Bale playing out of place in the second row.

Ireland were without the injured Hugh Greer, Des McCourt and Jackie Kyle, while Rees Stephens' being kept out of the Wales side on medical advice was the reason that Bale was called up.

Wales – Lloyd-Davies; (WE) Williams, +(BL) Williams, +(WLT) Williams (now Devonport Services), (DG) Jones; +Cleaver, *+Tanner (capt.); +(WJ) Evans, +(DM) James, +(C) Davies, Jack H. Bale (Newport), (DJ) Davies, (HE) Jones, *+Manfield, +(RT) Evans.

Tries: (WE) Williams, (BL) Williams.

Ireland – *+(CJ) Murphy (capt.); +(PJ) Reid, (GT) Quinn, +(KJ) Quinn, +(BT) Quinn; Carry, +Strathdee; +Corcoran, +(KD) Mullen, +Neely, +Callan, +Keeffe, +Hingerty, Dudgeon, R.E. Coolican (Dublin University).

DG: Carry.

Referee: Alan S. Bean (Sunderland).

WALES

John Henry (JACK) BALE – 2nd Row (later hooker). Born Newport 5/12/1916. Died Newport 17/10/1985, aged 68. Pill Harriers/Gwent Police/Newport

Tamplin kicks, Wales v Ireland, 'Victory' Series, 1946

(captain 1946-47, 126 games from 1939-40 until 1945-46 and again in 1949, but never scored a try). Police Officer (pre and post-war)/Army (Commandos). He was a PoW in North Africa during WW2 where 'Rommel saved his life' (Jack's own words) by disobeying Hitler's orders. Escaped three times from his Italian guards, being recaptured twice, but he eventually reached Switzerland, then returning to GB. After the war he returned to work in the Police and lived in a flat over a Police Station in Maindee, close to Newport's Rodney Parade. He married a Miss Elsie Bale (no relation before marriage) and was a detective-sergeant and later a coroner's officer, retiring and becoming an employee of Tovey Bros Funeral Directors. His brother, Alf, also played for Newport pre-war.

IRELAND

R.E.COOLICAN – Back Row. Dublin University.

March 16 – ENGLAND 12 SCOTLAND 8 (at Twickenham). (50,000).

Scotland started as favourites and led 8-0, but England caught them back at 8-8 and 10 minutes from time, the large crowd saw centre Keith Scott drop a winning goal. It was cold and the ball seemed to be over-inflated.

Once again, open-side wing forward Douglas Elliot was outstanding as first Russell Bruce sent 'Donny' Innes over and then Bruce caught Elliot's kick for a try that this time was converted by Keith Geddes.

In the second half England responded with a long penalty by Jack Heaton and then Scott and Heaton combined to send pre-war international wing Bobby Carr across with Heaton goaling from the touchline.

Scotland had to bring Ken Wilson to scrum half as Angus Black had examinations, while England lost Dickie Guest, who was refused leave from BAOR, so Harold Greasley played. Bill Moore was fourth choice at scrum half as Jack Ellis had to withdraw with a knee injury and both Nigel Stock and John Newton-Thompson were injured.

England – (HJM) Uren; Greasley, *+Heaton (capt.), +Scott, *Robert S.L. Carr (Manchester); +Hall, +William K.T. Moore (Leicester/Devonport Services); +Price, Fred C.H. Hill (Bristol), +Kelly, +Mycock, (HR) Peel, Thornton, +Vaughan, Bole.

Touch-Judge: Capt J.A.Haigh-Smith.

Try: Carr. Con/Pen: Heaton. DG: Scott.

Scotland – +Geddes (capt.); +Drummond, +Munro, +Bruce, *+Innes; +Lumsden, Capt Ken H.S.Wilson (Army); +(IC) Henderson, +Lyall, +Aitken, Kirk, +Watt, +Orr, +Deas, +Elliot.
Touch-Judge: R.K. Cuthbertson.
Tries: Innes, Bruce. Con: Geddes.
Referee: Ivor David (Neath).

ENGLAND

Robert Stanley Leonard (BOBBY) CARR, MC – Wing. Born Backlow, Timperley, Cheshire 11/7/1917. Died Macclesfield 3rd quarter 1979, aged 62. Cranleigh School/South Public Schools/England Public Schools (captain)/Rosslyn Park Public Schools/Old Cranleighans/Manchester/Moseley. 3 caps (1939). Company Director. Lieut. in the Manchester Regt. and was awarded the Military Cross when on attachment to the King's African Rifles in East Africa in 1943. Played hockey for Cranleigh and was outstanding as a school athlete.

William Kenneth Thomas (BILL) MOORE – Scrum Half. Born Leicester. 24/2/1921. Died Leicester 22/8/2002. Wyggeston School/Old Wyggestonians/Leicester/Devonport Services/Barbarians/Navy/Cornwall/Leicestershire. Shoe company sales manager. Navy in WW2 (HMS Defiance). 7 caps (1947-50).

FREDerick C.H. HILL – Hooker. Born 17/1/1917. Died 3/11/1997. Bricklayer. Army/Bristol. Played rugby despite having an artificial eye.

SCOTLAND

KENneth Horace Stephen WILSON – Scrum Half. Born in Calcutta, Bengal, India 7/7/1914, when his father was an engineer. George Watson's School (1930-31)/Watsonians/Manchester (1934)/Army/London Scottish/Barbarians/Kent/Combined Services. Captain, then Major, Lieut-Col. (1957) and finally Colonel (1961) in the Royal Sussex Regt.

England v Scotland, 'Victory' Series, 1946

Skippered Army and Combined Services. Good cricketer for Watsonians and in India before the war. He had worked in 1939 for a Lubriciating Oils firm in St. Pancras, London and was posted to Hong Kong after the war.

March 16 – FRANCE 9 KIWIS 14 (at Stade Colombes, Paris).

This was not strictly a 'Victory' match, and France, again awarding full caps, gave the tourists a terrific match, impressing the 'Kiwis' in the process. It was played on a Sunday, when heavy snow had been cleared. It was the tour's 28th match, in which the big wing, Jim ('Le Beau Cheval' – 'the Magnificent Horse') Sherratt, was given a huge ovation by the French supporters.

Sherratt opened the scoring and Bob Scott converted, but clever French passing saw left wing Elie Pebeyre score a try though Jean Prat failed to convert. Another tremendous try by Sherratt followed, but first Georges Baladie and then Pebeyre again scored treies to put France ahead at 9-8.

However, France lost their big second row forward Robert Soro with a broken arm early in the second half. The 'Kiwis' finished strongly, forward Alan Blake scored a try and Scott added a penalty to seal the win.

France - +Alvarez; +Baladie, +Michel Sorrondo (Montauban), +Junquas, +Pebeyre; +Terreau, +Bergougnan; +Prin-Clary, +Volot, +Buzy, +Soro, +Moga, +Matheu, +Basquet, +Prat.

Tries: Pebeyre 2, Baladie.

Kiwis – (team in next chapter).

Tries: Sherratt 2, Blake. Con/Pen: Scott.

Referee: Colonel George Warden (England).

FRANCE

MICHEL SORRONDO – Centre. Born Hendaye 16/7/1919. Died Montauban 24/7/1976. 6 caps (1946-48). Montauban Rugby Union and Rugby League sides.

March 24 – FRANCE 10 KIWIS 13 (at Stade Ernest-Wallon, Toulouse).

Again not part of the 'Victory' series, and once more France awarded full caps after surprising the 'Kiwis', who thought they were going to face a Southern France XV. This 31st tour match was played on a rock-hard pitch and the French led with a drop goal from centre Michel Sorrondo before

Kiwis on the attack against France, Colombes, 1946

France (three times) and the Kiwis (once) missed penalty shots. Then Bob Scott landed one just before the interval.

Soon after another French penalty miss, forward Guy Basquet scored a try, but the tourists replied with Neville Thornton going over and Scott converting. However, France were ahead again within two minutes as Jean Matheu crossed but the conversion failed and it was 10-8.

Then, when France interpassed just inside the Kiwis half, second-row forward Stan Young intercepted and tore down the other end to score with Scott adding the conversion. The final 25 minutes produced a lot of thrills, but no further scoring.

France - +Alvarez; +Lassegue, +Sorrondo, +Junquas, +Pebeyre; +Terreau, +Bergougnan; +Prin-Clary, +Volot, (?) Vidal, (?) Barris, +Moga, +Matheu, +Basquet, (?) Garrigue.

Tries: Basquet, Matheu. DG: Sorrondo.

Kiwis – (team in next chapter).

Stan Young, Kiwis' try scoring hero

Tries: Thornton, Young. 2 Cons/Pen: Scott.
Referee: Monsieur Barbe (France).

FRANCE

Forwards - Vidal, Barris and Garrigue were all new caps.

March 30 – SCOTLAND 13 WALES 11 (at Murrayfield, Edinburgh). (45,000).

Wales full-back Tyssul Griffiths suffered a broken rib when tackling Charlie Drummond after only three minutes and had to fully retire from the field eight minutes later. Wales brought out back-rowers Les Manfield and Hubert Jones in turn – the latter going to wing and Billy Cleaver to full back with Bleddyn Williams at fly half, but it was a severe handicap.

Jack Bale had moved back to hooker for Wales after being at second row in his previous match. It was a Jones try, converted by Cleaver, that saw Wales lead, but Manfield, who returned to the pack after being raked, lost the ball and Drummond scored with Keith Geddes converting.

Wales were to lead twice more, firstly when Billy Williams intercepted to score, but Haydn Tanner hit the post with the conversion from right in front and Geddes soon levelled at 8-8 with a penalty.

Then Tanner missed again with a conversion attempt after a Les Williams try had put Wales ahead for the third time, but when Ian Lumsden missed a drop shot, Russell Bruce followed up to score and Geddes converted to win it. A late Wales fightback just failed.

The father of Tyssul Griffiths turned on his radio to hear the broadcast of the second half of the game and could not understand why his son's name was not being mentioned. It was hours later that he found out why!

Scotland – +(KI) Geddes (capt.); +(CW) Drummond, +(WH) Munro, +(CR) Bruce, *+(JRS) Innes; +(IJM) Lumsden, +(AW) Black; +(IC) Henderson, +(GC) Lyall, (R) Aitken, +(FH) Coutts, +(AGM) Watt, +(JH) Orr, +(DW) Deas (capt), +(WID) Elliot.

Tries: Drummond, Bruce. 2 Cons/Pen: Geddes.

Wales – Tyssul Griffiths (Newport); (WE) Williams, +(J) Matthews, +(BL) Williams, +(WLT) Williams; +(WB) Cleaver, *+(H) Tanner (capt.); +(WJ) Evans, (JH) Bale, +(C) Davies, (DJ) Davies, +George W. Parsons (Abertillery/St Helen's RL), (HE) Jones, *+(L) Manfield, +(RT) Evans.

> Touch-Judge: Ivor Jones (Gorseinon).
> Tries: (HE) Jones, (WE) Williams, (WLT) Williams. Con: Cleaver.
> Referee: J.B.G. Whittaker (Lancashire).

WALES

TYSSUL ('Tal') GRIFFITHS – Full Back. Born 6/6/1919. Died 25/8/1978. Blaengarw/Newport/Monmouthshire. Hunslet, Doncaster, Halifax, Dewsbury and Wales RL.

GEORGE W. PARSONS – 2nd Row. Born Newbridge 21/4/1926. Died Llangynidr, near Crickhowell 24/11/2009. 1 cap (1947). Abertillery County School/Abertillery/Cardiff/Newport. St Helens, Rochdale, Salford, Wales RL. Army (Royal Fusiliers)/Police Officer/Glassworker. Played for a GB RL side against Australia and was player-coach at Rochdale and Salford RL.

Scotland v Wales, 'Victory' Series, 1946

April 13 – SCOTLAND 27 ENGLAND 0 (at Murrayfield, Edinburgh). (58,000).

This was the game originally due for January 5, but postponed due to bad weather. England lost Harold Uren late in the first half with Johnny Thornton going from the pack out onto the wing, Dickie Guest to centre and Keith Scott to full back. That, plus four penalties missed by Jack Heaton, gave England no chance.

Scotland led by 9-0 at half-time with Gordon Watt scoring the opening try and Keith Geddes placing a penalty before Russell Bruce crossed, though Geddes failed to convert either try.

The second half was a rout with Ian Lumsden, Watt again and Billy Munro crossing and now Geddes placed all three conversions. There was still time for a sixth try, scored by wing Bill MacLennan with no reply from England.

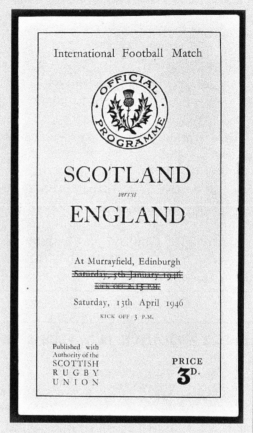

Scotland v England, 'Victory' Series, 1946

In front of a large crowd, wing forward Douglas Elliot was again outstanding with fine performances also from Geddes, MacLennan and the burly, powerful wing, Tom Jackson. At the age of 83, Russell Bruce recalled: "We were in their faces from the outset, and an audience of more than 60,000 offered us incredible support, so it was an uplifting afternoon.

We tackled as if our lives depended on it, we varied our angles of attack, and we never allowed them to develop any pattern, and we kept putting points on the board when we were in their territory. We were only in front 9-0 at half-time – I had managed to score a try after one of their lads booted the ball into my hands – but we were a confident bunch and we never relented for a second, to the stage where they were out on their feet.

It was all Scotland in the second period and there were tries for Lumsden, Gordon Watt, Billy MacLennan and Billy Munro and the last of these was an absolute beauty. He was released by Lumsden and shimmied and feinted his way past the English defence selling this lovely dummy, and touching down."

Scotland – +(KI) Geddes (capt); +(TGH) Jackson, +(WH) Munro, +(CR) Bruce, +(WD) MacLennan; +(IJM) Lumsden, +(AW) Black; +(IC) Henderson, +(GC) Lyall, (R) Aitken, +(FH) Coutts, +(AGM) Watt, +(JH) Orr, +(DW) Deas (capt), +(WID) Elliot.

Touch-Judge: R.M.Meldrum.

Tries: Watt 2, Bruce, Lumsden, Munro, MacLennan. 3 Cons/Pen: Geddes.

England – (HJM) Uren; *+(RH) Guest, *+(J) Heaton (capt.), +(EK) Scott, *(RSL) Carr; +(NM) Hall, +(WKT) Moore; +(TW) Price, (FCH) Hill, +(GA) Kelly, +(JS) Mycock, (HR) Peel, (JW) Thornton, +(DB) Vaughan, (E) Bole.

Touch-Judge: Capt H.A. Haigh-Smith.

Referee: N.H. Lambert (Ireland).There were no new players on either side.

April 22 – FRANCE 12 WALES 0 (at Stade Colombes, Paris). (25,000).

Easter Monday in Paris saw Wales fall to their fifth loss in eight matches in this final 'Victory' International. Wales were forced to make two changes. One was the injured Tyssul Griffiths at full back who was replaced by D. Glyn Davies. The other was officially never shown, but prop Cliff Davies had 'supposedly' suffered a colliery accident and could not travel.

Cliff's fellow Kenfig Hill and Cardiff prop W.G. (Bill) Jones, who was also Cliff's cousin, had no passport. So, Bill travelled on Cliff's passport and as Billy Cleaver said: "We all kept quiet and though Bill, who always wore a scrum cap, was photographed with the team, all reports stated - and still state – that Cliff played, but he had never left Wales. Well, they both had cauliflower ears!"

It was Bill's only appearance in a Wales shirt and soon after playing in the 1947 Cardiff side that beat Australia, he turned briefly to Rugby League, while Cliff carried on to Triple Crown success with Wales and a 1950 British Lions tour. France again awarded full caps and their pack, even without the injured Robert Soro, was too strong for Wales and well beat them up front and they were also surprisingly fast in support of their nippy backs.

Maurice Terreau, moved from fly half to centre, scored an opening try, though Jean Lassegue dropped the ball on the line soon afterwards. In the second half, Andre Alvarez, previously a full back, but now at fly half, dropped a goal and then Terreau scored again with wing forward Jean Prat converting.

The French Federation again awarded full caps.

France – +(LM) Rouffia (now Narbonne); +Jean Lassegue (Toulouse), +(M) Terreau (now Toulouse), +(L) Junquas (capt.), +(E) Pebeyre (now Brive); +(AJ) Alvarez (now Bayonne), +(YR) Bergougnan; +(JMG) Massare, +(M) Volot, +Eugene Buzy (Lourdes), +(J) Prin-Clary (now Cavillon), +(A) Moga, +(J) Matheu, +(G) Basquet, +(J) Prat.

Tries: Terreau 2. Con: Prat. DG: Alvarez.

Wales – David Glyn Davies (Neath); (WE) Williams, +(J) Matthews, +(BL) Williams, +(WLT) Williams; +(WB) Cleaver, *+(H) Tanner (capt.); +(WJ) Evans, (JH) Bale, W.G. (Bill) Jones (Cardiff), (DJ) Davies, +(GW) Parsons, (HE) Jones, *+(L) Manfield, +(RT) Evans.

Touch-Judge: R. Arthur Cornish.

Referee: Alan S. Bean (Sunderland).

FRANCE

JEAN LASSEGUE – Wing. Born Rieumes 15/2/1924. Toulouse/then switched to Rugby League. 9 caps (1946-49).

EUGENE BUZY – Prop. Born Benejacq 13/2/1917. Died Benejacq 19/5/2001. Lourdes. 17 caps (1946-49).

WALES

David GLYN DAVIES – Full Back. Born in 1919. Died 18/4/1981 at the Adelina Patti Hospital, Craig-y-Nos, Swansea Valley, aged 62. Cwmllynfell/ Neath/Swansea (captain 1948)/Wales Miners XV. His two brothers played for Cwmllynfell.

William Glyndwr (BILL, 'WG') JONES – Prop. Born 1924 Kenfig Hill. Died 24/3/1961 Kenfig Hill (aged 37). Kenfig Hill/Cardiff. He played in Cardiff's 1947 win over Australia, then moved to Rugby League with Hull Kingston Rovers/Hull. Cousin of Cliff Davies (Wales 16 caps 1947-51 & British Lions

France v Wales, 'Victory' Series, 1946 (Courtesy B Williams' family)

1950). NB: Bill was NOT the same player as the previous Services 'Cap', W.G. Jones of Newport.

Official NZ Services games played were:

Jan 3 – Dai R. Gent's XV 3 NZ Services 21 (at Chard).

Gent's XV was captained by F. Philip Dunkley and included hooker Rhys Davies (Somerset Police), the brother of the Wales and 1950 British Lions hooker Dai M. Davies, and fellow Welshmen (DH) Steer, (AR) Taylor and Elvet Jones in the pack, with Newport wing (WE) Williams and the Aberavon and Cheltenham full back, Stanley T.J. Walter.

Jan 5 – Bristol 0 NZ Services 23 (at the Memorial Ground, Bristol).

All Black and England cap Ian Botting scored two tries in each of his last three appearances for the NZ Services and 27 in

Swan & Carman's Services book

19 games in all. Morrie Goddard, later fully capped by NZ, scored tries in his last three games and 17 in 19 games overall. Bristol included Alun Meredith (later Wales) in the forwards.

Jan 19 – v United Services (at Portsmouth). The game was called off as the NZ Services were repatriated and returned home earlier than they had expected.

Other matches of note included:

Jan 1 – US Cognacaise 19 Cardiff 18 (at Cognac).

Jan 1 – France 10 Combined Services 0 (at Parc des Princes, Paris. Att: 15,000).

Tries: (Georges) Baladie, (J) Prat. DG: (YR) Bergougnan.

Jan 12 – Ireland Trial – Probables 18 The Rest 3 (at Cork).

Feb 16 – The Inter-Services Tournament was revived after seven years and the opener saw:

Royal Navy 6 RAF 9 (at Twickenham). (DB) Vaughan kicked two Navy penalties, but Welsh full-back (RH) Lloyd Davies gained a try and two penalties for the RAF.

Feb 28 – East Midlands 6 Barbarians 20 (at Northampton) in a revival of the Mobbs Memorial Match.

A late change in the forwards saw B.J.B. Hazell (Northampton) come in and he scored both tries for the East Midlands.

Barbarians - Lloyd-Davies; Marriott, *Hal S. Sever, (FG) Edwards, P.R. Graham (St Mary's Hospital); +(BL) Williams, *+Tanner (capt.); A.D. Bolesworth (Leicester/RAF), Gilthorpe, *+(IC) Henderson, +Mycock, (HR) Peel, +Steele-Bodger, C.H. Beamish (Leicester), Bole.

*Ken C. Fyfe (Sale) and *(HF) Wheatley had to withdraw with Francis Edwards and Arthur Denis Bolesworth coming in for the Barbarians.

Tries: Edwards 3, Gilthorpe, Mycock, Marriott. Con: Gilthorpe.

Referee: (RA) Beattie.

Mar 2 – Army 11 Navy 6 (Inter-Services Tournament, at Twickenham).

Mar 23 - Army 11 RAF 6 (at Twickenham). Army were winners of the Inter-Services Tournament.

April 19 – Penarth 6 Barbarians 27 (at the Athletic Field, Penarth).

Barbarians - *+(CJ) Murphy; P.H. Davies, *+(JRS) Innes, +W.A. (Billy) Meates (Kiwis), +Eric Boggs (Kiwis); +(I) Preece, +(AW) Black; +(GA) Kelly, *Longland, +Aitken, (HR) Peel, +Keeffe, +Steele-Bodger, (JB) Doherty, R.J.L. Hammond (Navy, captain).

Tries: Innes 3, Meates 2, Preece 2. Cons: Murphy 3.

Penarth – Try: E. Ronnie Knapp. Pen: A.C. Jones.

Their side included C. Derek Williams (Oxford University/London Welsh, later Cardiff/Wales wing forward) at centre. The referee was George Goldsworthy (Newport/Penarth).

April 20 – Cardiff 9 Barbarians 10 (at Arms Park, Cardiff).

Barbarians – Lloyd-Davies; +(TGH) Jackson, +Munro, +Meates, +Boggs; +Bruce, *+Tanner (captain); *+(IC) Henderson, Gilthorpe, +(TW) Price, +(C) Callan, +Mycock, (JW) Thornton, +(FH) Coutts, +(WID) Elliot.

Tries: Tanner, Meates. DG: Lloyd-Davies.

Cardiff – Try: (J) Matthews. Con: (DM) James. DG: (J) Matthews.

Referee: Ivor David (Neath).

April 22 – Swansea 6 Barbarians 11 (at St Helen's, Swansea).

Barbarians - +Trott; *+Innes, +Fred R. Allen (Kiwis), +John B. Smith (Kiwis), (PH) Davies; +Bruce (capt.), (KHS) Wilson; +Kelly, Gilthorpe, +Aitken, +Callan, R.D.B. Johnstone (Kiwis), Thornton, +Coutts, +Steele-Bodger.

Tries: (PH) Davies 2, Callan. Con: (JB) Smith.

Swansea – Tries: +R.L. Dobson (Kiwis), Guy Addenbrooke.

Referee: Trevor Jones (Llangynwyd, Maesteg).

Swansea included other Kiwis in Bert Cook and *Charlie Saxton (captain).

April 23 – Newport 11 Barbarians 6 (at Rodney Parade, Newport).

Barbarians – *+Murphy; +Meates, +Allen (capt), +Munro, +Jackson; +(IJM) Lumsden, +Black;

*+(IC) Henderson, *Longland, +Price, Doherty, (HR) Peel, Thornton, +Coutts, +Elliot.

Tries: Munro, Meates.

Newport – Tries: A. Hedley Rowland, Murrell Chatwin. Con/Pen: D. Ralph Morgan.

Newport included the 1938 British Lions forward A. Russell Taylor (Cross Keys/Wales) and the Wales centre (Les) Williams.

Referee: Vernon J. Parfitt (Newport).

Apr 27 – The official end of 'war-time rugby' came with the conclusion of the 1945-46 season at Twickenham, with the last 15 matches of the Middlesex Sevens. It brought the biggest-ever crowd and the highest receipts to that date, as 20,000 were present.

The NZ Kiwis entered late, so had to play in preliminary rounds a week earlier and won all three games, scoring 76-0 in total with J B Smith notching 4 tries, 11 cons, 2 pens – 40 points. They carried on in the fifth round and quarter-finals, tallying 26-0, thus gaining 102 points without reply.

Five of the eight games in the Fifth Round were played on a nearby Technical College Ground.

Fifth Round – London Welsh 8 Richmond/Blackheath 0; Nottingham 11 London Scottish 2nds 0; Harlequins 10 Old Blues 8; St Mary's Hospital 15 Sutton 0; Cardiff 8 Wasps 3; London Scottish 8 Metropolitan Police 3; Rosslyn Park 5 Middlesex Hospital 3; NZ 'Kiwis' 11 Guy's Hospital 0.

The quarter-finals saw Cardiff, Wales and 1950 British Lions prop forward Cliff Davies make a wonderful tackle to take the Welsh outfit through and St Mary's Hospital, Nottingham and the Kiwis joined them.

Quarter-finals – Nottingham 9 London Welsh 6 (after extra time); St Mary's Hospital 14 Harlequins 0; Cardiff 8 London Scottish 6; Kiwis 15 Rosslyn Park 0.

In the first semi-final, St Mary's Hospital beat Nottingham 11-0, thus scoring 40-0 in their three games.

The second semi was a thriller with prop Cliff Davies running from halfway and outpacing star Kiwi wing Jim Sherratt to score a superb Cardiff try in their 3-0 win.

The Middlesex Sevens, 1946

In the final, England fly half Nim Hall opened the scoring but Cardiff, those 1939 winners, replied with a brilliant Bleddyn Williams run and wing Dr. Glyn Jones crossed for 3-3 at half-time. However, Cardiff tired and the Hospital side, with Norman Bennett and Keith Scott rampant, scored further tries by Graham and Hall with Scott converting both.

Final – St Mary's Hospital 13 Cardiff 3.

St Mary's – P.R. Graham, +(NO) Bennett, +(Nim) Hall, +(EK) Scott; M.B. Devine, G. Robbins, W. Whittingham.

Cardiff – D. Glyn Jones, +(J) Matthews, +(BL) Williams, +Cleaver; Hubert E. Jones, +(Cliff) Davies, George Tomkins. (Cardiff lost scrum half Billy Darch in the fifth round and Cleaver switched to play there).

Referee: (CH) Gadney (Leicester).

May 1 – Cardiff Present 23 Cardiff Past 17 (at the Arms Park).

This was for the benefit of Cardiff Royal Infirmary with £1,400 being raised. Fittingly, and in more than a nod to continuity, tradition and the future, the returned PoW Wilf Wooller (Past) and the wartime medic and player Dr. Jack

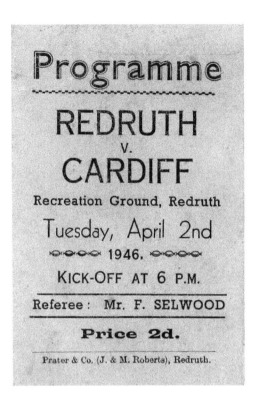

Programme
....

REDRUTH
v.
CARDIFF

Recreation Ground, Redruth

Tuesday, April 2nd

◦◦◦◦◦ 1946. ◦◦◦◦◦

KICK-OFF AT 6 P.M.

Referee : Mr. F. SELWOOD

Price 2d.

Prater & Co. (J. & M. Roberts), Redruth.

Cornish delights at the war's end

Matthews (Present) were the captains, with former Wales cap Arthur Cornish as referee.

Miscellaneous:

Cornish by name and Cornish by destination: as a month before the end of the war in Europe, something approaching normal Easter touring was back on the menu, with the visit of Cardiff to Redruth.

The Cardiff RFC team group for 1945-46 included Lieut. L.J. Callaghan, RNVR, MP. It was James (Jim) Callaghan, who much later became Chancellor of the Exchequer, Foreign Secretary and eventually Prime Minister. He was said to be 'an ex-Streatham player'.

Young Northampton wing forward DONald Frederick White of the Northants Regiment, appeared for an Army XV. He later won 14 caps for England from 1947-1953.

A splendid wing, John Lane (born 1927) made his Cross Keys debut from Pontywaun County School. He later moved to represent Newport and died in England in 2013.

'The History of Army Rugby' recorded that in a reversal of previous experience, at the end of the war two units of the Parachute Regiment played each other in Java: this time watched by a large number of Japanese Prisoners of War.

10
The 1945-46 'Kiwis' Tour

The vast majority of the original Kiwi players of 1945-6 returned to Britain some 47 years later. When asked why they had not gone back to their home country as soon as possible at the end of the war, their answer was the same as that given by their 1919 NZ Services predecessors and trailblazers – "Rugby was more important."

The firm intention that there should be a repeat of such a tour came years earlier in the war from legendary NZ commander, Surrey-born General Sir Bernard 'Tiny' Freyberg, later to become Lord Freyberg, VC, GCMCG, KCB, KBE, DSO, Governor-General of NZ 1946-52 and patron of the NZRU during his term of office in NZ.

In Cairo in 1940 he had not only stated as much, but selected then-Capt. Allan Andrews on the spot to arrange the players, the itinerary and the

Freyberg: Statue, Stamp and Cup

opposition. The NZ Division were, he said, to help both to put the game back on the map in the UK and provide a nucleus of experienced players to assist post-war rugby in New Zealand. Prophetic words indeed, though five war-ravaged years were to pass before, acted upon, they became triumphant and popular reality.

WO/1 Jack Hore (26th Infantry Battalion) selected soldiers from Egypt for trials, as did Lance Bombardier Ron T. Stewart (6th Field Artillery Regiment) and Major Victor C. Butler (21st Infantry Battalion) from Italy. Trials were held with 120 players involved. From those, 38 players were then shipped from Italy to England during the second week of September 1945 with now-Colonel Allan H. Andrews OBE as the manager, Hore as selector-coach and Charlie Saxton (the sole squad member capped prior to the war) as assistant-coach and captain.

On October 5, Stewart and Butler arrived in England with a further 23 players to play in final trials. They had come from 85 who had been in a training camp in Klagenfurt, Southern Austria.

The 61 players were then joined by three released Prisoners of War, who were already with the New Zealand Services team in Britain. Of these 64, a total of 31 were to play during the long tour of 38 matches in England, Wales, Scotland, Ireland, France, Germany and NZ that stretched from October 27, 1945 until August 3, 1946. There were 32 wins, 3 draws and 3 losses, with Points: 712-252.

The outstanding broadcaster Winston McCarthy joined the tour party while the 33 unlucky triallists **not** to make the tour (none of whom ever won full caps) were:

(From Italy) Full back – Trooper H.E. (Bert) Johns. Three-quarters – 2nd Lieut. W.B. Davis, 2nd Lieut. K. Rika, Lieut. R.L. Jones, 2nd Lieut. F.N. Rosenfeldt. Five-eighths – Trooper P.F. Furey, Cpl. A.S. Neighbours, Gnr. A.F. Bullick, WO/2 B. Kahotea, 2nd Lieut. C.C. Kjestrup. Half-back – 2nd Lieut. J.R. McCullough.

Forwards – Gnr. R.O. Bilkey, WO/2 R.J. Coupland, Sapper W.L. Gardiner, WO/1 C. Norris, Trooper H.G. Powell, Sgt.

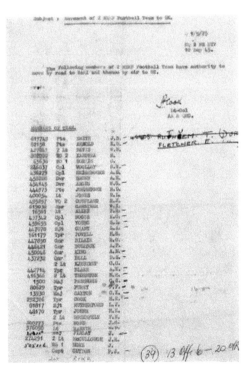

Movement Order for the Kiwis from Italy to the UK

L.J. Rutherford, Driver A.H. Brown, Pte. S.M. Gibb, Major C.S. Passmore, Lieut. K.D. Rankin.

(From Austria) Full back – Driver K.R. Sharland. Threequarters – R.F. Buckingham, Gnr. S.J. Gould, Sgt. A.I. McInnarney. Half-back – Pte. M.A. Dovell. Forwards – Pte. W.G. Butler, Gnr. C.L. Hardie, Lieut. S.J. Harvey, Cpl. B.A. McKenzie, Driver W.C. Porter, Sgt. D.R. Sapsford, Lance-Cpl. J.M. Thomson.

However, the chosen (inc. 2 replacements) were: (** denotes those NEVER capped for NZ):

(From Italy - 17)

**Trooper Herbert Errol (BERT) COOK – Full back. 19th Armoured Regt. Born Wairoa 24/12/1923. Died Leeds 19/12/1986. Hawke's Bay/7th Brigade Group/Marlborough/South Island/ Swansea. Then to RL with Leeds/Keighley/ Dewsbury/Other Nationalities. Coached Keighley/Dewsbury RL. Hotelier.

Driver Walter Garland (WALLY) ARGUS – Wing. ASC Tank Transport. Born Auckland 29/5/1921. Died 21/10/2016 Christchurch (aged 95). The oldest living All Black at the time of his death and the last of the 'Kiwis' to die. 4 tests (1946-47)

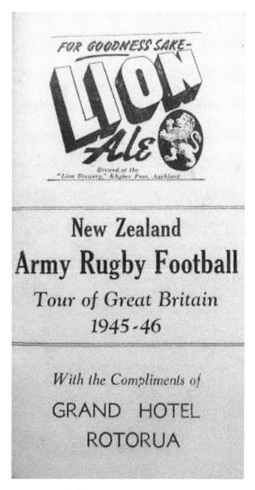

Fixture Card for the tour, issued back in NZ

plus 6 other games for the All Blacks. Pleasant Point District HS/Linwood RFC/ Canterbury/South Island. Market gardener and meat company worker.

Cpl. ERIC George BOGGS, QSM – Wing. 27th Infantry Battalion. Born Whangarei 28/3/1922. Died Auckland 16/10/2004. 2 tests (1946-49) plus 7 other games for the All Blacks. Horahora School/Papatopetoe School/Otahuhu Technical HS/Training College RFC/Auckland/Army/Ponsonby/Wellington/ North Island/Barbarians (GB). Queen's Service Medal 1980. Headmaster of Manukau Intermediate School.

Pte. John Burns (JOHNNY) SMITH – Centre. 21st Infantry Battalion. Born Kaikohe 25/9/1922. Died Auckland 3/12/1974. 4 tests (1946-49) plus 5 other matches for the All Blacks. Kaikohe Primary and District HS/Kaikohe/North Auckland/Maoris/North Island/Barbarians (GB). Previously in 1st Battalion

North Auckland Regt./12th Brigade Group/1st NZ Division. Baker. Brother of All Black Peter Smith.

Lieut. FREDerick (later SIR) Richard ('Needle') ALLEN – Five eighth. 27th Infantry Battalion. Born Oamaru 9/2/1920. Died Auckland 28/4/2012. 6 tests (1946-49) plus 15 other matches for the All Blacks. Knighted 7/6/2010. The oldest living All Black at the time of his death. Phillipstown School/Canterbury Primary Schools/Linwood/Canterbury/RNZ Air Force/Marlborough/Army/Waikato/Grammar RFC/Auckland/North Island/Barbarians (GB). Woman's dress manufacturer and New Zealand coach.

**Gunner Albert NORMAN KING – Five eighth. Anti-Tank Rgt. Born Wellington 18/10/1921. Died Wellington 28/4/1984. Centurions Club/Wellington B.

Major Charles Kesteven (CHARLIE) SAXTON – CAPTAIN. Scrum half. 19th Armoured Regt. Born Kurow 23/5/1913. Died Dunedin 4/7/2001. Cheviot and Arthur Street Primary Schools/Otago Boys HS/Pirates RFC/Otago/Timaru HSOB/South Canterbury/Southland/Army/South Island/Canterbury/Swansea/Barbarians (GB). 3 tests (1938) plus 4 other matches for the All Blacks. NZ tour manager 1967. Clothing firm traveller/Men's outfitter. Life Member NZRFU. Never played after the tour.

Pte. Keith Dawson ('Killer', 'KD') ARNOLD – Back row. 21st Infantry Battalion. Born Fielding 1/3/1920. Died Morrinsville 17/4/2006. 2 tests (1947) plus 6 other matches for the All Blacks. Cambridge School/Matamata RFC/Waikato/Hautapu RFC. Farmer.

**Gnr. DONald Stuart BELL – Prop/2nd Row. 4th Field Artillery Regt. Born Taumarunui 19/1/1922. Died Wairoa 21/7/1977. Hawke's Bay/Wairoa Athletic RFC. Worked for Wairoa Hospital Board; member of Wairoa Racing club executive and a farmer.

Trooper ALAN Walter ('Kiwi') BLAKE – Back row. 20th Armoured Regt. Born Carterton 3/11/1922. Died Masterton 31/10/2010. 1 test (1949). Wairarapa HS/Wairarapa/Carterton/Maoris/North Island/Wairarapa-Bush. Board walker, Freezing works.

Pte. Jack GARTH Parker BOND – Prop. 26th Infantry Battalion. Born Carterton 24/5/1920. Died Christchurch 29/7/1999. 1 test (1949). Hornby School/Albion RFC/Canterbury/South Island. Slaughterman in a freezing works and a racehorse owner and breeder.

Major JACK FINLAY, MC – VICE-CAPTAIN. Back Row. 25th Infantry Battalion. Born Normanby 31/1/1916. Died Fielding 30/6/2001. 1 test (1946). Christchurch Boys HS/Fielding Agricultural College/Fielding OB/Manawatu/Hutt Army/Wellington/North Island. Merchandise supervisor for Wright Stephenson Ltd.

Sgt. Lachlan Ashwell ('Goldie', LACHIE) GRANT – 2nd/Back Row. Div Cavalry Regt. Born Temuka 4/10/1923. Died Timaru 27/4/2002. 4 tests (1947-51) plus 19 other games for the All Blacks. Clandeboye School/Timaru Boys

HS/Temuka/South Canterbury/Hanan Shield Districts/South Island. Joined the team after Jack Maclean's injury. Farmer.

**Pte. RONald Desmond JOHNSTONE – 2nd Row/Prop. NZEME. Born Auckland 30/12/1922. Died Auckland 17/5/1992. Previously was a Driver in 1st Reserve Motor Transport. King Country/Auckland. His son was Bradley Ronald Johnstone (13 tests, 1976-79).

Lieut. NEVille Henry ('Nutcracker') THORNTON – No 8. 4th Brigade Headquarters. Born Otahuhu 12/12/1918. Died Auckland 12/9/1998. Otahuhu College/University RFC/Auckland/Grammar RFC/Otorohanga/King Country. 3 tests (1947-49) plus 16 other matches for the All Blacks. Principal of Papakura HS.

**Cpl. Stanley William (BILL) WOOLLEY – 2nd Row. 23rd Infantry Battalion. Born Mangawhata, Palmerston North (or Blenheim) 26/11/1919. Died Blenheim 20/11/2004. Marlborough/Moutere. Farmer. He had an appendicitis operation on the boat en route to NZ.

**Cpl. STANley Lake YOUNG, OBE – 2nd Row. 27th Infantry Battalion. Born Rawene 27/3/1923. Died Lower Hutt, Wellington 5/7/2013. Chief Traffic Officer for Nelson Transport Department. Kaikohe District HS/Northland/Wellington/North Island. He was a Weapons Instructor at Maadi Camp in Egypt, then a Sgt. in NZTS Trentham. Retired farmer (due to back injury received at Neath) and then a superintendent for the Ministry of Transport, being made an OBE for years of dedication in the latter job.

(From Austria – 11)

Driver Robert William Henry (BOB) SCOTT, MBE – Full Back. ASC Tank Transport. MBE 1945. Born Wellington 6/2/1921. Died Whanganita 16/11/2012. Oldest living All Black at the time of his death aged 91. 17 tests (1946-54) plus 35 other games for the All Blacks. Kapuni, Tangarakau and Ponsonby Schools/Ponsonby/Auckland/North Island/Petone. Ponsonby RL. Previously Motor Transport Pool/Divisional Ammunition Co in the Middle East. Warehouseman/painter/paper-hanger/men's outfitter.

Pte. William Anthony (BILLY) MEATES – Wing. Middle East Infantry. Born Greymouth 26/5/1923. Died Christchurch 1/2/2003. 7 tests (1949-50) plus 13 other matches for the All

The Kiwi Tourists' Badge

Blacks. Marist Brothers School/St Bede's College/Athletic-University RFC/ Canterbury/Teachers College RFC/University RFC/Otago/Ranfurly/South Island/Barbarians (GB). Schoolmaster and deputy principal of Aranui HS. Brother of Kevin Francis Meates (2 tests, 1952).

**Lieut. James Randall (JIM) SHERRATT – Wing. 22nd Infantry Battalion. 'Le Beau Grand Cheval'. Born Gisborne 11/5/1919. Died Katikati May 2011. Victoria University/Wellington/Grammar OB/Auckland. Farmer.

Lance-Bombardier RONald Leslie DOBSON – Five eighth. 6th Field Artillery Regt. Born Auckland 26/3/1923. Died Auckland 26/10/1994. 1 test (1949). Wellesley Street School/Ponsonby/Northcote/Auckland/Barbarians (GB)/ Swansea. House painter and textile production planner.

Trooper James Charles (JIM) KEARNEY – Centre/Five eighth. 18th Armoured Regt. Born Naseby 4/4/1920. Died Ranfurly 1/10/1998. 3 tests (1947-49) plus 19 other matches for the All Blacks. Ranfurly Public School/ St Kevin's College/Ranfurly/Otago/Brigade RFC/Canterbury/Canterbury Yeomanry Cavalry/Ashburton County/South Island. Farmer.

**Pte. Charles Tauwhanga (IKE) PROCTOR – Five eighth. 21st Infantry Battalion. Born Pawarenga 19/9/1921. Died April 2010 (aged 88). Northland RFC/12th Brigade Group/Auckland/Marist Brothers OB/Maoris. Played RL for Halifax/Leeds/Warrington. Previously a Trooper in the North Auckland Mounted Rifles.

**Pte. William Samuel ('Shorty', BILL) EDWARDS – Scrum half. NZEME. Born Devonport, Auckland 4/9/1921. Died 2005. Photo-engraver in Whitianga.

**Pte. Frank NEVille HAIGH – Hooker - Middle East Infantry. Born Silverstream 15/12/1920. Died Te Awamutu 16/11/1985. Wellington. Did not play rugby after the tour.

**Pte. Maurice Spencer ('MORRIE') INGPEN – Prop/Hooker. Middle East Infantry. Born Wanganui 15/6/1917. Died Lower Hutt, Wellington 5/6/1998. Wellington Athletic/Wellington. Joined the team on January 22, 1946 after Neville Haigh and Pat Rhind had received injuries.

**Major GEORGE Baillie NELSON, DSO – 2nd /Back Rows. 18th Armoured Regt. Born Ngaruawahia 13/8/1917. Died Auckland 31/3/2001. North Island/1st Tank Brigade/Ponsonby/Auckland. Previously Lieut. in the 1st Battalion NZATB. Worked in wholesale liquor.

Pte. John George (JOHNNY) SIMPSON – Prop. 25th Infantry Battalion. Born Roitorua 18/3/1922. Died Wellington 17/11/2010. 9 tests (1947-50) plus 21 other matches for the All Blacks. Riturua and Panmure Primary Schools/Ponsonby/Auckland/North Island. Auckland RLge. Motor Transport Pool team/Army in Egypt and Italy. Publican of Paraparaumu Hotel and a salesman. Previously a Corporal in the 7th Company, NZ Army Service Corps.

(Ex-Prisoners of War – 3) (So total eventually 31)

The Jerseys of the 1945-6 Kiwis

**Driver JACK ('Ghandi') MACLEAN – 2nd Row. NZASC. Born New Plymouth 21/12/1916. Died New Plymouth 27/3/1976. Taranaki/NZ Trials. He was in a wheelchair after the first game at Swansea and never played rugby again. Post and telegraph worker in New Plymouth.

**Capt. NEIL James McPHAIL – Prop. 20th Infantry Battalion. Born Christchurch 24/9/1913. Died Christchurch 7/11/1994. Christchurch Boys HS/Christchurch HSOB/Canterbury/NZ Trials. NZ assistant-manager to GB/France 1963-64. Retailer and worked in the family leather goods business.

Capt. PATrick Keith RHIND – Hooker/Prop. 20th Infantry Battalion. Born Lyttelton 20/6/1915. Died Christchurch 10/9/1996. 2 tests (1946). St Bede's College/Christchurch/Canterbury/Wellington/Army/South Island. Regular Army (Christchurch Area commander) then managing director of Rhind's Transport.

There were also:

Manager – ALLAN Huia ANDREWS, OBE. Regular Army (Lieut-Colonel, then Brigadier). Born New Plymouth 11/1/1912. Died Lower Hutt, Wellington 25/10/2002. Selected as a forward for NZ in 1934, but could not accept. Okato and Wharopoa Schools/New Plymouth Boys HS/University RFC/Canterbury/Hutt/Wellington/NZ Universities/NZ Trials/South Island. Was to work for an oil company.

Broadcaster – WINSTON John ('Winny') McCARTHY. Lieut., 2nd Wellington Regt. Born Wellington 10/3/1908. Died Auckland 2/1/1984. Mitcheltown, St Thomas's and Marist Brothers Schools/St Patrick's College, Wellington/

The Kiwis Touring Party, 1945-6

Palmerston North/Manawatu B/Bush Districts/Hamu/Kanini/Red Star (Masterton). Waiuta RL. Half back. Remembered for his "Listen…. It's a Goal" as well as "It's a try…. a Winning Try". A great broadcaster who thrilled all who ever heard his voice.

Selector Victor Claude Butler became Assistant Manager, while Percy James Guyton was the Kiwis masseur, James Arthur Glasson their press correspondent and Leighton McLeod Hill the official photographer.

1 - 27/10/1945 – Beat Swansea 22-6 (at St Helen's, Swansea).

Swansea – Gunner W. Gilbert A. Parkhouse; D.W. Samuel, D.J. Griffiths, Dan Griffiths, Guy Addenbrooke; Gwynne Griffiths, *+Haydn Tanner (capt.); John Phillips, *Harry Payne, Goronwy Williams, +Dai Jones, *Will Davies, Elvet Jones, D.J. Davies, +W.D. 'Dil' Johnson.

Parkhouse became a Glamorgan and England cricketer. (DJ) Davies was the father of future Wales skipper and 1971 and 1974 British Lion, Mervyn Davies.

Try: (Elvet) Jones. Pen: Parkhouse.

Kiwis – R. Scott; J. Sherratt, J.B. Smith, E. Boggs; I. Proctor, F. Allen, W.S. Edwards; N. McPhail, N. Haigh, P. Rhind, S. Woolley, J. Maclean, K.D. Arnold, J. Finlay (capt.), S. Young.

Tries: Sherratt 2, Arnold, Young, Smith. 2 Cons/Pen: Scott.

Referee: George Goldsworthy (Penarth).

2 - 30/10/1945 – Beat Llanelli 16-8 (at Stradey Park, Llanelli).

Llanelli – Fred Rees (capt.); +Peter Rees, Doug Thomas, +Les Williams, H.B. Miller; Ron Lewis, Rev John Henry T. (Jack) Evans; Elwyn Gwyther, Graham Jeffreys, +Griff Bevan, J. ('Tiny') Young, Doug Davies, +Ossie Williams, Hagen Evans, W.D. (Billy) Williams.

Gwyther, (L) Williams and (H) Evans all went to RL clubs.

Try: (Ossie) Williams. Con: (F) Rees. Pen: Bevan.

Kiwis – H.E. Cook; Boggs, J.C. Kearney, W.A. Meates; R.L. Dobson, Allen, Edwards; J. Simpson, Haigh, J. Bond, Woolley, D.S. Bell, A.W. Blake, Finlay (capt.), G.B. Nelson.

Tries: Allen, Nelson, Bond, Dobson. Cons: Cook 2.

Referee: Trevor Jones (Llangynwyd, Maesteg).

Swansea was the Kiwis' opening venue

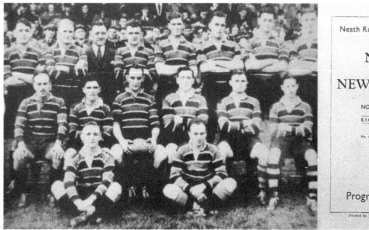

Neath v the Kiwis

3 - 3/11/1945 – Beat Neath 22-15 (at the Gnoll, Neath).

Neath – D. Glyn Davies; Roy Williams, T.D. James, John Thomas, Ken Hardwicke; Willie E. Jones, Harold Parker; Tom H. Bevan, Cliff Williams, +Les Anthony, Graham Hughes, George Hughes, Tom James (capt.), Morlais Thomas, +Rees Stephens.

Anthony went to play RL.

Tries: (TD) James, (Tom) James. Pens: (Willie) Jones 3.

Kiwis - Scott; Sherratt, Smith, W.A. Argus; Proctor, A.N. King, C.K. Saxton (capt.); Simpson, Rhind, Bond, Woolley, Young, Arnold, Finlay (capt.), N.H. Thornton.

Tries: Simpson, Sherratt, Argus, Proctor. 2 Cons/2 Pens: Scott.

Referee: George Goldsworthy (Penarth).

4 - 10/11/1945 – Beat Northern Services 14-7 (at Headingley, Leeds).

Northern Services – +Frank Trott; Albert Johnson, Gareth M. Price, Ernest Ward (all Army), Alan Edwards; Cliff Evans (capt.) (both RAF), W.J. Ellis; Emrys Evans, *J.D. Hastie, H.J. Reynolds, Doug V. Phillips, +J.B. Lees (all Army), Ike Owens (RAF), J.H. Fox, G.S. Brown (both Army).

(C) Evans, (E) Evans, Phillips, Owens, Price, Ward, Johnson and Edwards all RL.

Try/DG: (Cliff) Evans.

Kiwis – Cook; Boggs, Smith, Argus; Dobson, Allen (capt.), Edwards; McPhail, Haigh, Bond, Rhind, Bell, Simpson, Finlay (capt), Arnold.

Tries: Dobson, Boggs. Con/2 Pens: Cook.

Referee: J.B. Gordon Whittaker (Manchester).

5 - 14/11/1945 – Beat Ulster 10-9 (at Ravenhill, Belfast).

Ulster – Rev A. O'Connor; D.S. Hyndman, +Jack Monteith, Hugh Greer, +Des McKee; +Jack Kyle, +Ernie Strathdee; C. Finch, T.A. Cromey, H.G.G.

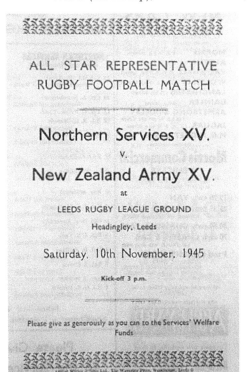

Northern Services v the Kiwis

Dudgeon, M.J. Wauchob, +Rob Agar, H. Martin, S.J. Edgar (capt.), +Des McCourt.

Try: Hyndman. Pens: Greer 2.

Kiwis – Cook; Sherratt, Kearney, Meates; Proctor, King, Edwards; McPhail, Simpson, Bell, L.A. Grant, Woolley, Blake, Finlay (capt.), Thornton.

Try: Finlay. Pen: Cook. DG: Kearney.

Referee: W. Shaw (Ulster).

6 - 17/11/1945 – Drew Leinster 10-10 (at Lansdowne Road, Dublin).

Leinster – *+Con Murphy (capt.); *F. George Moran, +Kevin Quinn, Terry Coveney, +Brendan Quinn; E.A. Carry, D. Thorpe; Jack Belton, +Karl Mullen, Hugh Dolan, K. O'Brien, +Colm Callan, J. Guiney, J. McAuliffe, E. Collican.

Tries: Coveney, Moran. DG: Carry.

Kiwis – Scott; Sherratt, Smith, Boggs; Proctor, Allen, Saxton (capt.); McPhail, Haigh, Bond, Bell, Woolley, Arnold, Finlay, Nelson.

Tries: Boggs, Arnold. Cons: Scott 2.

Referee: *Noel Hamilton ('Ham') Lambert (Leinster).

7 - 24/11/1945 – Beat ENGLAND 18-3 (at Twickenham, London).

England captain – Jack Heaton. (Team in 1945 chapter).

Pen – Heaton.

Ephemera, inc Mr de Valera, from the tour's Irish leg

England lose to the Kiwis

A 'Pirate' Programme for the England game

Kiwis – Cook; Roper, Smith, Sherratt; Proctor, Allen, Saxton (capt); Simpson, Haigh, McPhail, Woolley, Rhind, Arnold, Finlay, Blake.

Tries: Sherratt 2, Arnold. 3 Cons/Pen: Cook.

Referee: R.A. Beattie (Watsonians).

8 - 1/12/1945 – Beat British Army 25-5 (at Memorial Ground, Bristol).

British Army – +Frank Trott; Jack Anderson, Gus Risman, Ernest Ward, Albert Johnson; +Russell Bruce, K.H. Wilson (capt.); *Emrys Evans, *J.D. Hastie, W.G. Jones (Newport), Doug Phillips, *Harold Thomas, +J.B. Lees, H.M. Fenning, Elvet Jones.

(E) Evans, Phillips, Thomas, Risman, Ward, Anderson and Johnson to RL.

Try: Ward. Con: Risman.

Kiwis – Scott; Boggs, Smith, Argus; Dobson, Kearney, Edwards; McPhail (capt.), Haigh, R.D. Johnstone, Young, Woolley, Grant, Thornton, Arnold.

Tries: Argus 3, Smith, Young. Cons: Scott 5.

Referee: Ivor David (Neath).

A busy December away from home for the Kiwis

5/12/1945 - *The Kiwis played an 'extra' match. Why it was not counted on the tour nobody knows. It was played against REME (The Royal Electrical and Mechanical Engineers) at RAF Arborfield in Berkshire, with a complete Kiwis team beating the RAF station's side. The only player of note there at the time was Cardiff and Wales forward *+Les Manfield, but he was injured and did not play.*

The Kiwis won, but the score is not known, though Manfield remembered that Wally Argus scored a try. Their team was: - Scott; Argus, Kearney, Meates; Dobson, King, Edwards; Bond, Rhind (capt.), Johnstone, Young, Bell, Grant, Thornton, Nelson. The referee was the old England international H.L.V. Day.

The local side on the programme was: - Lieut. A.T.M. Addis; Sgt. E.(Joe) Starling, L/ Cpl. C. Morton, Capt. J. Woolacott; Capt. R. Ball, Sgt. T. Simms; Capt. Peter Wildman, Lt. R.J. Riorden, CMS A. Smith, Major Ian Priest, Capt. J.K.W. Slater, Major A. (Philip) Joy, Capt. N.K. Wiseman, Lieut. N. Jackson. REME won 22 of their 33 games that season but finished playing in 1950-51.

9 - 8/12/1945 – Beat Royal Air Force 11-0 (at Welford Road, Leicester).

RAF - +Keith Geddes (capt.); *G.E. Hancock, +Bleddyn Williams, +Morrie Goddard, +Ian Botting; P. Vallance, +Pat Sykes; Peter Plumpton, George Gilthorpe, *Dick Longland, R.H. Peel, H.P. (Nick) Hughes, Gordon Hudson, Cecil Beamish, John Thornton.

Flt-Sgt. Goddard and F/Officer Botting were New Zealanders with Botting (a 1949 All Black) later capped by England and Goddard (a Scotland Services cap) by New Zealand.

George Edward Hancock won three caps for England in 1939 and toured to the Argentine with GB in 1936.

'Extra' match v REME at Arborfield

Kiwis – Cook; Sherratt, Smith, Argus; Proctor, Kearney, Saxton (capt.); Johnstone, Haigh, Simpson, Rhind, Young, Arnold, Finlay, Nelson.

Tries: Argus, Finlay, Arnold. Con: Cook.

Referee: Cyril H. Gadney (Leicester).

10 - 15/12/1945 – Beat Royal Navy 6-3 (at Portsmouth).

Navy – F.T. Healy; E.A. Murray, +Les Williams, S. Peel, +W.D. MacLennan; Len Constance, +W.K.T. (Bill) Moore; J.K. Morrison, G.M. Bevan, +M.R. Neely, A.H. Dell, +John R.C. Matthews, M.A. Waller, Reginald J.L. Hammond (capt), +D. Brian Vaughan.

Try: (Les) Williams.

Constance and (L) Williams moved to RL.

Kiwis – Scott; Meates, Dobson, Boggs; Kearney, King, Edwards; McPhail, Simpson, Bond, Woolley, Bell, Blake, Finlay (capt), Young.

Pens: Scott 2.

Referee: R.A. Beattie (Watsonians).

11 - 22/12/1945 - Beat London Clubs 30-0 (at White City, London).

London Clubs – P.L.T. Lewis; Peter Graham, +E. Keith Scott, *Claud Davey, D.L. Marriott; +Nim Hall, V.J. Morris; Keith Chapman (capt.), J.H. Tyler, M. Shirley, +D. Brian Vaughan, D.J.B. Johnston, M. Hatton, +John R.C. Matthews, Victor Malempre.

Kiwis – Cook; Sherratt, Smith, Argus; Allen (capt.), Kearney, Proctor; Rhind, Haigh, Bond, Woolley, Johnstone, Arnold, Thornton, Blake.

Tries: Argus 2, Sherratt, Kearney, Thornton. 4 Cons/Pen/DG: Cook.

Referee: H.G. Lathwell (London).

For this game Welbecson Press (later Programme Publications) published British rugby's first-ever glossy magazine-type programme - a 24-page production (with a blue, black and white cover) of the sort that became standard for most of the home countries in the early 1950s.

12 - 26/12/1945 – Beat Cardiff 3-0 (at the Arms Park, Cardiff).

Cardiff – D. St John Rees; Basil V. Williams, +Bleddyn Williams, +Jack Matthews (capt.), Dr. Glyn Jones; +Billy Cleaver, Billy Darch; Gerry Blackmore, +Maldwyn James, W.G. Jones, Ray Bale, +Cliff Davies, Elvet Jones, *+Les Manfield, +Bill Tamplin.

The RAF entertain the Kiwis

Skipper Saxton: Invites, greetings & his later book

The Cardiff team that played the "Kiwis" at Cardiff Arms Park on 26th December, 1945.

Cardiff v the Kiwis

Newport v the Kiwis

(WG) Jones went to RL.

Kiwis – Scott; Sherratt, Smith, Argus; Allen, Kearney, Proctor; McPhail, Haigh, Bond, Johnstone, Woolley, Blake, Finlay (capt), Arnold.

Try: Kearney.

Referee: Trevor Jones (Llangynwyd, Maesteg).

13 - 29/12/1945 – Drew with Newport 3-3 (at Rodney Parade, Newport).

Newport – D. Ralph Morgan; W.E. Williams, Ross R. Johnson, A. Hedley Rowland, B. Roy J. Simpson; Alf R. Panting, Jim C. Hawkins (capt); Jack Bale, Tom Tamplin, Frank Morris, W.G. Jones, George Rogers, *A. Russell Taylor, Peter Davies, Wally Talbot.

(WE) Williams and (DR) Morgan went to RL.

Try: Hawkins.

Kiwis – Cook; Sherratt, Smith, Boggs; Dobson, King, Proctor; Bell, Haigh, Simpson, Johnstone, Woolley, Nelson, Finlay (capt.), Young.

Pen: Cook.

Referee: Ivor David (Neath).

14 - 5/1/1946 – Beat WALES 11-3 (at the Arms Park, Cardiff).

Wales captain – Bleddyn Williams. (Team in 1946 chapter).

Pen: Hugh Lloyd-Davies.

Lloyd-Davies, Les Thomas, William E. Williams and Les Williams switched to RL.

Kiwis - Scott; Sherratt, Smith, Argus; Proctor, Allen, Saxton (capt); McPhail, Haigh, Simpson, Young, Rhind, Blake, Finlay, Arnold.

Try: Sherratt. Con: Scott. Pens: Scott 2.
Referee: J.B. Gordon Whittaker
(Lancashire).

15 - 12/1/1946 – Beat Combined Services 31-0 (at Kingsholm, Gloucester).

Combined Sevices – Hugh Lloyd-Davies (RAF); Jack Anderson (Army), +Les Williams (Navy), +Bleddyn Williams, P.H. Davies (both RAF); Len Constance (RNVR), K.H.S. Wilson (Army, capt.); H.P. (Nick) Hughes, George Gilthorpe (both RAF), W.G. Jones (Newport,Army), +John R.C. Matthews (RNVR), Doug Phillips (Army), +D. Brian Vaughan (Navy), *+Les Manfield, John Thornton (both RAF).

Wales v the Kiwis

Wales' Hale hacks on

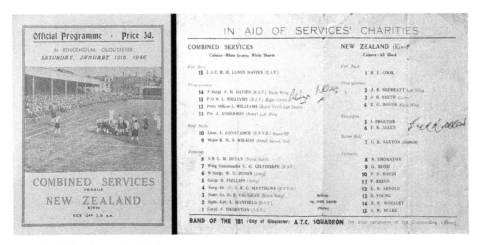

Combined Services v the Kiwis

Lloyd-Davies, (L) Williams, Constance, Anderson and Phillips all turned to RL.

Kiwis – Cook; Sherratt, Smith, Boggs; Proctor, Allen, Saxton (capt.); Bond, Haigh, Simpson, Woolley, Rhind, Blake, Thornton, Arnold.

Tries: Sherratt 2, Simpson, Proctor, Woolley, Thornton, Boggs. Cons: Cook 5.

Referee: Ivor David (Neath).

16 - 19/1/1946 – Lost to SCOTLAND 6-11 (at Murrayfield, Edinburgh).

Scotland captain – Keith Geddes. (Team in 1946 chapter).

Tries: Jack Anderson 2, Billy Munro. Con: Doug Smith.

Anderson signed to join RL the following day.

Kiwis – Cook; Sherratt, Smith, Argus; Allen, Kearney, Saxton (capt.); Simpson, Haigh, McPhail, Young, Woolley, Arnold, Finlay, Blake.

Try: Woolley. Pen: Cook.

Referee: (CH) Gadney (Leicester).

17 - 24/1/1946 – Beat Scottish Universities 57-3 (at Old Anniesland, Glasgow).

Scottish Universities – A.R. Murray; +Doug W.C. Smith, +D.D. Mackenzie, +Ranald Macdonald, G.D. Kay; +I.A. Ross, J. Stewart; F. Clark, Dr. K. Jack (capt.), A.D. Roy, A.N. Dowie, G.M. Howie, I.A. Buchanan, D.I.T. Wilson, R.D. Mills.

SCOTLAND 1946
Scotland 11 - New Zealand 6 - Murrayfield - 19th January 1946

C H Gadney (Referee)   D W C Smith   R Aitken   A G M Watt   W I D Elliot   J Kirk   J H Orr   D W Deas   I J M Lumsden

W H Munro   J Anderson   I C Henderson   K I Geddes (Captain)   C R Bruce   G Lyall   A W Black

NEW ZEALAND 1946
New Zealand 6 - Scotland 11 - Murrayfield, Edinburgh - 19th January 1946

C H Gadney (Referee)   F N Haigh   S W Woolley   S L Young   J R Sherratt   W G Argus   A W Blake   N H Thornton (Touch Judge)

J G Simpson   N J McPhail   J Finlay   C K Saxton (Captain)   F R Allen   J C Kearney   K D Arnold

H E Cook   J B Smith

Scotland lower the Kiwi colours

265

The Kiwis north of the border

Try: Smith.

Kiwis – Scott; Sherratt, Meates, Boggs; Dobson, Allen (capt.), Edwards; Bell, M.S. Ingpen, Bond, Johnstone, Woolley, Young, Thornton, Blake.

Tries: Dobson 3, Allen 2, Meates 2, Boggs 2, Ingpen, Young, Sherratt. 9 Cons/Pen: Scott.

Referee: M.A. Allen (Glasgow).

18 - 26/1/1946 – Beat a Midlands XV 24-9 (at Coundon Road, Coventry).

Midlands – Harry Pateman; Harold Greasley, +Logie Bruce Lockhart, H.D. Hollins, *R.S.L. Carr; P. Foster, Nigel J. Stock; P.J. Kilkelly, D. Salmon, +Harry Walker, R.L. Beckenham, G.F. Addison, +Micky Steele-Bodger, *Harold F. Wheatley (capt), J. Smith.

Try: Hollins. Pens: (Bruce) Lockhart 2.

Fred Allen, then & later; three tries in three days

Kiwis – Cook; Sherratt, Meates, Boggs; Dobson, Allen, Saxton (capt.); Johnstone, Ingpen, Bond, Woolley, Grant, Thornton, Finlay, Arnold.

Tries: Allen, Finlay, Sherratt, Dobson. 3 Cons/2 Pens: Cook.

Referee: Colonel George Warden (Northumberland).

19 - 31/1/1946 – Beat Leicestershire/ East Midlands 14-0 (at Welford Road, Leicester).

Leicestershire/East Midlands – Ernie Watkin; Robert O. Pell, Haydn Thomas, Francis G. Edwards, *A. Geoffrey Butler; John M. Pell, +W.K.T. (Bill) Moore; +Geoff Kelly, *Dick Longland, Denis Bolesworth,

Midlands XV v the Kiwis

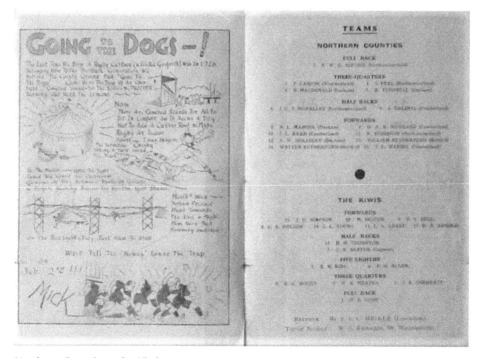

Northern Counties v the Kiwis

H.P. (Nick) Hughes, Rex Willsher, *J. Tom W. Berry (capt.), Cecil Beamish, M.M. Henderson.

Kiwis – Cook; Sherratt, Dobson, Boggs; Proctor, Kearney, Edwards; Bond, Ingpen, Rhind (capt.), Woolley, Johnstone, Grant, Thornton, Blake.

Tries: Sherratt, Rhind, Boggs. Con/Pen: Cook.

Referee: Cyril Gadney (Leicester).

20 - 2/2/1946 – Beat Northern Counties 25-8 (at the County Ground, Gosforth).

Northern Counties – B.W.G. Ritchie (capt.); K. Turnbull, S. Peel, +Ranald Macdonald, F. Casson; John G. Telford Moralee, A. Dalzell; J.L. Read, H.A.K. Rowland, N.L. Manuel, R. Robinson, T.W. Holliday, J.L. ('Pongo') Waring, William Rutherford, Walter Rutherford.

Tries: Peel, Ritchie. Con: Ritchie.

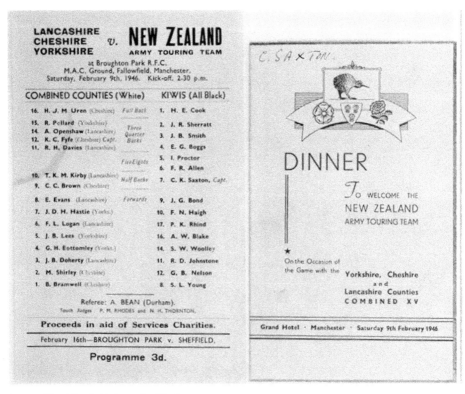

Lancs, Cheshire & Yorks v the Kiwis

Kiwis – Cook; Sherratt, Meates, Boggs; Allen, King, Saxton (capt.); Bell, Ingpen, Simpson, Grant, Young, Arnold, Thornton, Nelson.

Tries: Simpson, Thornton, Young, Meates, Boggs, Cook. 2 Cons/Pen: Cook.

Referee: *S.S.C. Meikle (Lancashire).

21 - 9/2/1946 – Beat Lancashire, Cheshire & Yorkshire 41-0 (at Fallowfield, Manchester).

Lancs/Cheshire/Yorks – H.J.M. Uren; Richard (Dick) Pollard, A. Openshaw, *Ken Fyfe (capt.), R.H. Davies; T.K.M. Kirby, C.C. Brown; F.L. Logan, *John D.H. Hastie, +Eric Evans, G.H. Bottomley, +J.B. Lees, J.B. Doherty, M. Shirley, B. Bramwell.

Kiwis – Cook; Sherratt, Smith, Boggs; Proctor, Allen, Saxton (capt.); Rhind, Haigh, Bond, Johnstone, Woolley, Blake, Young, Nelson.

Tries: Haigh 2, Saxton 2, Boggs, Allen, Sherratt, Rhind, Smith, Bond. 4 Cons/Pen: Cook.

Referee: Alan S. Bean (Durham).

22 - 14/2/1946 – Beat Oxford University 31-9 (at Iffley Road, Oxford).

Oxford Univ. – +Nigel Gibbs; +David W. Swarbrick, A.M. Stobie, J.E. Ramsden, J.K. Pearce; T.W. Cuff, +Martin Donnelly; M.P. Tahany, A. Harcourt (capt.), E.C.C. Wynter, B.W. Cole, M.W. Sutton, +C. Derek Williams, +Basil Travers, +Philip Moore.

Oxford University v the Kiwis

269

Martin Paterson ('Squib') Donnelly was an international for England rugby and New Zealand cricket. Though a centre, he played in this game as a scrum half. He was a major in the Fourth Armoured Brigade. Though born in Ngaruawahia (NZ), he died in Sydney (Australia).

Philip Brian Cecil Moore was later Lord Moore of Wolvercote, GCVO, KCB, CMG, PC. He was a prisoner of war in Germany 1942-45 having been in the RAF's 106 Sqdn Bomber Command. He became Private Secretary to Queen Elizabeth II from 1977 to 1986.

Basil Holmes ('Jika') Travers, OBE, was born and died in Sydney and was a Major in the Australian Infantry. Like Moore and Donnelly, he gained England rugby caps.

Pens: Donnelly 3.

Kiwis – Scott; Meates, Smith, Argus; Dobson, King, Edwards; Simpson, Ingpen, Bell, Johnstone, Grant, Nelson, Finlay (capt.), Thornton.

Tries: Argus 2, Meates 2, Thornton 2, Boggs. Cons: Scott 5.

Referee: Cyril Gadney (Leicester).

23 - 16/2/1946 – Beat Devon/Cornwall 11-3 (at the Recreation Ground, Torquay).

Devon/Cornwall – Frank Partridge; J. Roberts, +John M. Williams, T.E.R. Micklem, R. Gribble; Harry Oliver, +R.J.P. (Dick) Madge (capt.); W. Sanders, Les Semmens, R. Gove, +John T. George, W. Rowe, A.A. Brown, +Herbert A. Jones, William A. (Bill) Phillips.

Try: Phillips.

Kiwis – Scott; Meates, Smith, Argus; Allen, Kearney, Saxton (capt.); Bond, Haigh, McPhail, Rhind, Young, Arnold, Finlay, Blake.

Tries: Blake, Kearney, Haigh. Con: Scott.

Referee: *Edward ('Erb') Stanbury (Plymouth).

24 - 20/2/1946 – Beat Cambridge University 15-7 (at Grange Road, Cambridge).

Cambridge Univ. – Les R. Smith; J.E.C. Nicholl, +Logie Bruce Lockhart, Harold Kimberley, John F. Fairgrieve; T.K.M. Kirby, G.S. Lowden; A.V. Owen, +Alan P. Henderson, G.F.P. Mason, +John F. Bance, J. Fox, +Sam Perry, Eric Bole, +Micky Steele-Bodger (capt.).

Samuel Victor Perry, FRS, won seven England caps, 1947 and 1948, having been a PoW in both Italian and German camps after been captured while with the Royal Artillery in North Africa. He escaped and was recaptured on three

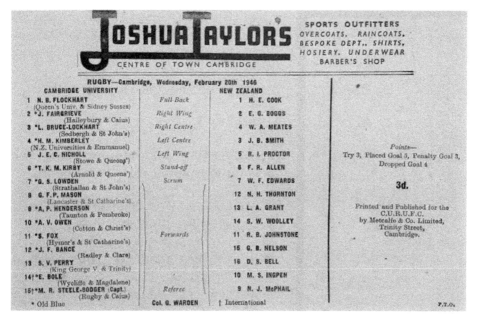

Kiwis v Cambridge University

occasions. Born in the Isle of Wight, he died in Pembrokeshire in 2009, aged 91, having been a pioneer in the field of biochemistry.

Harold Maynard Kimberley (born in 1918) was a New Zealander, who was a prisoner of war when a German ship sunk HMS Rangitane after leaving Auckland in 1940, but he returned to skipper Cambridge, lived in England and died in Nantwich, Cheshire in 2015, aged 96.

Pen: Kirby. DG: Smith.

Kiwis – Scott; Boggs, Smith (capt.), Meates; Proctor, Allen, Edwards; McPhail, Ingpen, Bell, Johnstone, Woolley, Nelson, Thornton, Grant.

Tries: Boggs, Meates. Pens: Cook 3.

Referee: Colonel George Warden (Northumberland).

25 - 23/2/1946 – Beat Gloucestershire/Somerset 11-0 (at the Memorial Ground, Bristol).

Gloucs./Somerset – Stanley T.J. Walter; Graham H. Edwards, Francis E. Edwards (capt.), Sidney F. Dangerfield, Gerry Hollis; *Ronnie Morris, D.L. Roberts; J. Hopson, Fred Hill, L.J. Griffin, +Alun Meredith, R. Morris, C.R. Murphy, D.H. Steer, *J.K. Watkins.

Glos/Somerset v the Kiwis

Kiwis – Scott; Sherratt, Smith, Argus; Dobson, Allen, Saxton (capt.); Simpson, Haigh, Bond, Young, Rhind, Blake, Finlay, Arnold.

Tries: Sherratt, Argus, Dobson. Con: Scott.

Referee: S. Skeels-Piggins (Bristol).

26-27/2/1946 – Lost to Monmouthshire 0-15 (at Pontypool Park, Pontypool).

Monmouthshire – Tyssul Griffiths; Ross Johnson, Hedley Rowland (all Newport), Ken Norman (Pontypool), W.E. Williams (Newport); Ben Southway (Ebbw Vale), Jim C. Hawkins (capt); Frank Morris (both Newport), Norman Davies (Cross Keys), +Wilf J. Evans (Pontypool), +Ernie Coleman (Newport), Ken Adams (Newbridge), Ken G. Venn (Cross Keys), +George Parsons (Abertillery), +R.T. (Bob) Evans (Newport).

Griffiths, Venn, Williams and Parsons moved to RL.

Monmouthshire down the Kiwis

Tries: Rowland 3. Con: Southway. DG: Hawkins.

Kiwis – Cook; Sherratt, Smith, Boggs; Dobson, Allen, Saxton (capt.); Simpson, Ingpen, Rhind, Johnstone, Woolley, Young, Thornton, Blake.

Referee: Vernon J. Parfitt (Newport).

27 - 2/3/1946 – Beat Aberavon 17-4 (at the Talbot Athletic Ground, Port Talbot).

Aberavon – Stanley T.J. Walter; Elwyn Bowen, Trevor Price, Joe Drew, Ivor John, Len Howard, Geoff Arnold; Dil Stanford, H. Morgan, Sedley Davies, W. Ivor Thomas, *Walter Vickery (capt.), David M. James, +Des Jones, *Allen McCarley.

DG: Howard, who went to RL.

Kiwis – Scott; Sherratt, Smith, Meates; Proctor, Kearney, Edwards; McPhail, Ingpen, Bond, Woolley, Rhind, Arnold, Finlay (capt.), Nelson.

Tries: Sherratt 2, Kearney, Nelson. Con/Pen: Scott.

Referee: Ivor David (Neath).

PORT TALBOT ATHLETIC GROUND
SATURDAY, MARCH 2nd, 1946

NEW ZEALAND
(KIWIS)
v.

ABERAVON

After the Match
Call at the

Mayfair Cafe
(MAYPHIL CAFE (Port Talbot) Ltd.

HIGH-CLASS
CONFECTIONERS
and CATERERS

31 STATION ROAD
PORT TALBOT
Telephone: Port Talbot 83.

Aberavon v the Kiwis Programme

Kiwi Jerseys & those exchanged in 'internationals'

28 - 10/3/1946 – Beat FRANCE 14-9 (at the Olympic Stadium, Stade Colombes, Paris).

France captain: Louis Junquas. (Team in 1946 chapter).

Tries: Elie Pebeyre 2, Georges Baladie. (A French report gave one of Pebeyre's tries to Maurice Terreau).

Kiwis – Scott; Sherratt, Smith, Boggs; Dobson, Allen, Saxton (capt.); Bond, Haigh, Rhind, Woolley, Young, Arnold, Finlay, Blake.

Tries: Sherratt 2, Blake. Con/Pen: Scott.

Referee: Colonel George Warden (England).

Lineout & Bob Scott kicking, Paris 1946

29 - 13/3/1946 – Beat British Army of the Rhine 12-0 (at Wuppertal Stadium, Germany).

British Army of the Rhine – Capt. G. Jenkins; Lieut. J.B. Richards, Gunner W.T. Davies, Cfn. Jimmy Stott, *+Capt. R.H. (Dickie) Guest (capt.); Lieut. T.B. Sale, Lieut. R.C. Murray; Major F.J. Leishman, Capt. Fred Goddard, Lieut-Colonel W.M. Jackson, Capt. C.G. Irwin, +Major Frank H. Coutts, Sgt. W.G. Chapman, CSM G.A. Bevan, Capt. C.H. Store.

Stott (also played in the next game) was with RL.

Kiwis – Cook; Meates, Smith, Argus; Proctor, Allen, Edwards; Simpson, Ingpen, McPhail, Johnstone, Young, Nelson, Finlay (capt.), Blake.

Tries: Meates, Allen, Smith, Young.

Referee: *Barney McCall, MC, the pre-war Wales wing.

30 - 16/3/1946 – Beat BAOR Combined Services 20-3 (at Bahrenfeld Stadium, Hamburg, Germany).

BAOR Combined Services – Capt. G. Jenkins; Lieut. J.B. Richards, Gunner W.T. Davies, Cfn. Jimmy Stott, *+Capt. Dickie Guest (capt.); Lieut. T.B. Sale, Lieut R.C. Murray; Major F.J. Leishman (all Army), Sgt. T. Gore (RAF), Lieut-Colonel W.M. Jackson, Capt C.G. Irwin, +Major Frank Coutts, Capt. Fred

Goddard, CSM G.A. Bevan, Sgt. W.G. Chapman (all Army).

Try: (WT) Davies.

Kiwis – Scott; Sherratt, Cook, Boggs; Smith, Allen, Edwards; Simpson, Haigh, Rhind, Johnstone, Woolley, Blake, Finlay (capt.), Arnold.

Tries: Sherratt, Boggs, Allen, Finlay. Con: Scott. Pens: Cook 2.

Referee: *Major Clifford W. Jones, the pre-war Wales outside half.

31 - 24/3/1946 – Beat FRANCE 13-10 (at Stade Ernest-Wallon, Toulouse).

France captain: Louis Junquas. (Team in 1946 chapter).

Tries: Guy Basquet, Jean Matheu. DG: Michel Sorrondo.

Kiwis – Scott; Sherratt, Smith, Argus; Dobson, Allen, Saxton (capt.); Bond, Haigh, Rhind, Young, Blake, Arnold, Thornton, Nelson.

Tries: Thornton, Young. 2 Cons/Pen: Scott.

Referee: Monsieur Barbe (France).

Wally Argus then returned to be married to Eileen Hogan in London with Bob Scott his best man, a compliment also

Dickie Guest plays host, and Yugoslav friends

returned. Scott was to be the oldest living All Black till his 2012 passing at 91, when Argus took over till his death at 95 in 2016.

32 - 27/3/1946 – Beat Selection Francaise 38-9 (at Sports Park, Bordeaux).

Selection Francaise - Bonnet; +Maurice Siman, +Lucien Rouffia, +Robert Geneste (capt.), +Michel Pomathios; Bacque, Lassalle; Buzy, Clave, Beheragaray, Albert Ferrasse, Moga, Deironde, Mulveau, *+Joseph Desclaux.

Buzy and Moga were brothers of French caps. Ferrasse became President of the FRF.

Pens: Beheragaray 3.

Wally Argus 1946 & with Richie McCaw 2015

Kiwis - Cook; Sherratt, Smith, Boggs; Proctor, King, Saxton (capt.); McPhail, Haigh, Simpson, Woolley, Grant, Young, Thornton, Arnold.

Tries: Sherratt 2, Smith 2, Thornton, King, Boggs, McPhail. Cons: Cook 5. DG: Thornton.

Referee: Monsieur Callede (France).

33 - 31/3/1946 - Beat L'Ile de France 24-13 (at the Olympic Stadium, Stade Colombes, Paris).

L'Ile de France – Alzate; Place, Ballouin, Ithurbide, Crouzet; Jorge, Lalie; Fonteille, +Marcel Volot, +Jean M.G. Massare, Crabos, Adami, Gascou, Phillips, Perrier (capt.).

Tries: Place, Adami. Pen: Jorge. DG: Ballouin.

Kiwis – Cook; Sherratt, Smith, Meates; Dobson, Allen, Saxton (capt.); Bell, Haigh, Rhind, Johnstone, Woolley, Blake, Grant, Young.

Tries: Sherratt 2, Woolley, Rhind, Meates. 3 Cons/Pen: Cook.

Referee: Jacques Delmas (France).

April 1 – The 'Kiwis' returned to England. Stan Young's back injury, suffered at Neath, flared up so he had treatment in St George's Hospital in London and he took up rowing on the Serpentine when it seems to assist his recovery.

May 20 – After delays, the team left Tilbury Docks bound for New Zealand on the *'Moreton Bay'*. Woolley, who had an appendicitis operation on board the ship, Kearney (hernia) and Young (injured back and damaged finger) were all ruled out from travelling yet, while Thornton, newly-married in England, was to arrive home too late for the Auckland match.

As with their post-WW1 predecessors, the much-admired team had no let up after their voyage of many weeks, but instead faced five good provinces in fifteen days in a homecoming 'welcome' internal tour. Doubtless the welcome prepared by those players (and potential rivals for All Black jerseys) who had not been on the tour, but had read or heard the very favourable UK and antipodean press coverage, was a warm one in more than one sense. No surprise maybe that, facing the determined hosts' variety of tactics, they didn't win them all.

(In New Zealand):

34 - 20/7/1946 – Drew Auckland 20-20 (at Eden Park, Auckland).

Auckland – R.G. Sorensen; +J.M. Dunn, C.M. Kingstone, D.T. Grace; R.P. McKey, D.A. Barchard, +Percy L. Tetzlaff (capt.); T.H. Pearce, A.J. ('Snow') Johnson, W.S. Edwards, +Morrie McHugh, P.B. Dignan, A.S. Taylor, +Des Christian, +Pat Crowley.

Tries: Dunn 2, Johnson, Sorensen, Grace. Con: Edwards. Pen: Sorensen.

Kiwis – Scott; Boggs, Smith, Sherratt; Allen, Proctor, Saxton (capt.); Rhind, Ingpen, Bond, Blake, Grant, Nelson, Finlay, Arnold.

Tries: Allen, Ingpen. 2 Cons/2 Pens: Scott. DG: Allen.

Referee: A.J. Lazarus (King Country).

Ephemera from the French leg of the tour

Auckland v Kiwis Programme

35 - 24/7/1946 – Beat Wairarapa/Bush 21-10 (at Solway Showgrounds, Masterton).

Wairarapa/Bush – P.B. Twentyman; A.J. Pinfold, +M. Ben Couch, J.L. Cross; O.J. Hatton, S.R. McKay, S.D. Tait; K. Matthews, B.S. Smith, Johnny T. Walker (capt.), D.H. Matheson, Doug Gunn, W.G. Thomas, P.J. Small, C.A. Hurndett.
Try: Hurndett. Pen: Walker. DG: McKay.
Kiwis – Cook; Sherratt, Meates, Argus; Dobson, Allen (capt.), Edwards; Simpson, Haigh, McPhail, Johnstone, Rhind, Nelson, Thornton, Blake.
Tries: Allen 2, Sherratt, Thornton. 3 Cons/Pen: Cook.
Referee: A.E. Ingram (Poverty Bay).

36 - 27/7/1946 – Beat Canterbury 36-11 (at Lancaster Park Oval, Christchurch).

Canterbury – P.R. Callanan; W.P. Hugh, Peter V. Kearney, R.S. Thomson; J.D. Morton, J.R. Roach, C.R.I. Monigatti; B.G. Miles (rep: P.T. Gilmour), A.P.H. Lee, S.M. O'Neill, K.N. Bain, J.H. Carroll, F.G. Hobbs, A.M. Henderson, Doug H. Herman (capt.).

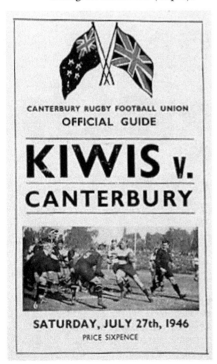

Tries: Henderson 2. Con/Pen: Morton.
Kiwis – Scott; Sherratt, Dobson, Argus; Proctor, Allen, Saxton (capt.); Bond, Haigh, McPhail, Grant, Blake, Finlay, Thornton, Arnold.
Tries: Finlay 2, Thornton, Argus, Grant, Allen, Arnold, Scott. Cons: Scott 6.
Referee: Arthur S. Fong (West Coast).

37 - 31/7/1946 – Beat Otago 19-8 (at Carisbrook Ground, Dunedin).

Otago – T.N. Kawe; A.D. Saul (rep: D.E. Collins), L.W. Deas, +Graham J.T. Moore; +Ron Elvidge, W.I. Perriam (capt.), +Jimmy S. Haig; Leo S. Connolly, A.H. Storer, T.G. Wallace (rep: C.J. Todd), W. Hay, +Charles Willocks, +John R. McNab, L.H. Aitken, A.E. Hellyer.
Haig went to RL.
Tries: Connolly, Haig. Con: Kawe.

Canterbury v Kiwis Programme

Kiwis – Scott; Boggs, Dobson, Argus; Proctor, Allen, Saxton (capt.); Rhind, Haigh, Simpson, Grant, Johnstone, Arnold, Thornton, Nelson.

Tries: Boggs 3, Johnstone, Argus. DG: Allen.

Referee: R. Ferguson (Southland).

38 - 3/8/1946 – Lost to Wellington 11-18 (at Athletic Park, Wellington).

Wellington – B.A. Wishnowsky; T.C. Svensen, D.R. Hayes, L.D.A. Abbott; M.D. Wickham, Ian A. Colquhoun, M.N. Paewai; +Ray Dalton, Richard B. Burke, +Des O'Donnell, R.E. Westerby, +Ken G. Elliott, G.R. Wales, E.L. Todd, +Roy M. White (capt.).

Tries: Elliott, Paewai. Con/2 Pens: Wishnowsky. DG: Colquhoun.

Kiwis – Scott; Boggs, Smith, Argus; Dobson (rep: Proctor), Allen, Saxton (capt.); Johnstone, Haigh, Rhind, Blake, Grant, Arnold, Thornton, Finlay.

Tries: Boggs, Arnold. Con/Pen: Scott.

Referee: J.G. Fitzpatrick (Wairarapa).

Wellington v Kiwis Programme

The Kiwis' final tally in official games: P 38; W 32; D 3; L 3. Pts For – 712; Pts Against – 252.

Leading Points Scorers: Cook 138; Scott 129. Most Tries - Sherratt 24; Boggs 15.

Most Appearances: 28 each by Sherratt, Allen and Smith; 25 by Arnold.

As noted in the previous chapter, the Kiwis had also competed in the Middlesex Sevens, the final rounds being on April 27, 1946. They beat Guy's Hospital 11-0 and Rosslyn Park 15-0, but lost 0-3 to that try by Cliff Davies of Cardiff in the semi-finals. They had won three Preliminary Round matches, scoring

Middlesex Sevens 1946

Kiwis play for the Barbarians and for Swansea!

70 points with Smith scoring 40 points from four tries, 11 conversions and two penalty goals.

Meates and Boggs played for the Barbarians against Penarth on April 19 and Cardiff on April 20. Smith and Allen played for the Barbarians against Swansea on April 22, while Dobson, Cook and Saxton (captain) all played in the Swansea team. Meates and Allen played for the Barbarians against Newport on April 23. Cook and Proctor turned to RL in England, while both Scott and broadcaster Winston McCarthy had played RL in New Zealand. Scott was to make the rugby union tour of the All Blacks to GB/France in 1953-54.

The clear objectives of the tour had been to help revive interest in rugby in the British Isles and to play bright, open football, with the winning of the game not necessarily the most important factor. The Kiwis proved hugely popular, on the park, and in the club, pub, home and press. Army, Navy, Air Force and other charities benefited by almost £40,000 as a consequence.

As well as the REME match mentioned earlier, there was it seems another, unofficial, clash: with a small west London rugby club on Sunday 12th May 1946. The intended donation of Bob Scott's Kiwis' jersey to Twickenham's World Rugby Museum by the family of one of the 1946 Osterley side prompted writer Huw Richards to delve deeper into the meeting.

It apparently followed an invitation, initiated by a contact in NZ House, for Fred Allen and Herb Cook to attend Osterley RFC's annual dinner. The club history says: "One of the highlights of the evening was the attendance of the two 'Kiwis'. Fred Allen said they would have been delighted to come along and coach us, or used our club for run-outs for their players after injury. They thoroughly enjoyed their evening and we literally had to carry them to Twickenham for next day's Middlesex Sevens.

You can imagine our surprise when, about ten days later, I received a telephone call from Fred Allen saying that, owing to a dock strike at Tilbury, their sailing for home on the SS *Moreton Bay* was delayed and could they come down and play us?"

After frantic out-of-season RFU permissions, post-hoisting and mowings, the game went ahead, previewed by the *Evening News* with 'This is why we like the Kiwis: here is a last chance to see in action the most popular of rugby visitors, players who have entertained so many rugby followers this winter. There is nothing competitive about the match. Osterley look upon it as a high honour, while the Kiwis are delighted to show their appreciation for the reception received'.

Some 2000 spectators turned up to the open field and small clubhouse for a most enjoyable game: result immaterial, score unknown. At half time some of the Kiwis switched sides and after the game Cook, Bob Scott and Co. were still on the field coaching the local players.

Both sides moved to the local "Lion and Lamb" to carry on the conviviality, and very late that night the Kiwis piled into two or three cars and were returned to their Fern Leaf Club base in Lowndes Square, Knightsbridge. A

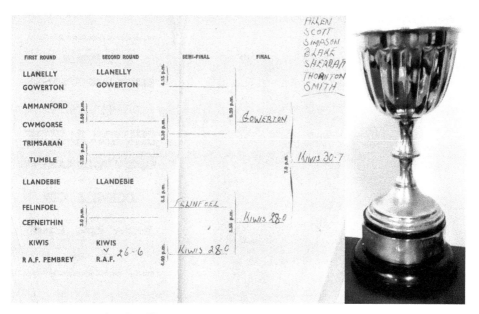

Programme & Trophy, Llanelli Sevens

couple of days later, just before they eventually sailed, the Osterley club and supporters were all invited to spend an evening there.

The teams that day were: 'Kiwis': H.E. Cook, R.W.H. Scott, E.G. Boggs, J.B. Smith, W.A. Meates, F.R. Allen, R.L. Dobson, I. Proctor, G.B. Nelson, A.W. Blake, J.G. Bond, W.S. Edwards, Hume, Urlich, Thayen, M.S. Ingpen. Three of the last four must have been 'temporary' Kiwis!

Osterley: J. Madath, W. Jones, G. Williams, E. McCormack, B. Nash, J. Nicholl, T.S. Davies, K.T. Eastman, J.M. Nicoll, R. Firman, G.L. Lewis, J. Holland, D.C. Morris, F. Yates, E. Cornwall.

Certainly this insight into the Kiwis' response to their frustrating additional sojourn before departure, and the way they were revered by those who saw and met them, would seem to add further credit to their deserved and enviable reputation.

As well as the Osterley game, while waiting to return home some of the side had an occasional outing for other local teams, including Torquay Athletic, and several took part as the Kiwis team in a Llanelli (then Llanelly)

Kiwis' Reunion, 1975

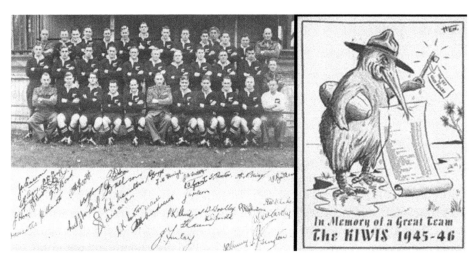

Signed Squad Picture & Admiring Cartoon, 1946

Sevens featuring RAF Pembrey and local clubs. Private Johnny Simpson was chosen on merit and in good democratic style to captain a side containing three officers, and duly raised the trophy.

The team's return from Wales was delayed, however, and arrangements for a squad photograph disrupted as full advantage was taken of the hospitality readily offered, gratefully accepted and, like the team themselves both off and on the field, most fondly remembered. The players, while enough survived, enjoyed their reunions, and observers have again come to realise the importance of their contribution and legacy.

So, with the Kiwis' departure, the curtain fell on the last acts and encore of wartime rugby - which, while inevitably disrupted, occasional, inconsistent and shot through with sadness and tragedy, importantly provided drama, skill, bravery, release, escape, entertainment, new and old friends, a sense of camaraderie and the hope of eventual normality for player and spectator alike.

Wairarapa-Bush entertained the Kiwis after their return home in 1946

AFTERWORD

The start of the 1946-47 season saw rugby return to normal – well, nearly, as France, expelled in the very early 1930s, were now back in the fold; and fully-capped international rugby for Britain returned on January 1, 1947 when France defeated Scotland by 8-3 in Paris. Teams were returning to full strength, although the memorial boards, plaques, arches and grounds being erected bore witness to those whose falling had stilled their talent and potential.

Down Under, Australia had already toured New Zealand and in the first test on September 14, 1946 New Zealand were 31-8 winners at Carisbrook, Dunedin. Several of the 'Kiwis' touring team had appeared and gained their full caps. South Africa had to wait a bit longer and it was 1949 before they entertained the touring All Blacks.

To a young boy there was the thrill of a world without war and visiting of Cardiff Arms Park, Ninian Park, Rodney Parade, etc. Down the streets I would march with a happy band of spectators –there were very few cars around in those days. In the doorways of Westgate Street on international days would be the 'pirate' programme sellers. On the Arms Park pitch the teams would run out of the North Stand, Taff End of the ground: but before that reserves, injured players, etc. would have walked behind the posts at the Taff End on their way to sit in the South Stand.

Next out was a little old man who carried a board, held high. He would march past the empty North Stand (bomb damaged,) around the Westgate Street end, past the greyhound totalisator board and down in front of the South Stand. I would scribble down the changes (from the board) and differences from the programme.

For international matches, if there was no stand ticket for me (though there usually was), my mother's uncle from North Petherton had made a little stool. "Let the lad hop over the rail," he would say to a policeman. And over I would go and sit on the track where the hare later ran – not a real hare of course! It was there at that corner flag the following season that Maurice Tonkin (Australia) vaulted over Frank Trott (Barbarians), right in front of me.

The players were all heroes to me, as was the St Alban's Band who played stirring marching tunes such as the Dambusters March. It was an era before

Some of rugby's war memorials: though the WRU's has now been changed to reflect the fact that Richard Thomas lost his life, not E.J.R. Thomas.

padding, gumshields, kicking tees, artificial pitches, referees 'miked up', etc. It was when hookers hooked and scrum halves put it in straight. Full backs stayed back and forwards dribbled with Stanley Matthews-like skill.

A collection of wartime programmes

I remember how we all stamped our feet in the grandstand to keep warm. Tries were three points, drop goals were four, you could kick the ball out on the full and the lineout would be formed where you had reached, while a mark was made by putting your heel into the ground and loudly shouting 'Mark' as you caught the ball. The wings threw the ball into the linesout; the touring teams played in numbers 1-30; injured players got up and played on – there were no replacements. How better the game seemed!

At half-time the teams stayed on the pitch, sucking oranges or lemons. The touch-judges were from clubs. The referee, despite often wearing a jacket, blazer or jumper and looking old, was almost always up with the play. In international matches the touch judges were not referees, but instead were officials of the two Unions whose teams were playing.

There were no floodlights, no TMOs, no artificial pitches, no Sunday rugby. To go to Rugby League was, rightly or not, to be ostracised. No Welsh newspaper would be likely to mention again those who left, and they were not allowed to enter a clubhouse.

Yes, the world was to change: but then, even the IRB were all ex-rugger men, not barristers and accountants. Again, how better the game seemed for all that. Sides being photographed – sometimes together – and the local papers supplying a supplement that sold out in minutes. Not any more.

Those days will never come back, of course. 2018 is a very different world from that of 1938 or 1948: but they were thrilling times of which to be a part. I hope they thrill you, the reader, as much as they did – and still do – me.

Howard Evans

SELECT BIBLIOGRAPHY AND THANKS

SELECT BIBLIOGRAPHY:

Files of *The Times* newspaper, 1939-1946
Playfair Rugby Football Annual 1948-9
Khaki-Clad Springboks: Gideon Nieman
Khaki All Blacks: A tribute to the 'Kiwis': Mike Whatman
Broadcasting with the Kiwis: Winston McCarthy
Five Seasons of (NZ) Services Rugby: A.C. Swan and A.H. Carman
The Complete Who's Who of International Rugby: Terry Godwin
The International Rugby Championship 1883-1983: Terry Godwin
The History of Army Rugby: John McLaren
The History of RAF Rugby: John Mace
Barbarian Football Club: A. ('Jock') Wemyss
Cardiff Rugby Club History and Statistics 1875-1976 'The Greatest": Danny E. Davies
The Skipper: A Biography of Wilfred Wooller: Andrew Hignell
The Red and The White: Huw Richards
A Game for Hooligans: Huw Richards
Rugger My Life: Bleddyn Williams
The Oval World: Tony Collins

THANKS:

In no particular order, for their support, practical or moral, obvious or unconscious, from collection or from memory, to our families, to Ashley Drake of St David's Press, Dai Richards of Rugby Relics, John Griffiths, Ray Ruddick, Dave Fox, Mark Hoskins, Gwyn Prescott & the family of the late Bleddyn Williams, the Friends of Newport Rugby Trust, Ron Palenski, Frederic Humbert, Phil McGowan of the World Rugby Museum, Twickenham, Stephen Berg and the NZ Rugby Museum at Palmerston North, Peter Owens (WRU), the late Gideon Nieman, Dave Dow (Swansea RFC), Tim Auty, Rob Cole and Tony Lewis, amongst others whom we may inadvertently have omitted. We are grateful!

St David's Press

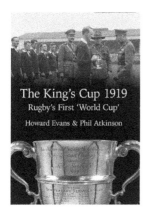

THE KING'S CUP 1919
Rugby's First World Cup

Howard Evans & Phil Atkinson

'An intriguing retelling of a significant but largely forgotten chapter of rugby union history, superbly illustrated.'   **Huw Richards**

'Howard is an authority on rugby's history and meticulous in his research'
                                        Andy Howell, *Western Mail*

After the Armistice in November 1918 – with the forces of the world's rugby-playing nations and many of their stars still stationed in Britain – and with the public desperate to see competitive rugby played again, an inter-military tournament was organised. King George V was so enthused by the proposed competition that he agreed to have the tournament named after him, and so The King's Cup was born.

The King's Cup 1919 is the first book to tell the full story of rugby's first 'World Cup' and is essential reading for all rugby enthusiasts and military historians.

        978-1-902719-44-3   192pp   £14.99   PB

THE WIZARDS
Aberavon Rugby 1876-2017

Howard Evans & Phil Atkinson

'I would rather have played rugby for Wales than Hamlet at the Old Vic. To that town, Aberavon and its rugby team, I pledge my continuing allegiance, until death.'   **Richard Burton**

One of the traditional powerhouses of Welsh first class rugby, Aberavon RFC has a long, proud and illustrious history, with 50 of its players being capped for Wales, the club winning many league titles and domestic cups, and - with Neath RFC - facing the might of South Africa, Australia and New Zealand. Aberavon RFC is a great rugby club and this is its story.

        978-1-902719-66-5   256pp   £19.99   PB

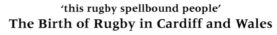

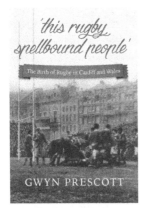

'this rugby spellbound people'
The Birth of Rugby in Cardiff and Wales

'...scrupulously researched [and] well written...Gwyn Prescott has given [rugby in Wales] a history to be proud of.' **Huw Richards, scrum.com**

'Prescott paints a meticulous picture of Welsh rugby's growth in Victorian Britain' **Rugby World**

'...a fascinating piece of research and a major contribution to the history of rugby.' **Tony Collins**

The Birth of Rugby in Cardiff and Wales is the essential guide to the importance of rugby in Cardiff and to the significance of Cardiff to the development of Welsh rugby in the nineteenth century.

978-1-902719-43-6   304pp   £16.99   PB

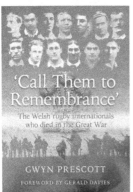

'Call Them to Remembrance'
The Welsh Rugby Internationals who died in the Great War

'This book is [an] acknowledgment of the sacrifice made by 13 Welshmen.... Theirs was a sacrifice which needs to be told....Gwyn Prescott, with meticulous and sympathetic attention to detail, tells the story. This narrative is an essential record.' **Gerald Davies**

'These humbling stories describe thirteen individual journeys which began on muddy yet familiar Welsh playing fields but ended in the unimaginable brutality of the battles of the First World War.' **www.gwladrugby.com**

'Call them to remembrance', which includes 120 illustrations and maps, tells the stories of thirteen Welsh heroes who shared the common bond of having worn the famous red jersey of the Welsh international rugby team.

978-1-902719-37-5   170pp   £14.99   PB

CRICKET IN WALES
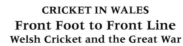
Front Foot to Front Line
Welsh Cricket and the Great War

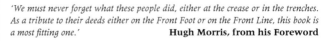

'We must never forget what these people did, either at the crease or in the trenches. As a tribute to their deeds either on the Front Foot or on the Front Line, this book is a most fitting one.' **Hugh Morris, from his Foreword**

Front Foot to Front Line commemorates Welsh cricket's contribution to the Great War by chronicling the lives of 55 professional and amateur cricketers who left the friendly rivalry of the crease for the brutality and horror of the trenches, and lost their lives as servicemen on the bloody battlefields of Europe.

The cricket clubs featured in Front Foot to Front Line include:
Blaina, Barry, Brecon, Bridgend Town, Briton Ferry, Cardiff, Cowbridge, Crickhowell, Denbighshire, Ferndale, Garth, Glamorgan, Llancarfan, Llandovery College, Llandudno, Llanelli, Monmouthshire, Neath, Newport, Pontypridd, Radyr, Swansea, Usk Valley, and Ystrad Mynach.

978-1-902719-42-9   209pp   £16.99   PB

ST DAVİD'S PRESS

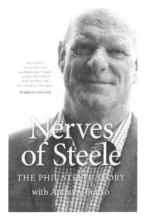

Nerves of Steele
The Phil Steele Story

'I've been lucky enough to get to know Phil during my time as Wales coach. He is an excellent broadcaster who genuinely wants Wales and Welsh players to excel and I respect his friendly and personal approach. I also admire the fact that he has been able to do this while facing personal and life changing challenges.'
Warren Gatland

'Phil Steele embodies all that is great about the culture of Welsh rugby. His strength of character and sense of fun are all the more impressive given some of the dark and devastating times he has endured.'
Caroline Hitt

Known to thousands of rugby fans as a knowledgeable, passionate and witty broadcaster, and as an entertaining and popular after-dinner speaker, Phil Steele's confident demeanour and humorous disposition mask a life-long battle against depression and anxiety heightened by heartbreak and tragedy in his personal life. Nerves of Steele is a remarkable story and reveals the real Phil Steele, a man known only by his very closest friends and family.

978-1-902719-50-4   208pp   £13.99   PB
978-1-902719-53-5   £9.99   eBook

2 Hard to Handle
The Autobiography of Mike 'Spikey' Watkins

'One of the most inspirational leaders that Welsh rugby has ever produced'
Mike Ruddock

'A great friend...also a great inspiration...he led from the front and his team mates could always rely on him when things got a bit rough, even though he'd probably started it!!'
Paul Turner

'No one trained harder, no one played harder...heart of a lion'
Terry Holmes

One of the most colourful and controversial characters in Welsh rugby history, Mike 'Spikey' Watkins remains the only player since 1882 to captain Wales on his debut, and win.

978-1-902719-40-5   251pp   £18.99   PB

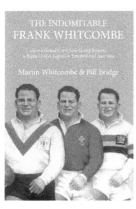

The Indomitable Frank Whitcombe
How a Genial Giant from Cardiff became
a Rugby League Legend in Yorkshire and Australia

'Frank Whitcombe was a rugby league cult hero in the days before there were cult heroes. An eighteen-stone battle tank of a prop forward, he graduated from Welsh rugby union to become a pillar of the great Bradford pack of the 1940s. In the process, he became the first forward to win the Lance Todd Trophy, a member of the 1946 'Indomitable' Lions touring team to Australasia and had even driven the team bus to Wembley when Bradford won the 1947 Challenge Cup Final. This book is his story - it is essential reading for anyone interested in the history of rugby and the amazing men who made the game.'
Prof. Tony Collins

'Frank Whitcombe became a Welsh international and a Great Britain tourist. He is widely regarded as an all-time great of rugby league.'
Fran Cotton

978-1-902719-47-4   256pp   £19.99   PB
978-1-902719-59-7   £9.99   eBook

Lightning Source UK Ltd.
Milton Keynes UK
UKHW030756181019

351839UK00004B/64/P